Professional Results

Microsoft® Office
Access 2003

D1372302

Professional Results

Microsoft® Office
Access 2003

McGraw-Hill/Osborne

New York   Chicago   San Francisco
Lisbon   London   Madrid   Mexico City
Milan   New Delhi   San Juan
Seoul   Singapore   Sydney   Toronto

Noel Jerke

The *McGraw·Hill* Companies

McGraw-Hill/Osborne
2100 Powell Street, 10th Floor
Emeryville, California 94608
U.S.A.

To arrange bulk purchase discounts for sales promotions, premiums, or fund-raisers, please contact **McGraw-Hill**/Osborne at the above address. For information on translations or book distributors outside the U.S.A., please see the International Contact Information page immediately following the index of this book.

Microsoft® Office Access 2003 Professional Results

1234567890 FGR FGR 019876543

ISBN 0-07-222965-9

Publisher	Brandon A. Nordin
Vice President &	
Associate Publisher	Scott Rogers
Acquisitions Editor	Nancy Maragioglio
Project Editor	Mark Karmendy
Acquisitions Coordinator	Athena Honore
Technical Editor	Greg Guntle
Indexer	Claire Splan
Composition	Carie Abrew, Tara A. Davis
Illustrators	Kathleen Fay Edwards, Melinda Moore Lytle, Lyssa Wald
Series Design	Mickey Galicia
Cover Design	Jeff Weeks

This book was composed with Corel VENTURA™ Publisher.

This book is dedicated to all our new friends we have made
since we have moved to Dallas.
You all have become very dear to us—God Bless!

About the Author

Noel Jerke is an independent consultant living in the Dallas–Fort Worth area. He is a 12-year veteran of the technology arena. Past clients include the Air Force, Mary Kay, the American Diabetes Association, and Martha Stewart. Noel's particular area of expertise is in technology operations management and building enterprise-level database applications. Noel is married to a wonderful wife and has three very special children, and can be reached at noeljerke@att.net.

Contents at a Glance

Contents

Acknowledgments

I would like to thank McGraw-Hill/Osborne for the support of this book. In particular, I would like to thank Wendy Rinaldi and Nancy Maragioglio, who supported the book concept and brought it to fruition. I would also like to thank Athena Honore, Greg Guntle, and Mark Karmendy for all of the great editing work on the book. Finally and most importantly, I would like to thank God for all of the many blessings in my life.

Introduction

Microsoft Access is sometimes viewed as a simple database application that isn't ready for prime time in the enterprise. While it certainly isn't a full-scale enterprise database, it does provide a robust relational database engine that can be useful for many enterprise purposes. And, for small to mid-level needs, it can be a perfect database development platform.

The audience for this book is literally any database developer—that is what makes Access so great. If you have requirements for a small database application, then Access is a great engine that is easy to learn and cost-effective. If you need a great "Swiss Army knife" for your enterprise database work, then Access is an excellent tool to utilize. It can be great for prototyping and manipulating enterprise data, and can function as a general database productivity tool. It is also a great platform for departmental databases and applications.

The goal of this book is to explore how professional database results can be achieved by using Microsoft Office Access. You will find tips, tricks, and explorations for the many capabilities of Access 2003. What you will not find is yet another book that covers the basics of Access. There is no extended coverage of building forms, reports, etc., found in these chapters.

In Chapter 1, the new features and capabilities of Access 2003 are explored. While there is nothing truly revolutionary about the new version, there are new capabilities that are important to be aware of.

Chapter 2 focuses on designing databases in Microsoft Office Access. One of the great things about Access is its graphical user interface (GUI) environment. Databases can be easily prototyped in Access 2003. Those database designs can then be easily upsized to a full enterprise implementation on Microsoft SQL Server.

In Chapter 3 and 4, we will explore the query building capabilities of Access. If the tools are leveraged properly they can significantly increase productivity by making complex and tedious queries easy to build. These chapters walk you step-by-step through getting professional results from the Access query capabilities.

Chapters 5 and 6 focus on programming within Access. In Chapter 5, Microsoft's free Web Matrix tool is utilized. Web Matrix supports the development of ASP.NET pages. In Chapter 6 we move into development with the full Visual Studio .NET and ASP.NET.

Working different types of data has always been one of the great features of Access. With its GUI interface, querying capabilities, and general ease of use, manipulating data is one of Access' great benefits. In Chapter 7, we explore examples of how to transform data through imports and exports. In Chapter 8, we explore the great new XML capabilities that have been added to Access 2003.

Chapter 9 and 10 focus on the Access Data Project (ADP) capabilities of Access. ADPs are great ways to combine enterprise databases with the capabilities of Access. In these two chapters, we explore how to set up and utilize ADPs. In Chapter 10, we build a sample ADP solution.

Finally, in Chapter 11 we explore some of the database management capabilities of Access. Topics include security, backups, and replication.

Understanding the capabilities and many uses of Access will show that it can be a powerful tool in the enterprise and a robust platform for small-to-midsize database applications.

Chapter 1

Introducing Office 2003

Office 2003 is Microsoft's office productivity software suite and is an upgrade from Office XP. Office 2003 focuses on enhancing the way individuals work together in a collaborative environment, including combining Office with Microsoft's enterprise portal technology—SharePoint. With this combination, individuals will be empowered to work together in groups, including being able to share documents, use group calendars, and conduct team meetings.

Another key technology integrated throughout Office is support for XML. With the new XML, support capabilities that are a part of Word, Excel, and Access, data can be easily shared and made available to workgroups throughout the enterprise.

Along with robust XML support, a major enhancement for Access is the ability to utilize Smart Tags in Access data and applications. Using Smart Tags, database developers provide data-sensitive links to external data such as accessing Microsoft Outlook, retrieving shipping data, and many other third-party supported features.

The good news is that the updates in Office 2003 are very focused on the corporate and professional marketplace. From a database perspective, that translates into even more reasons for considering Access as a useful tool in the enterprise database arsenal.

Office 2003 Overview

There is no doubt that when Office 2003 is released there will be a whole range of books published covering the depth and breadth of the product. In this book, we will focus on the major feature enhancements, the new components, and the importance for Access users.

Microsoft talks about three major improvements in Office. The first is in more efficient and effective communication. Outlook 2003 has several significant enhancements focused on controlling email flow, viewing communication more easily, and sharing information. Also, Outlook 2003 includes a new add-on called the Business Contact Manager. The Business Contact Manager allows you to track business contacts and accounts, active sales prospects, contact activity history, and generate reports collaboratively.

The second major focus is on collaboration. The key to the collaborative ability of Office 2003 is the leveraging of Windows SharePoint Services. With this integration groups can share and work on documents and manage versioning. The SharePoint technology creates ad hoc web sites for shared projects, documents, and meeting workspaces. With the workspaces, groups can share documents, calendars, and announcements, and conduct polls and implement other types of electronic collaboration.

The difference between this type of groupware collaboration from other technologies such as Lotus Notes or Groove is that collaboration can take place in any of the office products, not just in email.

The third major focus is in the area of business process improvement. The goal for these enhancements is focused on having the right information at the right time and in the right place (or application). The primary ingredient added to Office for this type of collaboration is XML support. With XML, any content in any of the Office suite of applications can be easily transformed to be used in another application.

From a product perspective, none of the applications have had a significant overhaul in core functionality. Table 1-1 provides highlights of some of the key changes in the core applications.

Application	Description
Microsoft Word	
Document Markup	The Document Markup features have been enhanced to make commenting and tracking changes easier.
XML	Word can save documents in XML as a standard format.
Microsoft Excel	
SharePoint Integration	Data in spreadsheets can be easily shared with other users via SharePoint services.
Smart Tags	The functionality and utilization of Smart Tags is more flexible and manageable.
Statistical Calculations	Enhancements have been made to the statistical functions of Excel. This will be useful as more and more users across the enterprise perform data analysis.
Microsoft PowerPoint	
CD Distribution	PowerPoint now supports saving PowerPoint presentations to CD for distribution.
Windows Media Player Integration	The full power of the Windows Media Player can now be accessed from within PowerPoint.
Smart Tags	They can now be utilized.
Microsoft Access	
AutoCorrect Smart Tag	This tag can now be used in Access.
Forms and Reports Error Checking	More errors are caught and flagged to the user for correction. This will make working and developing with Access easier.

TABLE 1-1   Key Office 2003 Enhancements

Office 2003 Overview

Application	Description
Identifying Dependent Objects	It will be easier for developers to identify object dependencies when developing Access-based applications.
XML Support	Importing and exporting XML files is far more flexible with Access 2003.
Database Backups	Backing up an Access database is now very simple from within the application.

TABLE 1-1 Key Office 2003 Enhancements *(continued)*

Those are the highlights of Office 2003. From an enterprise perspective, the collaborative and data-sharing capabilities will be a welcome addition to the Office suite.

Access 2003 Enhancements

Access 2003 is not a revolutionary upgrade from Access XP. Most of the changes are focused on tweaks and minor enhancements. The two major enhancements are focused on the use of Smart Tags and XML support.

XML

Access 2002/XP provided limited support for utilizing XML. With Access 2003, Microsoft has significantly enhanced the XML integration into Access 2003. Access 2003 does not require Access-specific schema that was utilized in Access 2002. Instead, the latest XSD standard format for XML data exchange with external data sources is supported.

For example, with Access 2003 users can browse related database tables and choose how data is exported by defining the data structure with an XSD. Access 2003 significantly enhances the importing and exporting of XML files. XML files provided in any schema format can be easily imported into Access. They can be transformed into an existing data structure or can continue using a structure defined by an XSLT that the developer or a third party provides.

Importing data into Access does not require an XSD. If there is no XSD, Access will infer a structure from the incoming data. If the XML data being imported has an accompanying XSD schema, Access 2003 will recognize defined data types based on the schema definition.

Exporting is also much more flexible. When data is exported from the database, a XSLT can be applied to transform the data from the Access table structure to a new format. Both the import and export features make integration with external data sources much easier.

These enhancements allow users within an organization or different organizations to share information more easily. We will be exploring the use of XML and Access in Chapter 8.

Smart Tags

Smart Tags add the ability to link external applications to your specific application. The key is to provide contextual help and links to data within the Office environment.

With Access 2003, developers can now easily embed Smart Tags into any Access field. Any control on a form, report, or data page will have a property for specifying Smart Tags. Any field or column on a table will also have this property. In addition, the columns in a query will inherit this property from the table the query is based on.

Access 2003 users who create forms for others can now attach Smart Tags to controls with no extra programming steps. This allows them to create solutions in Access that have the look and feel of other Office applications.

Let's build an example of using Smart Tags in Access. Start Access and create a new Access database. Save the database as Contacts.mdb.

Next, create a new table in the Design view by clicking the Create Table in Design View option. Create the table fields shown in Table 1-2.

NOTE   *If you are unfamiliar with building tables and data field types in Access, we will be exploring this in much more depth in the next chapter.*

Be sure to set the IDContact field as a primary key. Select the field and then click on the key icon on the toolbar. A primary key means that each IDContact field value in the table needs to be unique. Figure 1-1 shows the designed table.

Field Name	Data Type	Description
IDContact	AutoNumber – Primary Key	Unique identifier for each contact in the table
Name	Text	Contact's first and last name
EmailAddress	Text	Contact's address
BirthDay	Text	Contact's birthday

TABLE 1-2   Contact Table Fields

Access 2003 Enhancements

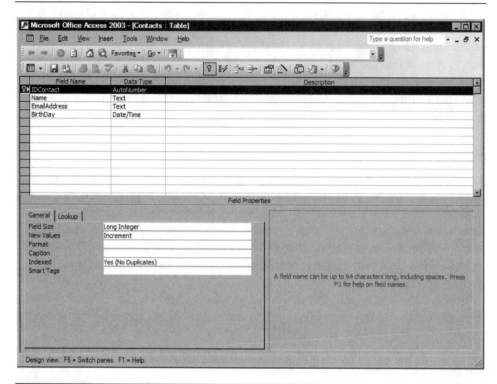

FIGURE 1-1 Contacts table

Now we are ready to set up our Smart Tags. Several Smart Tags for working with Outlook are installed with Outlook 2003. We will take advantage of these to see how the technology works in Access.

First, we will set up the Name field and set up a smart tag for it. Once the Name field is selected, note the Smart Tags property at the bottom of the screen. Select the property and note the "…" button that shows up next to the property. Click the button to pop up the Smart Tags dialog box. The dialog box is shown in Figure 1-2.

In this case we are going to use the Person Name Smart Tag to be able to work with the name data in our Contacts database. This Smart Tag will allow us to send mail, schedule a meeting with the contact, open a corresponding Outlook contact record, and add the contact to Outlook contacts. Click the OK button to set the Smart Tag for the field.

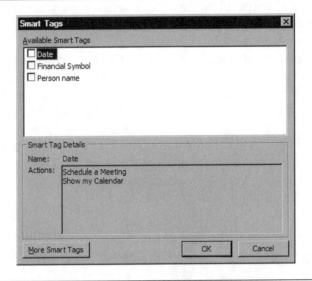

FIGURE 1-2   Smart Tags dialog box

When the Smart Tag is set for the field, a string of setting code is created as follows:

```
"urn:schemas-microsoft.com:office:smarttags#PersonName"
```

This code basically defines the Smart Tag to be utilized by Access. Fortunately, Access creates the Smart Tag references automatically. Next, let's add a Smart Tag for the EmailAddress field. Select the field and then click the Smart Tag property. Next click the "…" button. Again we will select the Person Name Smart Tag. The reference code is the same as for the Name field.

Now let's create a Smart Tag for the BirthDay field. Select the field and then select the Smart Tags property. Click the "…" button. Select the Date Smart Tag from the list. The tag references are created as follows:

```
"urn:schemas-microsoft.com:office:smarttags#date"
```

Now that the Smart Tags are created for our data, let's enter some data and see what options are provided to us. Switch to the View mode of the table by clicking the Design View button on the toolbar.

NOTE   *Be sure to save the table as Contacts.*

Enter a couple of contacts into the table. The first thing you will notice is the little triangle that shows up in the lower-right part of the fields where we added the Smart Tags. Figure 1-3 shows the table.

Now let's use the Smart Tags for each field. Click on one of the names in the Name field. You will see the Smart Tag icon pop up next to the field. It has a lowercase *i* with a circle around it. When you cursor over it, a drop-down arrow shows up. Click on the arrow to see the options for the field. Figure 1-4 shows the Smart Tag.

The drop-down list shows four options of how we can use the person's name in Outlook: an email can be sent to the contact; a meeting can be scheduled with the person; if the person is in your Outlook contacts, the contact record can be opened; and, finally, the person can be added to the contacts.

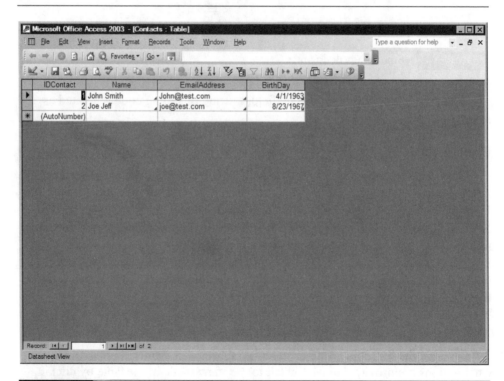

FIGURE 1-3 Contacts table Smart Tags

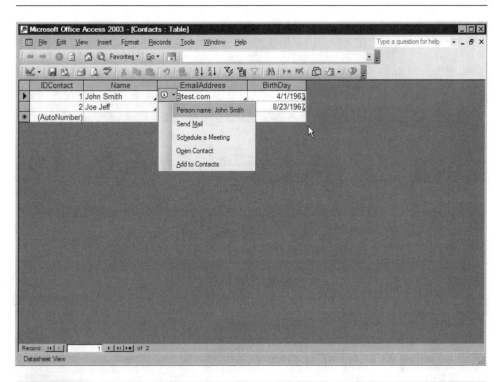

FIGURE 1-4   Person Name Smart Tag

Click the Add to Contacts option. This automatically opens up the Contacts dialog box from Outlook and fills in the Full Name field of the contact data. Figure 1-5 shows the Access table and the Contacts dialog box.

If you follow the same steps on the Email Address field, the same options will be available. Now let's look at the Date smart tag. Click the Smart Tag icon down arrow to see the options. In this case we have options to schedule a meeting in Outlook and look at the Outlook calendar. Figure 1-6 shows the Smart Tag dialog box.

Not only can Smart Tags be used in the table data sheets, but they can also be used on Access forms. Let's create a simple form for our Access table to see the

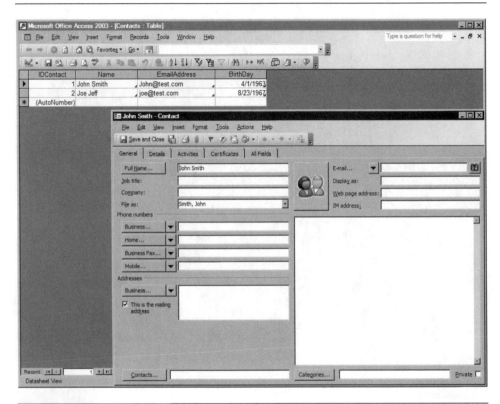

FIGURE 1-5   Contacts dialog box

Smart Tags in action in the programmatic interface of Access. Follow these steps to create the form:

1. Click the forms option of the Access database.

2. Click the Create Form by Using Wizard option.

3. Select all of the fields from the Contacts table by clicking the Double Arrow button. Click the Next button.

4. On the layout dialog box, leave the option on Columnar layout. Click the Next button.

5. On the style screen, keep the Standard style and click the Next button.

6. Keep the name of the form as Contacts and click Finish.

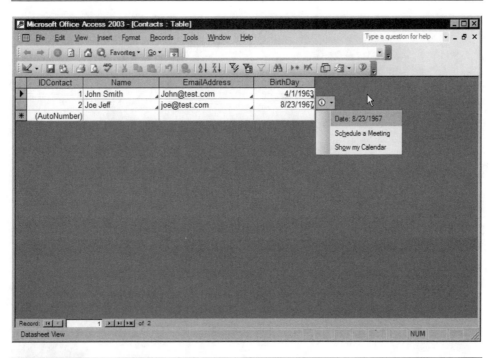

Access 2003 Enhancements

FIGURE 1-6	Date Smart Tag dialog box

The wizard creates a new form that allows for data entry of the Contacts table. The form is shown in Figure 1-7.

Note that the same field triangles show up in the lower right of the fields with Smart Tags. When you cursor over the field, the Smart Tag icon appears. When clicking on the Smart Tags, the same options appear as we saw in the datasheet view of the table.

For Access forms, the following controls can be enabled with Smart Tags:

■ Form controls:

   ■ Label

   ■ Text Box

   ■ Combo Box

   ■ List Box

■ Data Page controls:

   ■ Label

   ■ Bound Span

   ■ Text Box

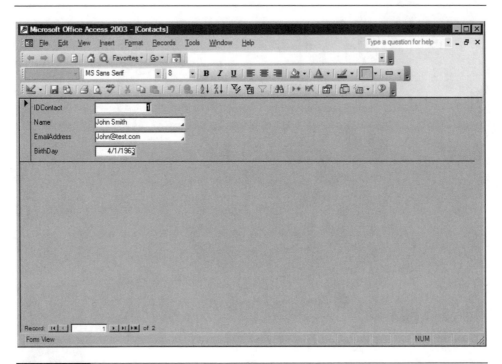

FIGURE 1-7   Contacts form

There are many additional Smart Tags available to utilize as well. If you click the More Smart Tags button on the Smart Tags dialog box, you will go to the Smart Tags references for Office. There, you can create Smart Tags. You can also visit http://www.officesmarttags.com/ to find many third-party Smart Tags to be added. Examples include adding FedEx® package tracking, ESPN® sport team references, MSNBC® news and weather, and many others.

Miscellaneous Enhancements

As mentioned, there are all kinds of minor enhancements in Access. Two additional ones to note include the increased integration with SharePoint and the ability to view object dependencies.

SharePoint Integration

Microsoft SharePoint is Microsoft's enterprise portal technology. It focuses on aggregating and collecting information into one interface. It also supports workflow and knowledge management capabilities to enable the enterprise to work in a collaborative environment on centralized data. SharePoint makes it easier for power users to pull in data from varied places—enterprise data, web data, text files, Microsoft Excel documents, and XML.

With Access in Microsoft Office XP, you can connect to a Microsoft SQL Server running with SharePoint Team Services 1.0 using Access projects (which connect to SQL). This works well for reporting and viewing data. However, that is not as useful for data entry tasks. In some cases, Access projects were the only way to move data in and out of SharePoint Team Services if you need to alter SharePoint Team Services data lists.

With the next versions of SharePoint Team Services and Access 2003, you can now perform the following operations:

- Export the contents of a table from Access to a list in SharePoint Team Services from Microsoft.

- Import the contents of a list in SharePoint Team Services from Microsoft into a table in Access.

- Link a table in Access to a SharePoint Team Services list.

There are a number of other advantages to using Access with SharePoint in the new versions. Most of these are related to updating and working with list grid data from SharePoint. The integration of an enterprise portal platform like SharePoint with Access 2003 is a great example of how Access can be utilized as a key tool in the enterprise database environment.

Object Dependencies

One useful feature of Access 2003 is the ability to see object dependencies. This view allows us to determine if a query or other type of object is dependent upon other objects. An example would be a query that is dependent upon other queries for its results.

To view the object dependencies for our Contacts Access database, click the View menu and click the Object Dependencies option. When that option is selected, a new pane is displayed that shows the dependencies for each object. Figure 1-8 shows the dependencies.

Access 2003 Enhancements

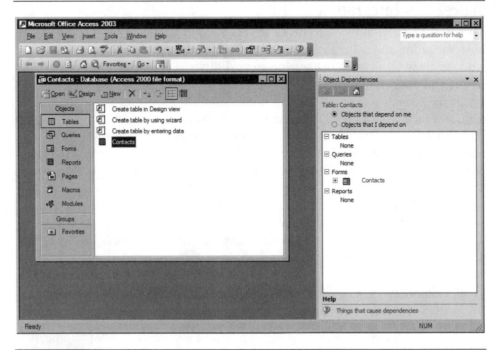

FIGURE 1-8 Object dependencies

For large and complex Access databases, this feature can be very useful and helpful when making changes to forms, queries, and other objects.

Summary

Office 2003 is revolutionary in its focus on integrating and extending the enterprise. From a day-to-day document and database utilization perspective, the applications have been spruced up and reworked based primarily on user feedback. Similarly, with Access, new features focus primarily on the increasing usability and programmability of Access.

In the next chapter we will explore designing and prototyping databases in Access. Access can be a great tool for prototyping database designs and applications before they are upsized to full enterprise databases. In addition, the GUI interface of Access can be a very useful environment for designing and testing databases.

Chapter 2

Designing and Prototyping Enterprise Databases with Microsoft Access

Thousands of Access databases, big and small, are in existence today. The sad reality is that many of these databases are poorly designed and very difficult to maintain. The goal of this chapter is to review basic database design techniques within the context of Access.

For those of you who are database veterans, this may seem a little remedial. But, if you have not done a lot of work in Access you may be surprised at how flexible Access is for database design. Its graphical interface is extremely easy to use and the data relationship building tools are very powerful. Access can be great for prototyping an early-stage enterprise database, after which the basic structure and data can be extended to SQL Server.

Database Design Refresher

There have been many books written on database design. We will not attempt to cover the entire topic in just a few pages. But, we can cover some of the basics and show how tasks are accomplished in Access. To get started, we need to be familiar with some key concepts related to designing databases.

Database Normalization

The goal of any database is to ensure that data is represented only once in the database. For example, if we are storing address data, we would want to store the address only once in the database and not in multiple locations, which could cause the data to get out of synch. In addition, we want to ensure that the database does not constrain the true representation of the data. For example, if we are storing multiple-choice test questions and answers, we would not want to limit the number answer choices for a question to an arbitrary number such as 4 or 5. Ideally, the database should be able to support an unlimited number of potential answer choices, even though the reality is the number of choices may be 4 or 5, 99 percent of the time. Ensuring that a database is normalized makes the data easier to manage and helps to maximize data integrity.

NOTE   *There are actually different levels of database normalization (first normal form, second normal form, and third normal form). The goal of database normalization is to ensure data is grouped properly and that it is nonredundant. For a more in-depth description of normalization, look at* Oracle9i: The Complete Reference *by Kevin Loney and George Koch (McGraw-Hill/Osborne, 0-07-222521-1).*

Keys

There are two types of "keys" that are defined when building a database. The *primary key* is a value that is unique for that set of data. A good example of a primary key is a social security number. No one has the same number and it uniquely identifies each person.

The second type of key is a *foreign key*. A foreign key is simply the storage of another set the of data's primary key. By storing the primary key value, it indicates that the two sets of data are linked. Using our social security example, let's say checks are being paid out to a social security recipient; in order to know who the recipient of the check is, we would want to store the check number, amount, and the social security number of the recipient. In this example the social security number acts as a foreign key. The following illustration shows the relationship.

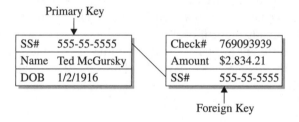

Relationships

Understanding how different sets of data relate to each other is critical to good database design. In our social security check example, there are in fact many checks that can be received by the person. This would define a one-to-many relationship (one person to many checks). There are three types of relationships that are found when designing a database.

- **One to one (1:1)**   A one-to-one relationship signifies that each instance of a given set of data relates to exactly one instance of another set of data. For example, a student will have one final grade for a class/course.

- **One to many (1:M)**   A one-to-many relationship signifies that each instance of a given set of data relates to one or more instances of another set of data. In this case a teacher may teach multiple classes, and multiple classes are taught by one teacher. Note that you can also have zero or one to many, which indicates that you don't have to have a related instance, but if you do you can only have one instance. In our example, you might have classes in the database that are not yet being taught by a teacher.

■ **Many to many (M:M)**   A many-to-many relationship signifies that many instances of a given entity relate to many instances of another entity. For example, a student can take many tests and many tests can be taken by many students. The many-to-many relationship is also called a cross-reference relationship.

NOTE   *There are diagramming standards for showing these relationships. In this chapter we are keeping the diagramming simple. Many reference texts provide extended details on database diagramming.*

Data Types in Access

When designing a database, it is important to define the type of data being worked with. For example, numbers such as 1, 2.6, and -23.98 can be stored in the database differently than standard text such as "abc", "the quick brown fox", etc. If a field is defined as number, mathematical operations can be performed on the data. Access supports the nine different primary data types outlined in Table 2-1.

Access also supports the concept of a Lookup data type. Lookups allow you to choose a value from another table or from a list of values by using a list box or

Data Type	Description
Text	Stores up to 255 characters.
Memo	Stores up to 65,535 characters. In certain cases, can store an unlimited amount of data (see Access help for further information).
Number	Used for storing numbers and can be set to store different sizes of integers, including byte (0 to 255), integer (−32,768 to 32,767), long integer (−2,147,483,648 to 2,147,483,647), and decimal.
Date/Time	Stores date and time values.
Currency	Used for storing monetary values up to four decimals, and all math operations operate on the data with that level of precision.
AutoNumber	With each new record, the value increments by 1. This field is often used to create a primary unique key for a table. For example: When storing name information, if there are two John Smiths, the value of this field would ensure the record is unique (e.g., 1, John, Smith versus 2, John, Smith)
Yes/No	Contains only two values (yes, no) and is used as an indicator field. For example, is the student actively taking the course—yes or no.
OLE Object	Stores objects such as Excel spreadsheets and other binary type data.
HyperLink	Stores URL links.

TABLE 2-1   Access Data Types

combo box in the Access interface. This is unique to Access and should not be used if you are developing your application outside of the Access environment or intend to upsize the database to SQL Server.

It is important to pick the right data types to represent your data. If you need to perform math functions, storing numbers in a text field is not going to work well. And, trying to store text in a number field will not work at all. In addition, think about the size of the data. If you are storing a two-character abbreviation of a state, using a memo field would be overkill.

Querying and Reporting

What use would a database be without the ability to query for and report on data? Access, like most all databases, provides a powerful engine for querying data. It provides built-in wizards that make building simple queries easy. And, it provides a query designer environment where queries can be visually built. Finally, Structured Query Language (SQL) statements can be built directly as well. In Chapters 3 and 4 we will explore building queries in Microsoft Access in depth.

From a database design perspective, it is important to keep in mind what consumers of the data will want to know. For example, in our social security data example, if one of the purposes of collecting the data is to be able to review payments to individuals historically, the database better track each payment.

There are cases where we don't necessarily want to store every small detail about the data. A good example is storing web ad views (impressions) and clicks. If the database were to store a record every time an ad pops up on a web page, given high traffic site distribution, the database could be storing millions of records an hour. Trying to query and sift through that much data is probably not reasonably feasible and not useful to the end user.

In cases like this, it is helpful to "roll up" the impression and click data into an aggregate form. A count of the impressions over a period of time (e.g., every 10 minutes or an hour, etc.) could be stored instead of one record for each impression. Then the queries would be based on time-interval increments instead of on single impressions.

When designing a database it is very important to be aware of what the data will be utilized for and to ensure that the data structure is optimized to support the user's querying and reporting needs.

Prototyping for Enterprise Databases

Before we dig into designing a real database structure in Access, it is important to understand one of the more powerful uses of Access. Access provides the ability to prototype databases rapidly. In today's software development environment where rapid application development is the norm, building a prototype before developing the full enterprise database can provide an effective method of presenting the potential application to end users.

Easy Database Design

As we will see, Access provides a relatively easy graphical database design environment—changes and tweaks can be quickly made. Oftentimes the requirements for a database are not clear up front and require several iterations to complete the design. Access provides a very interactive environment for design that can be easily coupled with a functional interface.

Of course, traditional tools such as Erwin, Visio, etc., can be utilized for database design. This may be the appropriate route for more sophisticated database design requirements and can be done in conjunction with prototyping in Access. Table 2-2 provides some guidance techniques for prototyping in Access.

SQL Server Upsizing

A prototype design in Access can be easily upsized to SQL Server, as will be demonstrated in the "Upsizing to SQL Server" section of this chapter. The upsizing process is fairly simple. The beauty of this is that it allows the prototype to be utilized and not discarded. Once upsized, the database can then be extended as appropriate.

Rapid Interface Prototyping

This book will not cover explicitly building forms and reports in Access, but one of the benefits of prototyping in Access is the ability to create a sample user

Technique	Description
Table Design	Build only core tables that are required for demonstrating the database. Lookup tables (e.g., country, state, etc.) do not necessarily need to be created in the prototype.
Data Type Selection	Pick data types that are closely aligned to SQL or your enterprise database. Note that Access doesn't provide as finely-grained data typing as most enterprise databases.
Query Creation	As shown in the next two chapters, Access can be an excellent tool for rapidly building queries. Take full advantage of the querying capabilities in Access. The SQL code can be copied from the query design environment.

TABLE 2-2   Access Prototyping Guidelines

interface quickly. If you are building a web-based solution, prototype web pages can be built and then retargeted to the upsized enterprise database.

NOTE   *If you would like more in-depth information on building forms and reports in Access, see* Access 2002®: The Complete Reference *by Virginia Andersen (McGraw-Hill/Osborne, ISBN: 0-07-213241-8).*

Sample Database Design

Now it's time to build a real database design in Access. Our sample data domain will be automotive-related data. The task is to build a database that will store make, model, and year data for all of the automobiles on the market.

Designing the Data Structure

The primary goal for the database is to be able to retrieve a listing of automobiles by model and retrieve applicable data about the particular model. Here are the "facts" about the data that need to be incorporated:

- Categories define groups of like automobiles (e.g., SUV, Compact, etc.).
- Categories can be made up of subcategories (e.g., Sedans: Compact, Luxury).
- Automobiles can be classified in only one category.
- Automobile models have a maker (e.g., Lexus®, Honda®, GMC®, etc.).
- Automobile models have a fuel efficiency rating (e.g., miles per gallon).
- Automobile models have a set of color options (e.g., Stardust Red, Baby Blue, Forest Green, etc.).
- Automobile models have a manufacturing year.

Given these facts, we can come up with a database design to capture the data. The data breaks down into three major entities as follows:

- **Models**   Stores the fact data for the car model.
- **Makes**   Indicates the manufacturer of the model.
- **Category**   Defines the categorization structure for classifying or grouping the models.

Given these primary entities, a database diagram could be built, as shown here:

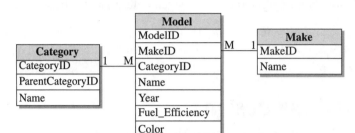

In this diagram, three tables have been created. The first is for category. The primary key is the CategoryID. The second table is for storing the model information. It relates to the Category table in that each model can be classified in one category. Note that categories can contain many models.

The last table is for the make of the model. Each model is made by only one maker. And, each maker can make multiple models.

But wait, there is a flaw in the design. Did you catch it? In our current design the color option of the model is stored in the Model table. This is going to pose several problems. If a model comes in multiple colors, there are only two options for storing that data. The first would be to put a record in the Model table for each color. An example is shown in Table 2-3.

Of course, the problem with this is that most of the data for the model is being stored more than once. This violates the rules of normalization and potentially can lead to bad data if the records get out of synch.

The second way to store the data would be to put all of the colors in the Color field, as shown in Table 2-4.

This presents problems on two fronts. The first is that having all of the colors in one field doesn't make the data easy to work with. In the user interface, listing all of the colors in a drop-down box would require the field data to be parsed. And, it will be difficult to query for the data (e.g., find out if there was a 2003 Anatari Side Winder LX made in Green).

ModelID	MakeID	CategoryID	Name	Year	Fuel Efficiency	Color
1	1	1	Side Winder LX	2003	1.5 MPG	Pink
1	1	1	Side Winder LX	2003	1.5 MPG	Chartreuse
1	1	1	Side Winder LX	2003	1.5 MPG	Aqua Green

TABLE 2-3   Sample Model Data for Non-Normalized Color Data

ModelID	MakeID	CategoryID	Name	Year	Fuel Efficiency	Color
1	1	1	Side Winder LX	2003	1.5 MPG	Pink, Chartreuse, Aqua Green

TABLE 2-4   Sample Model Data for Non-Normalized Color Data

The second major problem is that those colors may be used with other models built by the maker of the Side Winder LX. The manufacturer may also make a Side Winder L vehicle that comes in the same Pink and Chartreuse but not in Aqua Green.

To resolve these issues, the color data needs to be broken out into its own table. Reasonably, it can be surmised that each manufacturer/maker of automobiles will have its own selection of colors that will be available on some of its models. This entails a many-to-many relationship because many colors will be used on many models. The following reflects this change in the data structure.

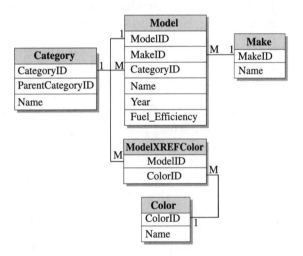

Many-to-many relationships are set up in what are called cross-reference tables. The cross-reference table stores the primary keys of the two related entities. In our example that is the Color table and the Model table. The best way to illustrate this is with actual data. Tables 2-5, 2-6, and 2-7 show sample data for each table.

ModelID	MakeID	CategoryID	Name	Year	Fuel Efficiency
1	1	1	Side Winder LX	2003	1.5 MPG
2	1	1	Side Winder L	2003	1.5 MPG

TABLE 2-5   Sample Model Data for the Model Table

ModelID	ColorID
1	1
1	2
1	3
2	1
2	2

TABLE 2-6 Sample Model and Color Cross-Reference Data for the ModelXREFColor Table

In this set of data, the Side Winder LX comes in all three colors. Note the ModelID and ColorID combinations. The Side Winder L comes in two colors as defined in the Model and Color cross-reference data. Thus, we have many models (L and LX) that come in many colors (Pink, Chartreuse, and Aqua Green). Also note that the combination of ModelID and ColorID is always unique because it would not make sense to show a model coming in the same color twice. Thus the two foreign keys combined make the primary key of the ModelXREFColor table.

NOTE *By no means is this simple design meant to truly capture all of the aspects of tracking automobile model-related data. It is for illustrative purposes only, given the list of facts that are provided.*

That completes the data structure for the example and all of the data facts are met. Next, the database will be implemented in Access.

NOTE *An astute database designer probably noted one potential flaw in our design. The categorization of automobiles may change over time. For example, many years ago minivans didn't exist. And, when they first came out they were likely categorized as vans instead of minivans. Once they caught on and became popular, a new category was probably set up specifically for minivans. Right now, our category structure doesn't allow for tracking categorization changes over time. In other words, there is no way to see that at one point in time there was no minivan category and certain models were classified as vans versus minivans.*

ColorID	Name
1	Pink
2	Chartreuse
3	Aqua Green

TABLE 2-7 Sample Color Data for the Color Table

Implementing a Database Design in Access

At last we are ready to get started in Access by implementing the database design for the automobile model data. Start up Microsoft Access and let's begin.

Building the Table Structures

When Access starts up, you will need to create a blank database. Under the New tab on the right startup pane, click on Blank Database. Name the database Models.mdb and save the database in an appropriate directory. Your screen should look like Figure 2-1.

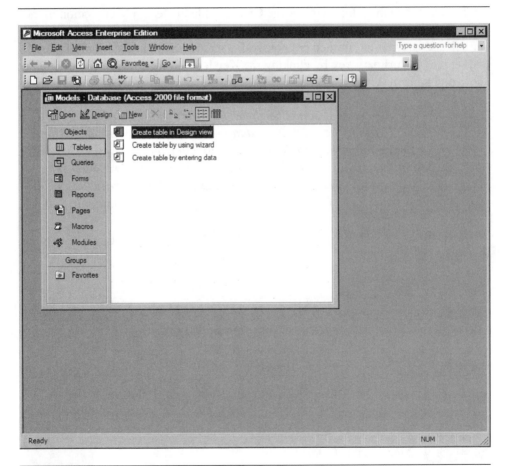

FIGURE 2-1   Blank database created in Access

The next step is to create the tables per the database design. In order to create the tables, it is important to determine what data type is needed for each field.

To get started, the Models table will need to be created. Table 2-8 shows the appropriate data types for each of the fields in the table.

NOTE *In general, it is a good idea to have foreign keys that are generated from an autonumber field be stored as long integer numbers. This helps to eliminate any size restrictions. And, in order to create SQL joins with autonumber fields, the foreign key must be a long integer.*

To create the table, double-click the Create Table in Design View option in the Table Objects window. That brings up the Table Design view. Enter the field names and select data types as outlined previously. Be sure to highlight the ModelID field and set it as the primary key by clicking the Key Icon on the toolbar. Figure 2-2 shows the table in Access.

NOTE *When setting up an autonumber field, there are options for having the data indexed. Indexing means that the data is sorted for fast searching. There is an option to have the table indexed with duplicates; however, since we want these fields to be a primary key, by definition there will be no duplicate values. When a field that is set as an autonumber field is set to be a primary key, it is automatically set to be indexed without duplicates.*

Next, the Makes table can be created. Table 2-9 shows the fields and data types for the table.

Field	Data Type
ModelID	Autonumber – Primary Key
CategoryID	Number – Long Integer
MakeID	Number – Long Integer
Name	Text – size 50
Year	Date/Time
Fuel_Efficiency	Number – Integer

TABLE 2-8   Models Table Fields

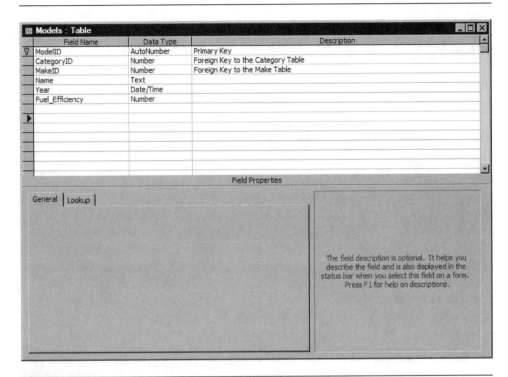

FIGURE 2-2   Models table

Now create the new table in Access. Be sure to set the MakeID as the primary key. Figure 2-3 shows the design of the table.

Next, create the Category table. Table 2-10 shows the data types for the table. Be sure to set the CategoryID as the primary key. Figure 2-4 shows the designed table.

Field	Data Type
MakeID	Autonumber – Primary Key
Name	Text – size 50

TABLE 2-9   Makes Table Fields

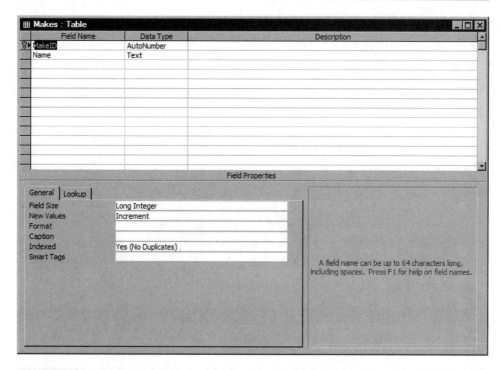

FIGURE 2-3   Makes table

The last implementation is for the cross-reference structure of the color data. As the previous diagram shows, two tables will be created. The first will be ModelXREFColor, which holds the color and model IDs. The second table will hold the color data. Tables 2-11 and 2-12 show the data types for the fields.

Next, create the tables in Access. For the ModelXREFColor table, the primary key is the combination of the two fields: ModelID and ColorID. Highlight both

Field	Data Type
CategoryID	Autonumber – Primary Key
ParentCategoryID	Number – Long Integer
Name	Text – size 50

TABLE 2-10   Category Table Fields

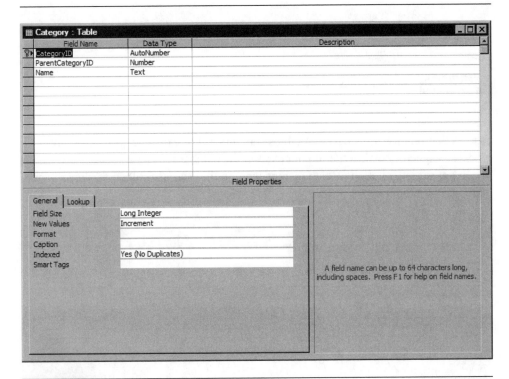

FIGURE 2-4   Category table

and then set the primary key. Finally, set the ColorID field on the Colors table as the primary key. Figure 2-5 shows the two tables.

That does it for creating all of the tables from our database design. Next, the relationships between the tables need to be set up.

Implementing the Table Relationships

The tables are now defined, but we can do more to ensure that the referential integrity of the database stays intact when data is being updated. Referential integrity

Field	Data Type
ModelID	Number – Long Integer – Primary Key
ColorID	Number – Long Integer – Primary Key

TABLE 2-11   ModelXREFColor Table Fields

Field	Data Type
ColorID	Autonumber – Primary Key
Name	Text – size 50

TABLE 2-12   Colors Table Fields

ensures that relationships between tables stay intact. For example, you can't have models assigned to makes that do not exist in the database.

To get started, click the Relationships icon on the Access toolbar, as shown here:

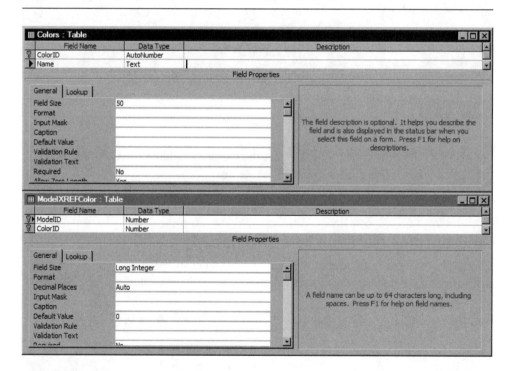

FIGURE 2-5   The Color and ModelXREFColor tables

The Relationship Designer then pops up. Because relationships have not been previously designed, the tables need to be selected, as shown here:

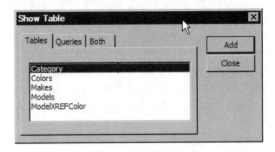

Select each of the tables to be added to the designer. When this is complete, each of the tables will be shown in the Relationship Designer:

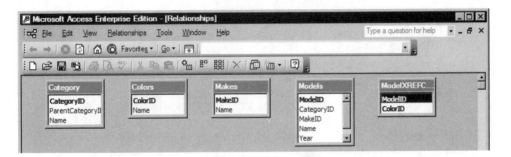

When building relationships between tables, the focus is on the primary and foreign keys. A primary or foreign key is dragged from one table to the same key on the target table. To demonstrate, let's build the relationship between the Category table and Models table.

First, click on the CategoryID field on the Category table. Then drag the field over to the Models table. When your cursor is over the table, it will change from the circle with the slash to a droppable icon. Figure 2-6 shows the Drop icon next to the CategoryID field in the Models table.

Sample Database Design

Now drop the CategoryID on top of the CategoryID field in the Models table. When you do that, an Edit Relationships dialog box pops up, as shown in Figure 2-7.

The first thing to note is the relationship type shown in the dialog box. As was designed into our diagram, the relationship between the two tables is one-to-many. There are many models for one category.

The second thing to note is the option to Enforce Referential Integrity. If this check box is selected, Access will not allow a foreign key to be entered for any records that do not exist in the related table. For example, a CategoryID value cannot be entered into the Models table if the CategoryID value does not exist in the Category table.

If the Enforce Referential Integrity check box is selected, there are two options to consider. The first, Cascade Update Related Fields, will change any related data

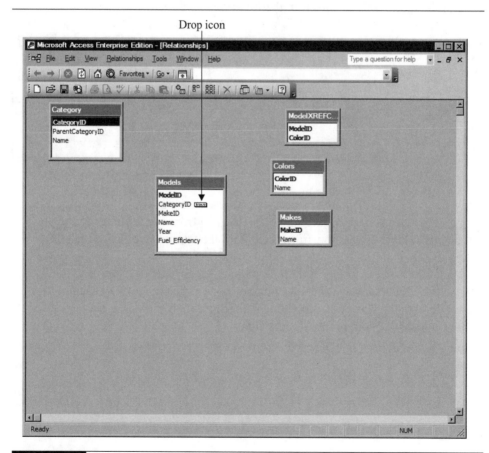

FIGURE 2-6   Building the CategoryID relationship

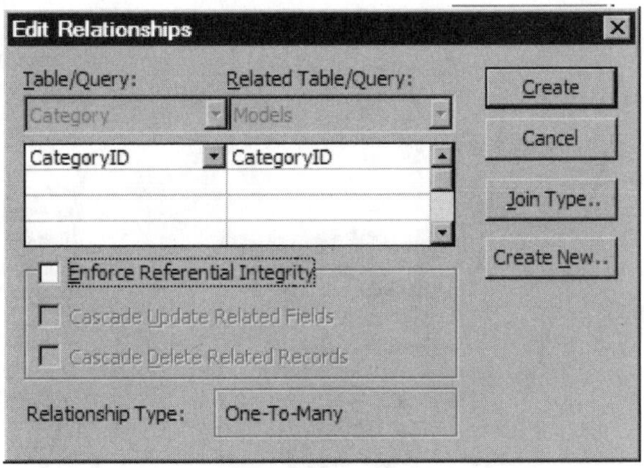

FIGURE 2-7   Edit Relationships dialog box

when the primary key value has changed. For example, if the primary key of a color field changes to a new value, the ID will be changed in all related fields. In most cases, primary keys are autonumber-generated values and the values do not change. So, this will only be implemented in unique cases.

The second option, Cascade Delete Related Records, is much more powerful. If a category of vehicles is deleted, then any models in that category will also be deleted. That might not be the desired effect in this case, so we will not select it. But, there are cases where cascading deletes are useful. For example, if you are storing address data for a customer in a table unique to the core customer data, and if the customer is deleted, it makes logical sense to always delete their address data.

Select the Enforce Referential Integrity check box and then click the Create button to create the relationship. Figure 2-8 shows the updated relationship diagram.

Note the line drawn between the two tables. Next to the Category table there is a 1 and next to the Models table an infinity sign (sideways 8). This indicates the one-to-many relationship.

Next, the relationships between Models and Makes can be created in the same fashion by dragging the MakeID of the Makes table on top of the MakeID in the Models table. Again there is a one-to-many relationship since each model belongs to only one maker and makers can make many different models. With regard to enforcing referential integrity, here we want to enforce it. With regards to cascading deletes, it is hard to imagine when a maker would be deleted given that this database will historically store model data. So, it is probably safer not to enforce a cascading

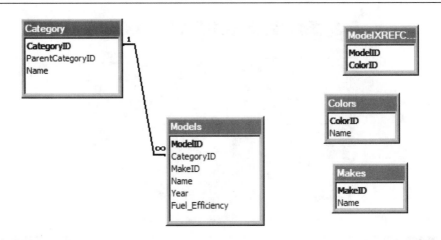

FIGURE 2-8 Created relationship between Category and Models

delete of models if a maker is removed. Figure 2-9 shows the relationship between Makes and Models.

The final set of relationships to create is between Models and Colors. The relationship is set up between the Models table and the ModelXREFColor table, and the Color table and ModelXREFColor table.

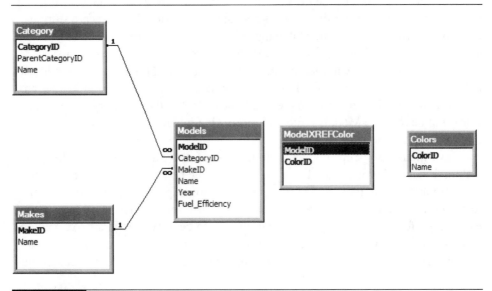

FIGURE 2-9 Makes to Models relationship

First, drag the ModelID field from the ModelXREFColor table to the ModelID field in the Models table. Then create the relationship. In this case it makes sense to enforce a cascading delete referential integrity. If a model is incorrectly set up in the database and color relationships were set up, then if the model is deleted, any colors set up for that model should also be deleted. Note that only the relationship is deleted, not the colors as well.

Second, drag the ColorID from the Colors table to the ModelXREFColor table and drop it on the ColorID field. It is hard to imagine when a color would be deleted from the database. If it is, we also want to delete any relationships to models since any existing records would point to an invalid color. We would not want to leave any dangling records in the ModelXREFColor table that do not point to an existing color. Figure 2-10 shows the relationship among the tables.

This three-way relationship depicts the many-to-many relationship between colors and models. Many models relate to many colors.

With that, we have completed the design of our database and implemented it in Access. Overall, this makes for a very simple database implementation and the application prototyping can begin.

Upsizing to SQL Server

Now for the gravy ... the database built in Access can be upsized to an enterprise SQL Server database with just a few clicks. Access provides a built-in Upsizing Wizard that makes the process very simple.

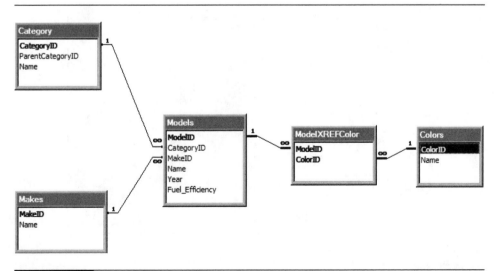

FIGURE 2-10   ModelXREFColor, Models, and Colors relationships

You will need to have SQL Server available either on the network or on your local system. As mentioned in the book introduction, it is assumed you have basic SQL Server skills for exercises involving the use of SQL Server.

We will first walk through the wizard and then talk about the ramifications of the upsizing. On the Tools menu select Database Utilities, then Upsizing Wizard. Figure 2-11 shows the startup of the Upsizing Wizard.

In this case a new database is being created, so select that option. Click the Next button to continue.

The next screen requires that you select your server where the database will be created. Select the appropriate server and security. The database will be named Models (you can keep the ModelsSQL that is defaulted). Figure 2-12 shows the wizard screen.

Next, you are given the option of selecting the tables to export. In this case we want to export all of the tables to the new database. Figure 2-13 shows the selection.

The next step in the wizard is to set the table attributes you would like to export to the new database. If you select the Indexes check box, the Upsizing Wizard upsizes all indexes. The Upsizing Wizard converts Microsoft Access primary keys

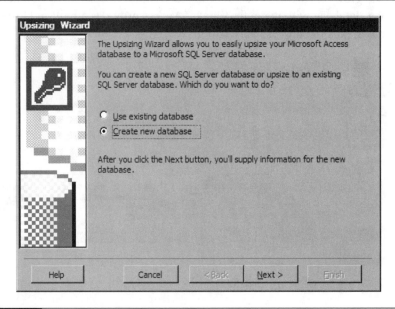

FIGURE 2-11   Upsizing Wizard startup

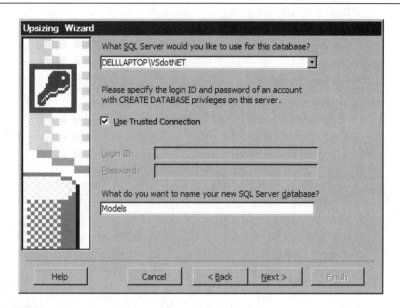

FIGURE 2-12   Selecting the SQL Server database

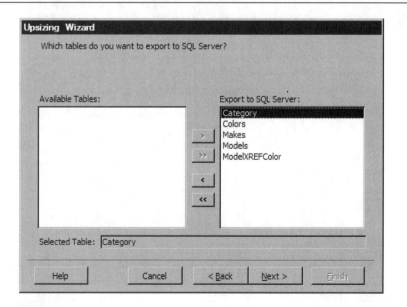

FIGURE 2-13   Selecting tables for export

to Microsoft SQL Server nonclustered, unique indexes, and marks them as SQL Server primary keys.

Validation rules, which can be set up on the table fields, are uploaded as update and insert triggers in SQL Server. And, referential integrity set up for the table relationships can be uploaded either as triggers or by using declared referential integrity (DRI). Triggers are a good option if you are using the cascading update or delete capability of Access. In this case we are, so that option will be selected. Additional details on how Access handles the upsizing of table attributes can be found in the Access Help documents.

The next option relates to whether you want to keep Access' built-in timestamp data that tracks when a record has changed. In general, you probably do not want to keep this data unless you are going to manage timestamp data explicitly in the enterprise application.

The last option is to indicate if only the table structure should be uploaded or if data should be uploaded as well. The fact that Access can upload data provides a powerful tool for manipulating data in Access and then easily exporting it to SQL Server. In this example we have no data to upsize, so the option will not be selected. Figure 2-14 shows the Table Attributes dialog box.

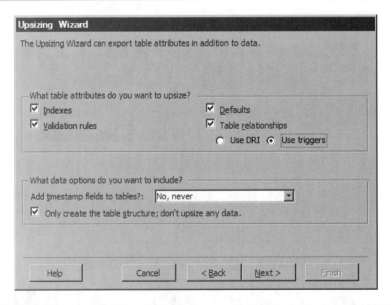

FIGURE 2-14   Upsize Wizard Table Attributes dialog box

The next dialog box provides options for working with the new SQL Server database. An Access client/server application or ADP front end to the database can be created. The tables can be linked in Access, or no application can be created. In this case, we are only interested in the creation of the new database in SQL Server. So, no application changes should be selected. Figure 2-15 shows the dialog box.

The last dialog box simply confirms that you are ready to upsize the database. Click Finish to start the process.

When the upsizing is completed, a report is generated that indicates what was upsized and how it was upsized. Tables created, fields, and any triggers that are created are all detailed in the report.

Now let's take a look at what was created by going into SQL Enterprise Manager. Or, alternately, you can view the database tables in Visual Studio .NET if you do not have the SQL Enterprise tools. Figure 2-16 shows Enterprise Manager with the Models database expanded. Note the highlighted table fields.

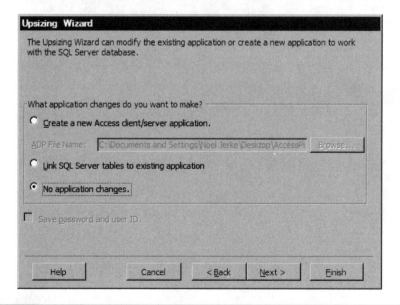

FIGURE 2-15   Upsizing Wizard Application Changes dialog box

Upsizing to SQL Server

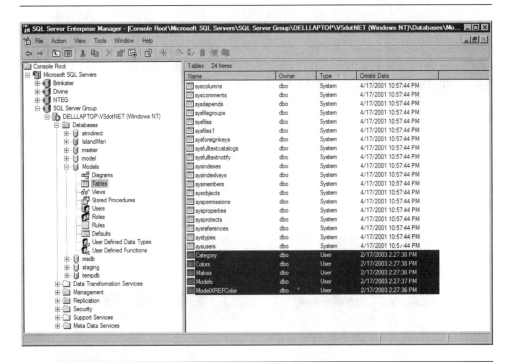

FIGURE 2-16   Models database

Select the ModelXREFColor table, right-click, and select Design Table. Remember that the primary key of the table is the two fields combined. Note the Key icon next to each field in Figure 2-17.

Finally, let's look at one of the triggers created. Remember that we enforced referential integrity on all of the tables. And, for the Colors and Models tables, we enforced a cascading delete in ModelXREFColor if a model or color was removed. Right-click on the Colors table and select All Tasks, then select Manage Triggers. In the Trigger window that pops up, select the T_Colors_DTrig trigger. Figure 2-18 shows the trigger.

If you look at the other tables, you will note that triggers are in place that ensure a foreign key cannot be entered that doesn't exist in the related table.

The last thing to look at is the translation of data types from Access to SQL Server. All of the text values are converted to nvarchar with the equivalent character lengths. The primary keys are all converted to int data types. In general, there isn't too much to worry about when converting data to SQL Server. Note that the Upsizing Wizard does convert all text to Unicode format.

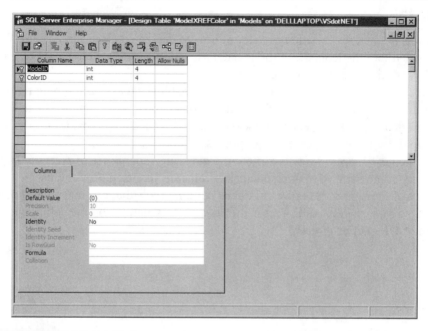

FIGURE 2-17   ModelXREFColor Table

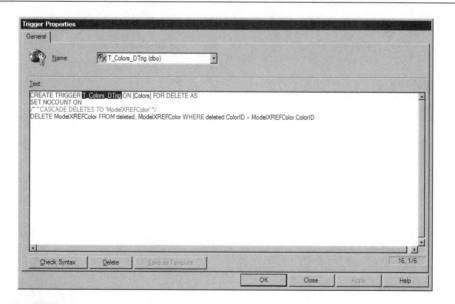

FIGURE 2-18   Colors cascading delete trigger

Summary

That was a quick review and refresher of how to design databases in Access. While Access isn't a full-fledged enterprise database, all of the key components of good database design can be implemented in Access.

Access also provides for a powerful and flexible database prototyping platform that can be utilized during the software development process. It can then be uploaded to a full-fledged SQL Server enterprise database. This capability provides for flexibility and rapid development in the design process.

In the next chapter we will explore the querying capabilities of Access. Queries are a key component of making databases valuable and useful for end users. As we will see, Access provides powerful query building tools that can make rapid query development possible. And, Access imposes few restrictions on the complexity of writing SQL queries directly.

Chapter 3

Building Advanced Queries with the Query Wizard

Access provides several tools for achieving professional results when it comes to building database queries, including the Simple Query Wizard, pivot tables, and the Crosstab Query Wizard. In this chapter and the next we are going to look at how the Access query engine can be leveraged to build complex queries quickly and effectively.

The Access Query Engine

Access provides a powerful querying engine that is based on the Structured Query Language (SQL). In general, queries that are built in Access follow the same rules and structure of the ANSI 92 SQL standard. There are extensions to the language that Access utilizes, such as its method for embedding variable values into the SQL query and certain Access-specific keywords. Queries written for SQL Server should, for the most part, work fine in Access. Likewise, basic queries generated in Access can be used in ANSI 92 SQL–compliant databases.

The Access Query Wizard provides a very useful tool for building SQL queries. It is by no means a super SQL generator that allows you to define and build any type of query. But, for very specific tasks, it can be an incredibly useful tool for query generation. In the context of building prototype applications in Access, once again we will see that these queries will not have to be thrown away, but can also be used in an enterprise-level database.

As we are going through this chapter, keep a couple of things in mind. The first is that the query Design view provides even more flexibility in building queries. We will not be exploring the Design view in this chapter, but in Chapter 4 it will be explained in detail. The second thing to remember is that any of the SQL generated by the wizard or the Design view can be modified and extended using standard SQL syntax.

Reviewing the Data Sample

Before we get into the details of building queries with the wizard, we are going to need a data sample that we can query against. In the last chapter, an Access database was designed for holding automobile data. That same structure will be used for the examples in this chapter.

The tables will now need sample data. Download the database with sample data from www.osborne.com before digging into the examples in this chapter.

Introducing the Simple Query Wizard

The Query Wizard is just that—a step-by-step process for selecting data to query and defining characteristics of the query. There are four steps that take place in the Simple Query Wizard, as follows:

1. Selecting tables and fields to be included in the query.

2. Determining if the query should return row-by-row results or if it should provide summary data.

3. For summary results, the fields to summarize are selected.

4. Naming and viewing the query.

That is it for the steps. As we will see, the real power is hidden under the covers. We will review several examples of what the Query Wizard will produce and how these queries can be leveraged as a useful tool in your database arsenal.

NOTE *The Query Wizard only builds select queries where data is returned. It does not build insert, update, or delete queries.*

Quickly Create Joins

At times, there can be nothing more tedious then building multiple joins of tables, especially when you have a lot of named fields to return. In this author's experience, this is where working with the Query Wizard to whip out a quick query can be quite useful.

TIP *When working with SQL Server databases, consider keeping an Access database handy that has the SQL tables linked to it. You can use Access to build complex queries quickly and copy the SQL right into a stored procedure in SQL Server. Writing the SQL queries from scratch can be very time-consuming, whereas using Access can reduce the frustration of building handwritten queries.*

For our first look at the wizard, we are going to build a query that will join together the color and model data. To get started, open the Access database and switch to the Queries objects. Next, run the Create Query by Using Wizard option.

The first screen of the query, shown in Figure 3-1, allows us to pick the data fields we want to show in our query.

As you will see, queries also show up in the Tables/Queries drop-down box. Select queries in Access can be thought of like views in SQL Server. The returned fields from the query can be in turn queried against.

To join together the color and model data, the fields from each table will need to be selected. Select the Models table from the Tables/Queries drop-down box. Then click on the double arrow to add all of the fields to the Selected Fields list box.

Next, select the Colors table from the Tables/Queries drop-down box. Again click on the double arrow to select all of the fields and place them in the Selected Fields list box. Now your dialog box should look like Figure 3-2.

That is it for this step. Click on the Next button to continue. The next screen gives us a couple of options. The first is to show a Detail view, which just means that all of the rows from the joined tables are returned. The second option is Summary, which will instruct the wizard to aggregate data on fields. An example of how to use the Summary option will be shown later in the chapter. For this example, select the Detail option. Then click on the Next button to go to the last screen of the wizard.

This last dialog box, shown in Figure 3-3, simply allows you to name the query and choose whether to go into design mode or to execute/open the query. Keep the defaults and click Finish to see the query results.

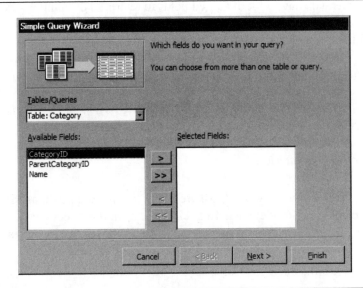

FIGURE 3-1   Field Selection Wizard dialog box

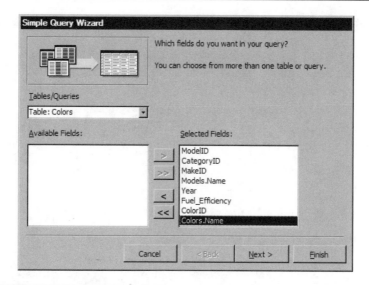

FIGURE 3-2   Colors and Models data fields selected

The query is opened and the results are displayed, as shown in Figure 3-4. All of the fields selected are returned, and basically we see all of the models and color options displayed.

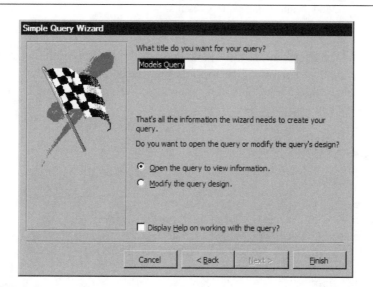

FIGURE 3-3   Query Wizard final dialog screen

Introducing the Simple Query Wizard

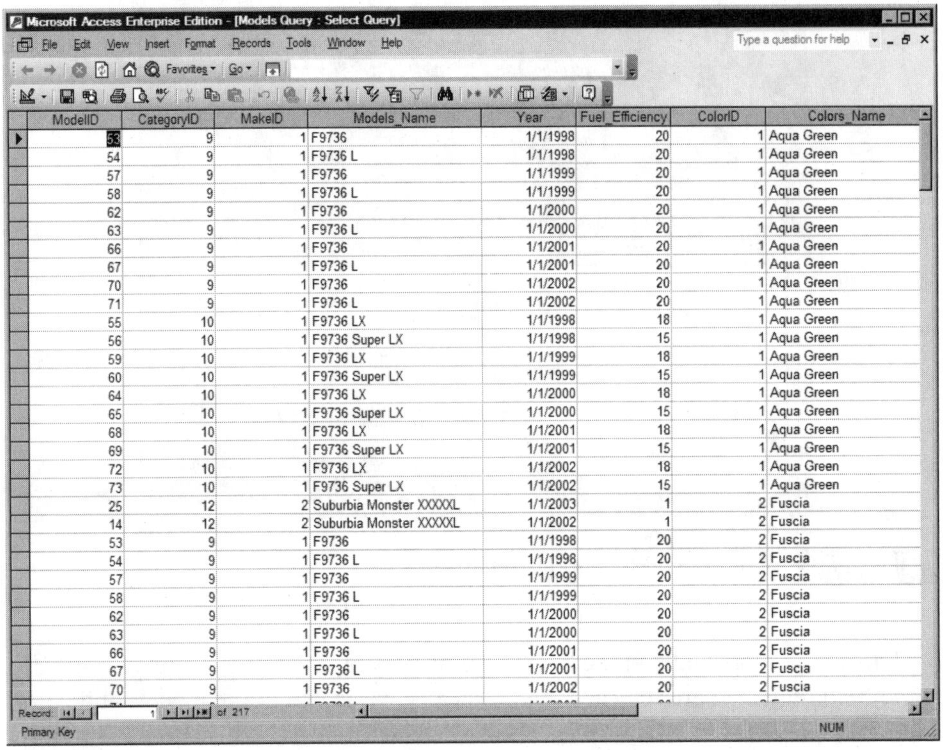

ModelID	CategoryID	MakeID	Models_Name	Year	Fuel_Efficiency	ColorID	Colors_Name
53	9	1	F9736	1/1/1998	20	1	Aqua Green
54	9	1	F9736 L	1/1/1998	20	1	Aqua Green
57	9	1	F9736	1/1/1999	20	1	Aqua Green
58	9	1	F9736 L	1/1/1999	20	1	Aqua Green
62	9	1	F9736	1/1/2000	20	1	Aqua Green
63	9	1	F9736 L	1/1/2000	20	1	Aqua Green
66	9	1	F9736	1/1/2001	20	1	Aqua Green
67	9	1	F9736 L	1/1/2001	20	1	Aqua Green
70	9	1	F9736	1/1/2002	20	1	Aqua Green
71	9	1	F9736 L	1/1/2002	20	1	Aqua Green
55	10	1	F9736 LX	1/1/1998	18	1	Aqua Green
56	10	1	F9736 Super LX	1/1/1998	15	1	Aqua Green
59	10	1	F9736 LX	1/1/1999	18	1	Aqua Green
60	10	1	F9736 Super LX	1/1/1999	15	1	Aqua Green
64	10	1	F9736 LX	1/1/2000	18	1	Aqua Green
65	10	1	F9736 Super LX	1/1/2000	15	1	Aqua Green
68	10	1	F9736 LX	1/1/2001	18	1	Aqua Green
69	10	1	F9736 Super LX	1/1/2001	15	1	Aqua Green
72	10	1	F9736 LX	1/1/2002	18	1	Aqua Green
73	10	1	F9736 Super LX	1/1/2002	15	1	Aqua Green
25	12	2	Suburbia Monster XXXXXL	1/1/2003	1	2	Fuscia
14	12	2	Suburbia Monster XXXXXL	1/1/2002	1	2	Fuscia
53	9	1	F9736	1/1/1998	20	2	Fuscia
54	9	1	F9736 L	1/1/1998	20	2	Fuscia
57	9	1	F9736	1/1/1999	20	2	Fuscia
58	9	1	F9736 L	1/1/1999	20	2	Fuscia
62	9	1	F9736	1/1/2000	20	2	Fuscia
63	9	1	F9736 L	1/1/2000	20	2	Fuscia
66	9	1	F9736	1/1/2001	20	2	Fuscia
67	9	1	F9736 L	1/1/2001	20	2	Fuscia
70	9	1	F9736	1/1/2002	20	2	Fuscia

FIGURE 3-4 Models and Colors query results

Now let's take a look at the SQL code that was generated by the wizard. To do this, click on the down arrow of the top-left View button on the toolbar. In the list of options, select SQL View. This view shows the SQL code created by the wizard. The code is shown in Listing 3-1.

Listing 3-1

```
SELECT
    Models.ModelID, Models.CategoryID,
    Models.MakeID, Models.Name AS Models_Name,
    Models.Year, Models.Fuel_Efficiency,
    Colors.ColorID, Colors.Name AS Colors_Name
FROM
     Models INNER JOIN
```

```
(Colors INNER JOIN ModelXREFColor
ON Colors.ColorID = ModelXREFColor.ColorID)
ON Models.ModelID = ModelXREFColor.ModelID;
```

The wizard did a good job creating the appropriate SQL for the query. The first thing to note is that both the Models and Colors tables have fields named "Name." The wizard used the SQL AS statement to return their values in unique names.

Because three tables are being joined together (remember, this is a many-to-many relationship), two joins are required to pull the data together. And, as expected, the wizard built the double inner join.

As this small demonstration shows, in a just a few clicks the wizard can spit out SQL code that would normally take some time to write by hand. Just consider if the tables had many more fields to be returned and required joining more than three tables. This is often the case in complex enterprise databases, so keeping the Access Query Wizard in your toolkit can be very useful and productive.

Before we move on to our next example, let's make a slight modification to the query and then execute it again. Let's suppose we just want to see model and color data for Sports Coupes, which is category 11, and order by the model name. In the SQL view, modify the query to include the where and order by clauses, as shown in Listing 3-2.

Listing 3-2

```
SELECT
    Models.ModelID, Models.CategoryID,
    Models.MakeID, Models.Name AS Models_Name,
    Models.Year, Models.Fuel_Efficiency,
    Colors.ColorID, Colors.Name AS Colors_Name
FROM
    Models INNER JOIN
    (Colors INNER JOIN ModelXREFColor
    ON Colors.ColorID = ModelXREFColor.ColorID)
    ON Models.ModelID = ModelXREFColor.ModelID
Where models.categoryid = 11
Order By Models.Name;
```

Once the modification is made, click the down arrow of the View button and select Datasheet view. The new query is shown with only models in category 11 displayed and sorted by the model name. Note that you have *not* saved the query yet. You can make modifications to the query until you are happy with it and then save it.

Building Complex Queries and PivotTable Views

One of the more powerful uses of the Access query capabilities is the ability to build complex queries quickly and then build a PivotTable view of the data. This is extremely useful when working with data imports or data exports. As we will see in Chapter 7, the ability to view import/export data relationships and verify data quickly is yet another of the great features of Access.

> **TIP**   *For an introduction to PivotTables and PivotCharts, see Appendix B.*

In our automobile model database, we have multiple sets of data combined to provide the model data. One logical view of the data is by category, by year, by make. Building the query to view this data in SQL would not be a trivial task given the multiple joins. And, if we want to double-check the validity of the data returned by the query as well as the integrity of the data itself, it would be hard to do with just a row-by-row listing because a hierarchical view is not returned from standard query results.

The Query Wizard

To build a query quickly that allows us to view the data, the query wizard will be utilized to create the query, and then a Pivot Table view of the query data will be created. To get started, click the Create Query by Using Wizard option on the Queries window.

For this query, we are essentially going to view data from all of the tables. But, to make the view useful, we really don't need primary and foreign keys showing up in the returned data.

For the Category, Colors, and Makes tables, add only the Name field to the Selected Fields list box. Do not add the ID fields.

> **TIP**   *If you are working on importing or exporting data and want to ensure IDs match up properly, consider adding the appropriate ID fields to validate against the original data.*

For the Models table, add all of the fields except MakeID, ModelID, and CategoryID. Because we set up the relationships between the tables in the last chapter, the Query Wizard is smart enough to know how to build the joins even if the primary and foreign key fields are not selected. And, for that reason, you do not need to select either of the fields from the ModelXREFColor table.

Click the Next button to go to the next dialog screen. We are not going to do any summarizing of the data at this stage, so click Next again. Finally, keep the defaults on the last dialog screen and click Finish. Your final query results should look something like Figure 3-5.

Basically, every model in every color for every year is listed with its corresponding make and category. The SQL query that was generated is shown in Listing 3-3.

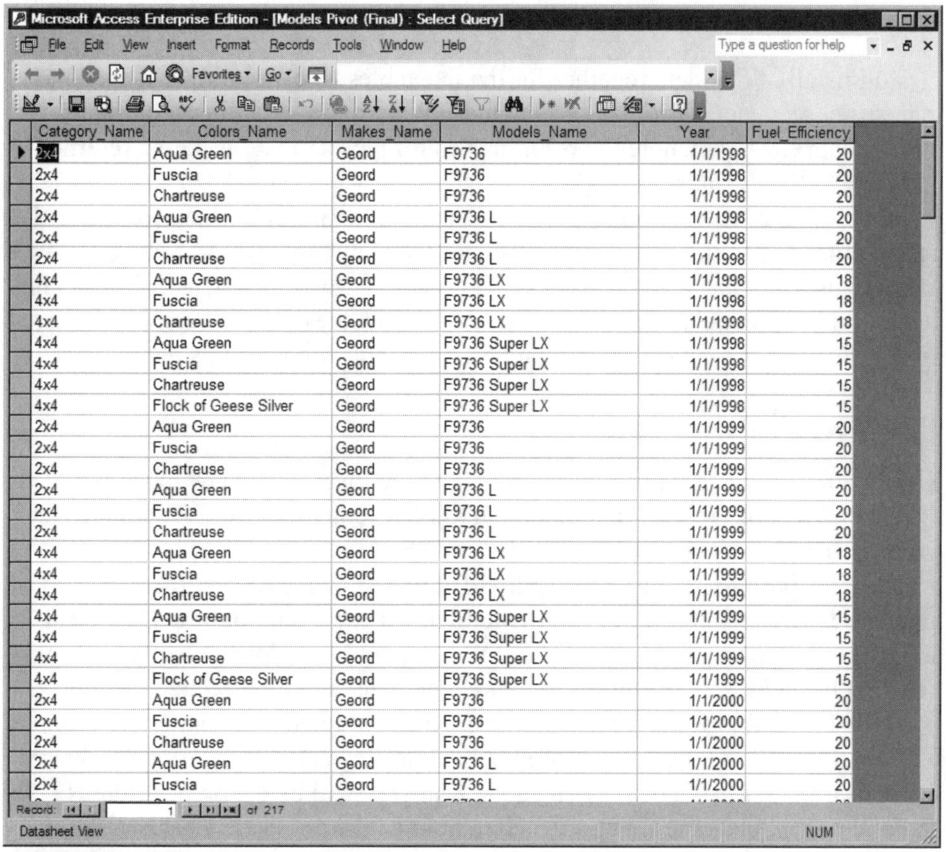

Category_Name	Colors_Name	Makes_Name	Models_Name	Year	Fuel_Efficiency
2x4	Aqua Green	Geord	F9736	1/1/1998	20
2x4	Fuscia	Geord	F9736	1/1/1998	20
2x4	Chartreuse	Geord	F9736	1/1/1998	20
2x4	Aqua Green	Geord	F9736 L	1/1/1998	20
2x4	Fuscia	Geord	F9736 L	1/1/1998	20
2x4	Chartreuse	Geord	F9736 L	1/1/1998	20
4x4	Aqua Green	Geord	F9736 LX	1/1/1998	18
4x4	Fuscia	Geord	F9736 LX	1/1/1998	18
4x4	Chartreuse	Geord	F9736 LX	1/1/1998	18
4x4	Aqua Green	Geord	F9736 Super LX	1/1/1998	15
4x4	Fuscia	Geord	F9736 Super LX	1/1/1998	15
4x4	Chartreuse	Geord	F9736 Super LX	1/1/1998	15
4x4	Flock of Geese Silver	Geord	F9736 Super LX	1/1/1998	15
2x4	Aqua Green	Geord	F9736	1/1/1999	20
2x4	Fuscia	Geord	F9736	1/1/1999	20
2x4	Chartreuse	Geord	F9736	1/1/1999	20
2x4	Aqua Green	Geord	F9736 L	1/1/1999	20
2x4	Fuscia	Geord	F9736 L	1/1/1999	20
2x4	Chartreuse	Geord	F9736 L	1/1/1999	20
4x4	Aqua Green	Geord	F9736 LX	1/1/1999	18
4x4	Fuscia	Geord	F9736 LX	1/1/1999	18
4x4	Chartreuse	Geord	F9736 LX	1/1/1999	18
4x4	Aqua Green	Geord	F9736 Super LX	1/1/1999	15
4x4	Fuscia	Geord	F9736 Super LX	1/1/1999	15
4x4	Chartreuse	Geord	F9736 Super LX	1/1/1999	15
4x4	Flock of Geese Silver	Geord	F9736 Super LX	1/1/1999	15
2x4	Aqua Green	Geord	F9736	1/1/2000	20
2x4	Fuscia	Geord	F9736	1/1/2000	20
2x4	Chartreuse	Geord	F9736	1/1/2000	20
2x4	Aqua Green	Geord	F9736 L	1/1/2000	20
2x4	Fuscia	Geord	F9736 L	1/1/2000	20

Record: 1 of 217

FIGURE 3-5   Query results for the Model data

Listing 3-3

```
SELECT
    Category.Name AS Category_Name, Colors.Name AS Colors_Name,
    Makes.Name AS Makes_Name, Models.Name AS Models_Name,
    Models.Year, Models.Fuel_Efficiency
FROM
    (Makes INNER JOIN (Category INNER JOIN
    Models ON Category.CategoryID = Models.CategoryID) ON
    Makes.MakeID = Models.MakeID) INNER JOIN
    (Colors INNER JOIN ModelXREFColor ON Colors.ColorID =
    ModelXREFColor.ColorID) ON Models.ModelID = ModelXREFColor.ModelID;
```

Pulling all of that data together for the five tables takes four inner joins done in the right sequence. Fortunately, the Query Wizard did all of the right things to make it happen. Again, note the result names for the Name fields being returned using the SQL AS statement.

If we were trying to proof our data to ensure it is valid, we likely would need to add an order by parameter and might also need to view subsets of the data by adding where clauses. Fortunately, Access has a built-in Query Pivot view that makes looking at the data in a hierarchical structure easy to do. And, the data can be quickly filtered as well. In the next section we will build a PivotTable view for this query.

The PivotTable View

Keeping the same query open, get started with the PivotTable view by clicking on the down arrow of the View button on the top-left toolbar. Select PivotTable View from the list. The PivotTable view is shown in Figure 3-6.

Note the pop-up toolbar with the field names showing. Also note that it automatically provides options on the toolbar for exploding out the Date field and looking at subsegments of the date. We will not be exploring that functionality here, but it can be very useful for working with date- and time-related data.

For a PivotTable view, we need to create the row and column structure of the view. In this case we want to explore the data starting at the category level. From there we want to see the data by category. Category will be the pivot columns across the top. Select the Category_Name field on the pop-up toolbar. On the bottom of the toolbar, select Column Area from the drop-down list. Then click the

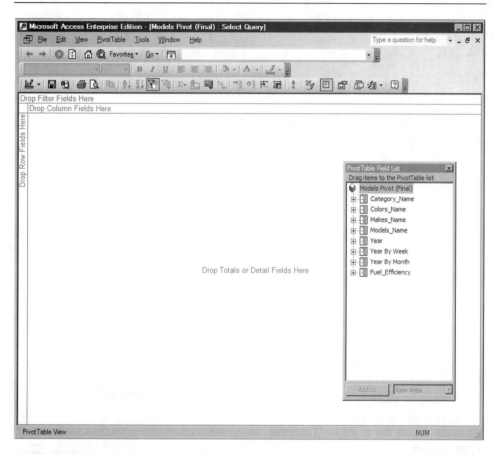

FIGURE 3-6   PivotTable view

Add To button. That will place the Category_Name field in the column area.
Figure 3-7 shows the updated pivot table.

Next we will want to view the models by year within the category. So, the Year
field will become a subcolumn under the category name. Select the Year
field and add it to the column area. Figure 3-8 shows the updated PivotTable.

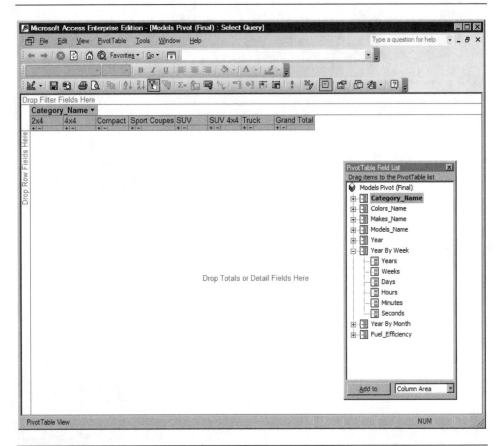

Category_Name added to the PivotTable

Now we are ready to show the model data, which is the detail data of the PivotTable. Select the Models_Name field and select Detail Data in the drop-down list. Then click the Add To button. Follow the same steps for the Makes_Name, Colors_Name and Fuel_Efficiency fields. You may not see these appear immediately. To see the data, click on the + sign below the year value and the make, model, and color data will be displayed for that category for that year.

It might also be helpful to do some counts for the model data for that year. Right-click on the Models_Name column and select AutoCalc. In the drop-down

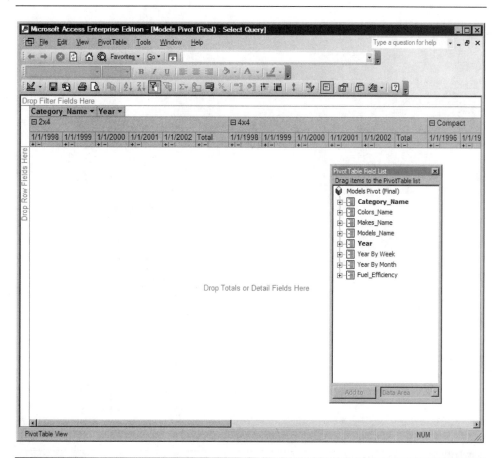

FIGURE 3-8   Updated PivotTable category name and year

list, select Count. When you do that a count of the number of models is calculated. Figure 3-9 shows the resulting PivotTable.

Now suppose you just want to see model data by category for the year 2000. Click the drop-down arrow by the Year column. A drop-down list of all of the Year values is shown. Uncheck the All option and check the 2000 option. For each category, only the Year 2000 models are shown. If you scroll to the end of the PivotTable, a count of all the models for all categories is given for the year 2000.

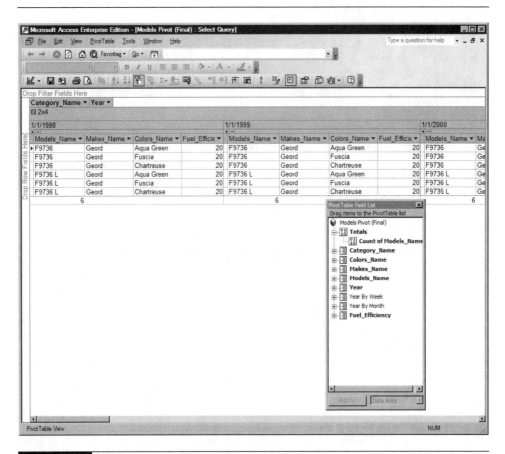

FIGURE 3-9 PivotTable with model, make, and color data by year by category

This is a great example of how using the built-in query capabilities and graphical nature of Access can make working with complex data much simpler. Keep in mind that all of these features are available when working with linked SQL tables or Access Data Projects.

NOTE *Working with PivotTables and data is a complex topic in and of itself. If you are interested in learning more, consider looking at* Access 2002®: The Complete Reference, *by Andersen (McGraw-Hill/Osborne, ISBN 0-07-213241-8).*

Building Summary and Crosstab Queries

Two additional areas where the Access Query Wizards can be particularly useful are in building summary and crosstab queries. These are queries that calculate values including sums, averages, etc. Earlier we noted the Summary option on the Simple Query Wizard. We will now build a quick example based on that functionality. There is also a Crosstab Query Wizard that can be utilized for creating summary results.

Summary Queries

Let's first build a summary query using the simple query wizard. Click the Create Query by Using Wizard option. In this example, a query will be built that counts the number of models by category and averages the fuel efficiency for the category. From the Category table, select all of the fields. From the Models table, select the Fuel_Efficiency field. Click the Next button to continue.

On the next screen, select the Summary option. When that option is selected, the Summary Options button becomes active. Click the button. A new screen is shown that provides options for summarizing the data, as shown in Figure 3-10. In this case, for Fuel_Efficiency, select the Avg, Min, and Max options. On the lower right of the screen, select the Count Records in Models check box. Note that the wizard is smart enough to recognize the one-to-many relationship between categories and models and will provide the option to count the number of models.

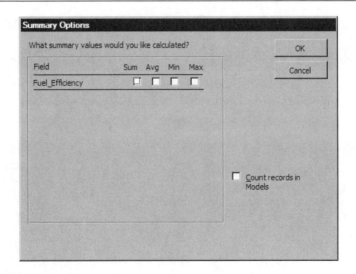

FIGURE 3-10   Summary Options dialog screen

Building Summary and
Crosstab Queries

Click OK to continue and then click the Next button. On the final screen, keep the defaults but name the query "Models Summary By Category". Then click Finish. Figure 3-11 shows the results using the provided sample data.

Note that for each category with assigned models, the average, minimum, and maximum fuel efficiencies are calculated, as well as the number of models in the category. Listing 3-4 shows the SQL code generated by the query.

Listing 3-4

```
SELECT
       DISTINCTROW Category.CategoryID,
       Category.ParentCategoryID, Category.Name,
       Avg(Models.Fuel_Efficiency) AS [Avg Of Fuel_Efficiency],
       Min(Models.Fuel_Efficiency) AS [Min Of Fuel_Efficiency],
       Max(Models.Fuel_Efficiency) AS [Max Of Fuel_Efficiency],
       Count(*) AS [Count Of Models]
FROM
       Category INNER JOIN Models ON Category.CategoryID = Models.CategoryID
GROUP BY
       Category.CategoryID, Category.ParentCategoryID, Category.Name;
```

The generated SQL code is another great example of why using the Query Wizards can be extremely useful. From a SQL standpoint, the query isn't overly

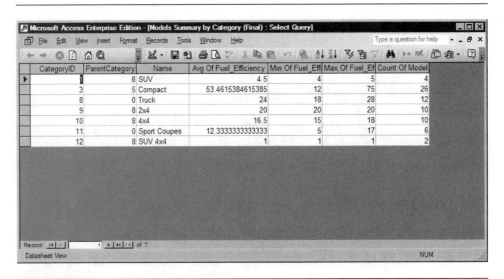

CategoryID	ParentCategory	Name	Avg Of Fuel_Efficiency	Min Of Fuel_Effi	Max Of Fuel_Ef	Count Of Model
1	8	SUV	4.5	4	5	4
3	5	Compact	53.4615384615385	12	75	26
8	0	Truck	24	18	28	12
9	8	2x4	20	20	20	10
10	8	4x4	16.5	15	18	10
11	0	Sport Coupes	12.3333333333333	5	17	6
12	8	SUV 4x4	1	1	1	2

FIGURE 3-11   Access summary query results

complex—yet at the same time, it isn't simple either. But, the code was generated in just a few seconds, which definitely makes life easier. To double-check that everything makes sense in the query, take a look at the SUV 4x4 category (id 12). Note that the average fuel efficiency is 1. Let's change the average. Add a new record to the Models table as follows:

- CategoryID: 12

- MakeID: 1

- Name: Hydrogen X3498

- Year: 1/1/2004

- Fuel_Efficiency: 95

NOTE   *If you are using the sample data from the download site, this row of data will already be added.*

By adding this new hydrogen-powered vehicle to the SUV 4x4 category, we should see the average fuel efficiency for the category increase dramatically. Now run the query. The fuel efficiency for the SUV 4x4 category has now increased to 32.33 and the number of vehicles in the category to 3.

Crosstab Queries

The crosstab query is another Query Wizard that can be useful when reviewing and working with summary data. For example, if we were importing model data into our database, we might want to look at certain counts to verify the data imported properly. A crosstab query would be a perfect tool for the verification. In this example, a query will be built to summarize what years each model was available on the market.

TIP   *If you want to combine multiple tables of data and build a crosstab query, you will first have to create a standard query, and then select that query in the Crosstab Wizard.*

To launch the Crosstab Wizard, from the query screen, click the New toolbar button. A dialog box appears with several options— select the Crosstab Query Wizard option. Figure 3-12 shows the initial dialog box for the wizard.

Select the Models table and click the Next button to continue. The next screen is where the left column of the results is set. Think of this like a spreadsheet—we

Building Summary and Crosstab Queries

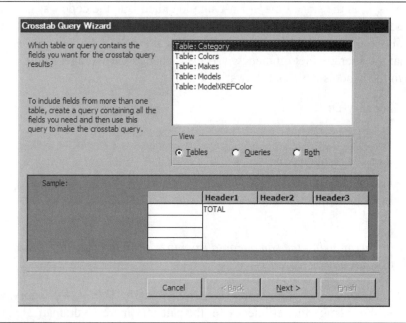

FIGURE 3-12   Crosstab Query Wizard dialog box

are setting the label for each row. In this case, it will be the model name. Add the Name to the Selected Fields column. The preview sample is updated to show what the result will look like. Figure 3-13 shows the Wizard dialog screen.

> **TIP** *To create a crosstab query, you need to have at least three fields of data. Two fields will display as column and row headings in the crosstab query. The remaining field will supply the data to be calculated.*

Click the Next button to continue. In this screen we are going to set the columns of the query. In this case, it will be the model years. Select the Year field. When you do so, the preview sample is updated to show the column heading. Figure 3-14 shows the Wizard dialog screen.

Click the Next button to continue. The wizard is smart enough to recognize that the columns are based on date data. It gives us options to break down the date data in our query. In this case, we are only interested in year-by-year data, so select Year. Then click the Next button to continue.

The last screen defines what calculation should be shown for each model year. In this case, we don't really have anything specific we want to be calculated other than a count indicator that a model exists for that year. So, select the ModelID field

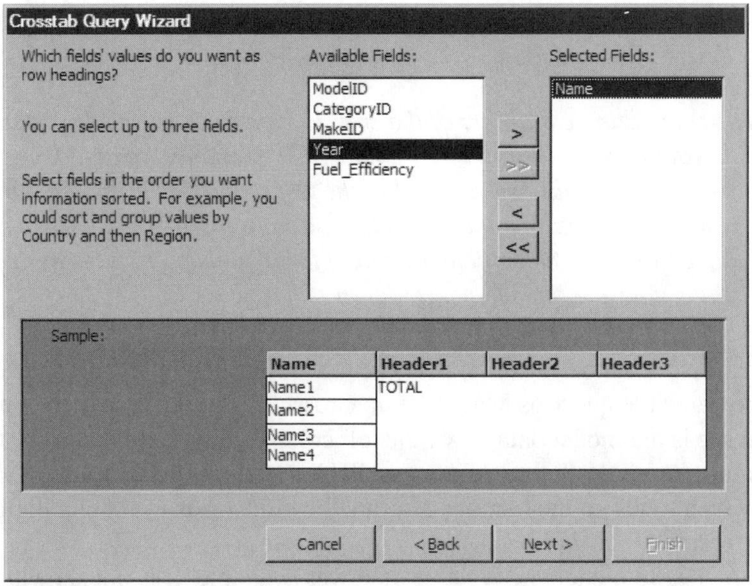

FIGURE 3-13   Setting the crosstab query row headings

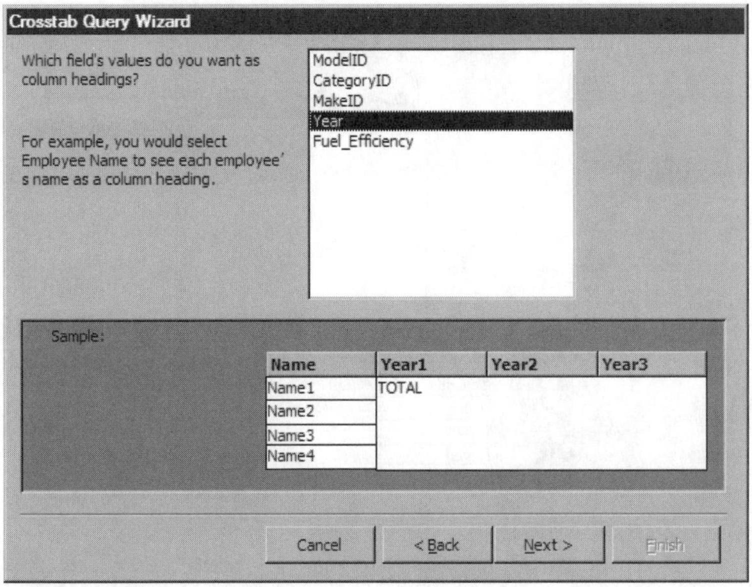

FIGURE 3-14   Setting the crosstab query column headings

and the Count function. We also want to summarize each row. By doing that, the query will total the number of years the model was available on the market. Figure 3-15 shows the Wizard dialog screen.

> **NOTE** *The calculating capability of the crosstab query is extremely useful when you want to report on or verify counts. For example, we could create a crosstab query that averages all of the test scores for a student. Or, in our car models example, if the example data were more extensive, we could build an average fuel efficiency rating for a model across multiple years (as it is now, the fuel efficiency doesn't change).*

Click the Next button to continue to the next screen. Keep the defaults on this screen and name the query as Model-Years Crosstab. The query is then generated. What you see is the model data down the left column, the years across the top, and a 1 indicating each year the model was available. There is also a Total of ModelID column, which totals up the number of years the model was available. Figure 3-16 shows the result.

Note the F9736 model and what years it was available. It is not showing up for years 1996 and 1997, and a quick check of the table data shows that to be correct. Listing 3-5 shows the SQL generated by the query.

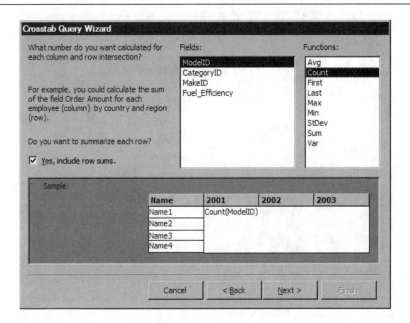

FIGURE 3-15 Setting the calculated values for the crosstab query

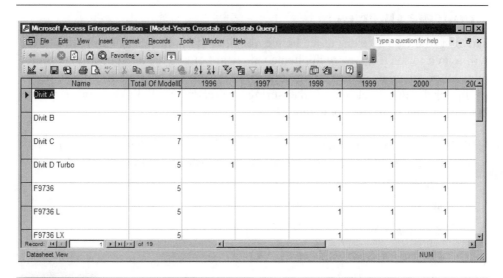

FIGURE 3-16   Models by Year crosstab query

Listing 3-5

```
TRANSFORM
    Count(Models.ModelID) AS CountOfModelID
SELECT
    Models.Name, Count(Models.ModelID) AS [Total Of ModelID]
FROM Models
GROUP BY Models.Name
PIVOT Format([Year],"yyyy");
```

If you upsize the database to SQL Server, including the data, and try to run this query, you will find that the syntax isn't supported. In particular, Access' use of Transform and Pivot are not supported in the SQL engine. But, you can run this query against linked SQL Server tables. So, if you have need of a quick crosstab querying capability, Access is a handy tool to have.

Duplicates and Unmatched Queries

There are two additional Query Wizards available for use. Both can be found by clicking the New toolbar button on the Query window. These final two Query Wizards allow us to analyze our data further to ensure it has appropriate referential integrity.

Duplicate Queries

The first of the queries discussed here is for finding duplicates. Running this query will search to see if there are duplicate values in fields. This is especially helpful when importing data and ensuring duplicate keys are not entered. It can also be useful for doing data cleanup and ensuring that records with different primary keys but similar field data are not entered.

TIP

You can also find duplicates in the results of an existing query. To run a quick test of this query, build a duplicate model record in the Models table as follows:

- *CategoryID: 12*
- *MakeID: 2*
- *Name: Suburbia Monster XXXXXL*
- *Year: 1/1/2003*
- *Fuel_Efficiency: 1*

This duplicates all of the values of an existing Models record except for the ModelID value, which is autogenerated. Now let's build the query. Click the New button of the Query Window toolbar. Select the Find Duplicates Query Wizard. On the first screen, select the Models table.

The next Wizard dialog screen gives us options to indicate what fields we want to check for duplicates. Note that it will check all of the fields together (using AND logic) to see if there are any duplicates. In our case, let's check the Name, Year, and Fuel_Efficiency fields. Click the Next button to continue.

This screen gives the option of picking fields we would like displayed in addition to the fields that are checked for duplicates. In this case, it would be very helpful to show the ModelID as well. Add the ModelID field to the Additional Fields list. Click the Next button to continue.

On the last screen, accept the default values and keep the suggested query name. Click Finish to show the query results. The query results are shown in Figure 3-17.

As expected, our two duplicate records appear in the results. The SQL generated by the query is shown in Listing 3-6.

Listing 3-6

```
SELECT
    Models.Name, Models.Year, Models.Fuel_Efficiency, Models.ModelID
```

```
FROM
     Models
WHERE
     (
        ((Models.Name) In
           (SELECT [Name] FROM [Models] As Tmp
            GROUP BY [Name],[Year],[Fuel_Efficiency] HAVING Count(*)>1
            And [Year] = [Models].[Year] And
        [Fuel_Efficiency] = [Models].[Fuel_Efficiency])))
ORDER BY
     Models.Name, Models.Year, Models.Fuel_Efficiency;
```

In this example, we see one of the more sophisticated queries created in the chapter examples. The where clause actually executes a subquery that looks for grouped duplicates.

Unmatched Queries

The last query option looks for unmatched or "dangling" records. If, for example, we had a model CategoryID foreign key that pointed to a category that didn't exist, we could use this Query Wizard to find the unmatched model record. Because we built the database to have strong referential integrity in the last chapter, it would be pretty hard for this to happen in our database. But, as we all know, when importing data or working with suboptimized databases, this can occur all too often. This wizard can be extremely helpful in ferreting out dead or improperly built data.

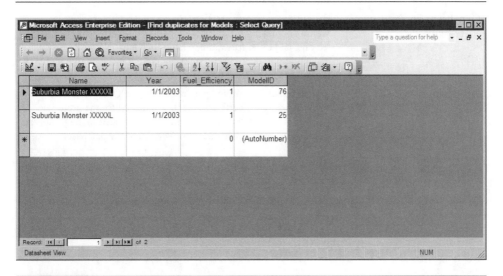

FIGURE 3-17 Duplicate query results

Access Query Wizard Best Practices

By now you have seen in this chapter that Access can be a very powerful tool for building queries for application development use, as well as for building queries to validate data. Table 3-1 provides some guidelines for when to consider leveraging the Query Wizards presented in the chapter.

Case	Description
Data mining	The pivot features and crosstab query features of Access can make simple data mining easy to perform. The wizards and GUI interface can support quick querying and viewing of results. Of course, Access certainly doesn't replace full-featured data mining tools. But, in a pinch they are easy to use.
Data import	When importing data, especially from nonrelational sources, the Query Wizards can be very helpful in building views of the data that target a designated structure. Then the SQL query can be modified to insert the data into the new structure. Also, with the macro and VBA programmatic interfaces of Access, massaging data for import can be easily done. The duplicate and unmatched Query Wizards can also be used to validate the data integrity quickly.
Data export	If you need to export data in a particular structure, the Query Wizards can be utilized to create the structure. In particular for exporting in spreadsheet-like formats, the Crosstab Query Wizard can be useful because it allows you to view the data structurally and filter it easily.
Complex or lengthy queries	Having a rapid query creation tool can help with productivity. Writing complex SQL queries by hand can be time-consuming, tedious, and often frustrating. Using the Query Wizard tools can make building queries with multiple table joins and large numbers of fields a much easier task.
Prototyping	If you are building prototypes in Access, the Query Wizard tools come in handy for getting at the data required for the prototype quickly. As noted, the SQL generated and utilized in the prototype can then be used in the enterprise version of the database.

TABLE 3-1   Access Query Utilization Guidelines

Summary

In this chapter we explored the various Access Query Wizards and query building features of Access. These straightforward tools can be very useful and productive for your enterprise development efforts. Whether you are prototyping, validating, importing, exporting, or just need quick queries, the Query Wizards should always be considered as an option for achieving professional results.

In the next chapter, we will explore the Query Design view and how to build more complex queries in Access, including insert, update, and delete queries. We will also discuss techniques for moving the queries to SQL Server.

Summary

Chapter 4

Building Advanced Queries with the Query Design View

In the last chapter we explored how to leverage the Access Query Wizards to create complex queries and work with data. In this chapter, we are going to explore the Query Design view, which allows us to construct queries in a visual designer. As with the Query Wizards, the SQL code created by the Design view is always accessible and can be modified. In addition, with the Design view, update and appends (e.g., insert) queries can also be created.

Introducing the Access Design View

The Design view in Access provides a graphical interface for creating SQL queries. From a relational view of the tables, the database fields can be added to the query and the SQL is generated behind the scenes.

NOTE *For our examples in this chapter, we are going to be using the models database constructed in Chapter 2 with the added sample data used in Chapter 3.*

To get started working with the Design view, on the Queries window double-click the Create Query in Design View option. This will bring up the Design view and a dialog box for selecting what tables you want to use in your query. Figure 4-1 shows the screen.

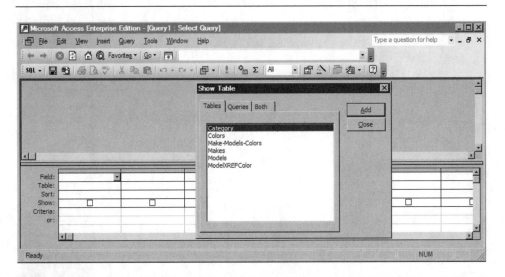

FIGURE 4-1   Access Design view with Table Selection dialog box

In this case, let's build a query that shows all of the models, in their respective categories, with all of the color options. In other words, a join between Category, Models, ModelXREFColor, and Colors. Select those four tables and close the Table Selection dialog box. You will note that the tables are added into the Design view and the relationships between the tables are shown. Figure 4-2 shows the Design view.

Now that the tables are added, we are ready to define what fields we would like to have shown in our query results. As with the Query Wizards, the primary and foreign keys do not have to be selected because the Design view SQL generated is smart enough to see the relationships and build the SQL query appropriately.

For this query, let's show the category name, model name, year, fuel efficiency, and color name. To add those fields to the query, simply select the field name from the appropriate table and drag it down to the grid at the bottom of the Design view. Drag all five fields to the grid. Figure 4-3 shows the updated Design view.

That is it—now the query is created. To see the results of the query, click the View toolbar button and select Datasheet View. The results of the query are then shown with all of the appropriate records by category, by model, by color. The

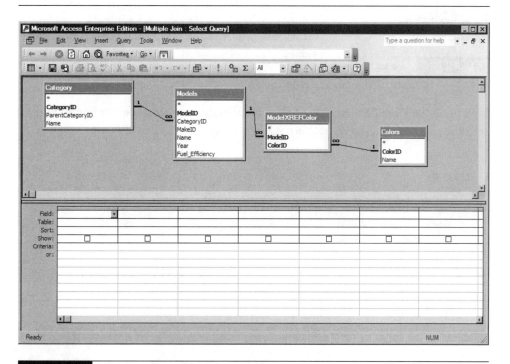

FIGURE 4-2   Design view with tables added

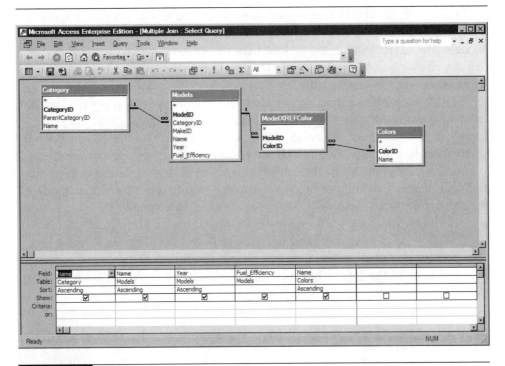

Design view with selected fields

SQL generated for the view can be seen by clicking the View toolbar button and selecting SQL View. The generated SQL code is shown in Listing 4-1.

Listing 4-1

```
SELECT
    Category.Name, Models.Name, Models.Year,
    Models.Fuel_Efficiency, Colors.Name
FROM
    (Category INNER JOIN Models ON Category.CategoryID=Models.CategoryID)
    INNER JOIN (Colors INNER JOIN ModelXREFColor ON
    Colors.ColorID=ModelXREFColor.ColorID) ON
    Models.ModelID=ModelXREFColor.ModelID
ORDER BY
    Category.Name, Models.Name, Models.Year, Colors.Name;
```

The query includes the appropriate inner joins to combine the tables and return the results. This was created pretty easily given the Design view. Using the Design view, we can also modify the query—for example, suppose we want to see only models for the year 2000. The grid interface on the Design view makes this easy to set the sort order for the fields.

Switch back to the Design view for the query. On the design grid there is a row labeled Criteria. For the Year column, we will want to set the value to 1/1/2000. When the value is set, the date value is enclosed by # symbols, which are used to delimit dates in Access.

You can also set the sort criteria as well by selecting Ascending or Descending on the various columns. Note that the sort order will be from left to right. You can highlight a column and drag it left or right to change the column order. In this case, set all of the name fields to be sorted in ascending order.

Now execute the query and you'll see that only year 2000 models are listed. The SQL for the query is updated as showing in Listing 4-2.

Listing 4-2

```
SELECT
      Category.Name, Models.Name, Models.Year,
      Models.Fuel_Efficiency, Colors.Name
FROM
      (Category INNER JOIN Models ON Category.CategoryID =
      Models.CategoryID) INNER JOIN
      (Colors INNER JOIN ModelXREFColor ON Colors.ColorID =
      ModelXREFColor.ColorID) ON Models.ModelID =
      ModelXREFColor.ModelID
WHERE (((Models.Year)=#1/1/2000#))
ORDER BY Category.Name, Models.Name, Models.Year, Colors.Name;
```

Note the where and order by clauses that are now added to the query. While this example seems simple, if you are building complex queries where a number of criteria need to be set, using the Design view can make life a lot simpler. As we will see in later examples, the criteria clause can include Ands, Ors, and subselects.

Building Complex Queries with Design View

Now that a moderately complex multiple table join has been built using the Design view, let's get a little more complicated and see how we can leverage the Design view, and yet also mix in a little SQL to create a fairly complex query.

Our example will utilize the Models table. Let's suppose we need to build a query that will show all models that do not have a ModelID greater than or equal to 10 and whose model name does not contain "monster" in it. To show a little more complexity, we want to do this using the Not In SQL statement and use some subqueries to select the records we don't want. We can then return all of the records not in the records that we don't want. Confused? Things will become clearer in a minute.

First, create a new query in the Design view by clicking on Create Query in Design View. Add the Models table to the query. Next, drag the ModelID and Name fields to the Design view grid. These will be the two columns returned in the query. Also set the sort for ModelID to be ascending. At this stage, your query should look like Figure 4-4.

The next step is to build the criteria for our query. We have two criteria: we don't want models with an ID of less than 10, and we don't want models with "monster" anywhere in the name.

First let's build a quick query by hand that will return all models with an ID of less than 10. Listing 4-3 shows the SQL code.

Listing 4-3

```
select modelid from models where modelid < 10
```

This simple select returns all of the ModelIDs with a value less than 10. Next let's build a quick query that will return all models with "monster" in the name. Listing 4-4 shows the query.

Listing 4-4

```
select modelid from models where name like "*monster*"
```

In this query, all of the ModelIDs are returned where the model name has "monster" in the name.

> **TIP** *The * symbol is used in Access instead of the % symbol in SQL for wild carding the like match criteria. For example, "*monster" would return records that have "monster" at the end of the name (e.g., bigmonster) but not "monster" at the beginning (e.g., monstertruck).*

Next, we want to retrieve all of the records that are not found in the records returned by our two queries. So, these two queries become criteria for our main query. The final SQL where clause criteria is shown in Listing 4-5.

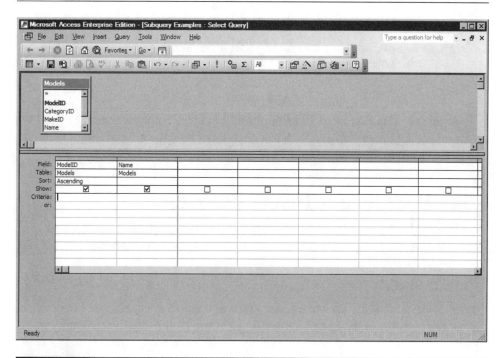

FIGURE 4-4   Models query setup

Listing 4-5

```
Not In (select modelid from models where modelid<10) And
Not In (select modelid from models where name like "*monster*")
```

Thus we want all records returned where the modelID is not found in either of the select statements in our criteria. To enter this into the Design view, the above SQL code goes into the criteria field for the ModelID column. Figure 4-5 shows the setup of the query.

Note the criteria in the ModelID column. The Access SQL engine then adds the criteria appropriately into the overall SQL query. Listing 4-6 shows the full query code.

Listing 4-6

```
SELECT Models.ModelID, Models.Name
FROM Models
WHERE
```

```
((
(Models.ModelID) Not In (select modelid from models where modelid<10)
And
(Models.ModelID) Not In (select modelid from models where name like
    "*monster*")
))
ORDER BY Models.ModelID;
```

Admittedly, this example makes things a little more complex than they need to be for retrieving the example data, but it does show how the query Design view can be extended to do more complex select queries.

Building Update and Insert Queries

So, the next thing you are probably wondering is how update and insert queries can be built in the Design view. These are fairly easy to create as well.

Update Query

To demonstrate building update queries, we will create a query that will update the name of a color in the Colors table. To get started, click the Create Query in

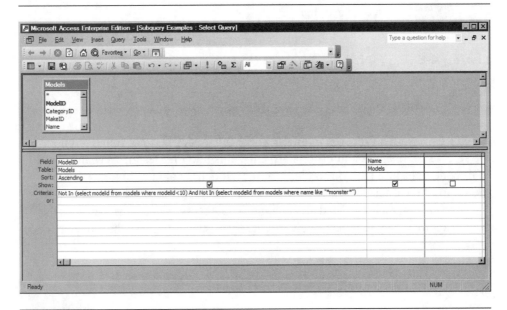

FIGURE 4-5   Adding the SQL criteria

Design View option on the Queries window. When the Design view comes up, select the Colors table to add to the query.

At this stage the Design view is set to create a standard select query. To change it to an update query, click the Query menu, and then select Update Query. Figure 4-6 shows the menu option.

Note that in the Design View grid, a new row option has become available—Update To. Add the Name field from the Colors table to the Design grid.

For this example, we want to update the Fuscia color to Vibrant Fuscia. In the Update To row field for the Name column, type **Vibrant Fuscia**. If the query were run now, then all of the color records would be updated. That isn't what we want—we only want Fuscia updated.

We have a couple of options here. The first is to add the ColorID field into the grid and set a criteria of 2 so that only records with an ID of 2 (Fuscia) are updated. Or, we can get a little more creative and use the SQL Like command. In this case, we want to update all color names where the name is like Fuscia. So, for the Name criteria we will enter the following SQL snippet:

```
Like "*Fuscia*"
```

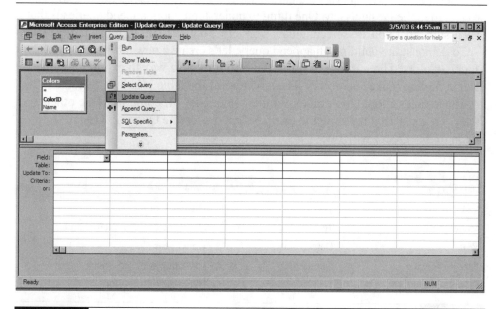

FIGURE 4-6   Setting the query to an update query

That does it for setting up the query. Now run the query. You should get a message indicating you are about to update 1 row(s) in the table. Click Yes to continue. Now, if you look at the data in the Colors table you will see that the Fuscia record has been updated. The SQL code generated is shown in Listing 4-7.

Listing 4-7

```
UPDATE Colors
SET Colors.Name = "Vibrant Fuscia"
WHERE (((Colors.Name) Like "*Fuscia*"));
```

As we can see, a simple update query has been created that does the work for us. This simple example is probably easier to write by hand than by using the Design view to create. But imagine if the update query involved multiple joins and several matching criteria—in that case, using the Design view can be a powerful way to construct queries quickly.

Insert/Append Queries

In Access, SQL insert queries are called append queries. Append queries can also be created in the Design view. One thing to understand about append queries is that they assume that you are selecting data from other tables to insert into a target table.

To demonstrate building an append query, let's create a new table called Makes-Models-Colors. The purpose of this table is to provide a way to export all model data, including make and colors. The structure of the table is shown in Table 4-1.

These fields should look pretty familiar since they all come from the other tables. To get started building the query, select the Create Query in Design View option on the Query window.

Field	Type	Description
Make_Name	Text	The name of the make
Model_Name	Text	The name of the model
Year	Date/Time	Model year
Fuel_Efficiency	Number	The model's fuel efficiency
Color_Name	Text	The name of the color

TABLE 4-1   Makes-Models-Colors Table Structure

We are going to be combining data from the Makes, Models, ModelsXREFColors, and Colors tables for the insert into the Makes-Models-Colors table. So, select all four tables and add them into the query.

As with the update query, we need to make this an append query. On the query menu, select Append Query to change it. Once you've done that, a dialog box pops up that asks what table the data should be appended to:

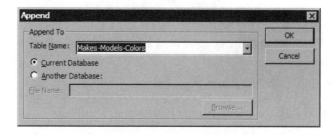

In this case we want it to be the Makes-Models-Colors table that we just created. Select that table and then click on OK.

The next step is to select the fields that we want append to our target table. In this case it is the Makes Name, Models Name, Models Year, Models Fuel_Efficiency, and Colors Name fields. Drag each of those onto the design grid.

For each column in the Design view, we need to select the target table field that we want the data appended to. Select the corresponding field for each. The query is now set up and ready to run. Figure 4-7 shows the Design view for the query.

Now run the query. A dialog box will pop up indicating that an append query is being run and that data will be modified. Click Yes to continue. Now look at the data in the Makes-Models-Colors table. You will see that 217 rows of data were inserted—a row for each make, model, and color combination. Listing 4-8 shows the SQL created by the query engine.

Listing 4-8

```
INSERT INTO
    [Makes-Models-Colors] ( Make_Name, Model_Name, [Year],
                            Fuel_Efficiency, Color_Name )
SELECT
        Makes.Name, Models.Name, Models.Year,
        Models.Fuel_Efficiency, Colors.Name
FROM
```

```
(Makes INNER JOIN Models ON Makes.MakeID=Models.MakeID)
  INNER JOIN (Colors INNER JOIN ModelXREFColor ON
  Colors.ColorID=ModelXREFColor.ColorID) ON
  Models.ModelID=ModelXREFColor.ModelID;
```

We find an insert statement has been built that utilizes data from a select of our joined tables. Now let's suppose we want to place some criteria on the export. Let's focus on only exporting data for the model year 2003.

In the Design view for the query, we will place a criteria value for the Year column. Type **1/1/2003** into the criteria row. Now run the query. Note that you will want to clear out the previously appended data before running this query.

When you look at the results in the Makes-Models-Colors table, you will see that there are only 15 rows that have been appended and all are for 2003 models. The SQL generated by the query engine is shown in Listing 4-9.

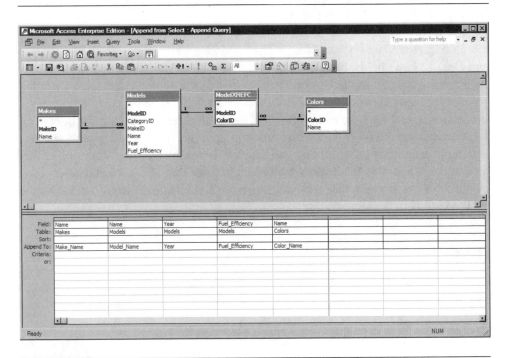

FIGURE 4-7   Append Query Design view

Listing 4-9

```
INSERT INTO [Makes-Models-Colors]
    ( Make_Name, Model_Name, [Year], Fuel_Efficiency, Color_Name )
SELECT Makes.Name, Models.Name, Models.Year,
    Models.Fuel_Efficiency, Colors.Name
FROM (Makes INNER JOIN Models ON Makes.MakeID = Models.MakeID)
    INNER JOIN (Colors INNER JOIN ModelXREFColor ON
    Colors.ColorID = ModelXREFColor.ColorID) ON
    Models.ModelID = ModelXREFColor.ModelID
WHERE (((Models.Year)=#1/1/2003#));
```

Note that we now have a where clause added to our query that only pulls year 2003 matching rows.

You are probably wondering how you would do an insert where you are inserting nontable values. For example, how would you insert a new color into the Colors table? Let's build a quick example of how this type of insert would be created.

Create a new query. In this case we do not want any tables added to the Query view. Switch the query to be an append query and select the Colors table as the target.

In the first column in the Design View grid, type the color **Yellow** in the field row. When you click out of the field, note that the field changes to Expr1: Yellow. This indicates that an expression instead of a field name is being inserted.

Next, select the field for the data to be appended to. In this case, select the Name field. Figure 4-8 shows the query setup.

Now if we look at the SQL being generated by the query engine, we will see that it isn't quite a traditional insert query with listed values. Listing 4-10 shows the SQL code.

Listing 4-10

```
INSERT INTO Colors ( Name )
SELECT Yellow AS Expr1;
```

Instead, we once again see a select with an insert. But, in reality this is equivalent to the following query in Listing 4-11.

Listing 4-11

```
INSERT INTO Colors ( Name ) Values("Yellow")
```

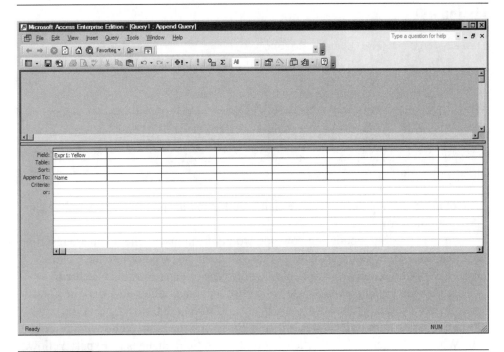

Append Query setup

TIP *You can actually copy the Listing 4-11 query into the SQL view and see that the Design view shows the same setup.*

While these types of inserts can be done in the Design view, it is frankly much easier to just go to the Table view and type in the new color. Or, simply go into the SQL view and build the SQL code directly.

That is it for creating update and append queries in Access. Now let's build a more complicated example using multiple queries and the Design view.

Building SQL Unions

One thing that we can't easily do in the Access Design view is build a union of multiple result sets from queries. In this case, we are going to need to do some work directly in SQL coding. But, we can leverage the Design view to build the components of our union.

NOTE *In general, you can always use the SQL view to create any type of standard SQL query. You do not always need to use the Design view or wizards.*

In this example, we are going to build two similar queries in the Design view and then join them together in a third query. The two queries will return all of the model data for a particular make.

To get started, create the first query in the Design view. Add the Category, Models, and Makes tables to the query. The returned values for the query include the make ID, make name, model ID, model name, and category name. Drag each of those fields to the Design View grid.

In this case we want all of the models from the Geord line, which has a makeID of 1. So, set the makeID criteria to 1. Figure 4-9 shows the setup for the query.

If you run the query, you will see that only model data for the Geord make is returned. The SQL generated for the query is shown in Listing 4-12.

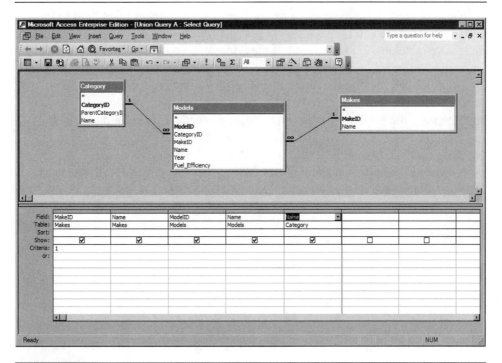

FIGURE 4-9   Make Query setup

Listing 4-12

```
SELECT Makes.MakeID, Makes.Name, Models.ModelID,
       Models.Name, Category.Name
FROM Makes INNER JOIN (Category INNER JOIN Models ON
        Category.CategoryID = Models.CategoryID) ON
        Makes.MakeID = Models.MakeID
WHERE (((Makes.MakeID)=1));
```

In this case, the inner joins on the tables are created and the where clause is created to only retrieve the Geord models. Save this query as Union Query A.

Now we are going to repeat the same process and create a second query that retrieves all of the model data for the Hevy make, which has a makeID of 2. In this case, though, we only want models for the year 2002.

Create a new query in the Design view and add the Categories, Makes, and Models tables. Add the same fields as for the previous query to this query, and set the MakeID criteria to 2.

Now we need to set the criteria for the year. We need to add that field to the design grid, but we can't have it show up in the returned results. Union queries must have matching fields returned; if they do not, then the two queries cannot be unioned together.

Drag the Year field to the Design View grid. Set the criteria to 1/1/2002. In order to not have the values for Year returned, uncheck the Show check box. To double-check the results, quickly run the query to ensure the right data is being returned. You should see all of the Hevy Suburbia Monster series models and not see any year data. Figure 4-10 shows the setup of the query.

Now save the query as Union Query B. The SQL generated for the query is shown in Listing 4-13.

Listing 4-13

```
SELECT Makes.MakeID, Makes.Name, Models.ModelID,
       Models.Name, Category.Name
FROM Makes INNER JOIN (Category INNER JOIN Models ON
     Category.CategoryID = Models.CategoryID) ON
     Makes.MakeID = Models.MakeID
WHERE (((Makes.MakeID)=2) AND ((Models.Year)=#1/1/2002#));
```

The where clause of the query contains both of the criteria for pulling back the make data.

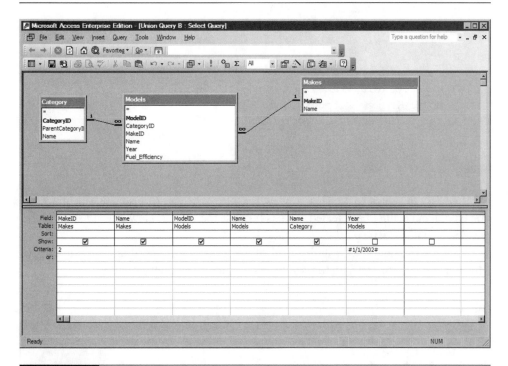

FIGURE 4-10   Make Query setup

Now we are ready to combine the two queries and union together the results. The simplest way to do this is to create a third query. Go ahead and create a third query in the Design view.

Do not add any tables to the query. In this case, we simply want to go to the SQL view and build our SQL union. Copy the SQL code from our Union A and Union B queries into the SQL view of the new query.

Now place the SQL keyword Union between the two queries. Your final query should look like Listing 4-14.

Listing 4-14

```
SELECT Makes.MakeID, Makes.Name, Models.ModelID,
       Models.Name, Category.Name
FROM Makes INNER JOIN (Category INNER JOIN Models ON
        Category.CategoryID = Models.CategoryID) ON
```

```
        Makes.MakeID = Models.MakeID
WHERE (((Makes.MakeID)=1));


UNION


SELECT Makes.MakeID, Makes.Name, Models.ModelID,
        Models.Name, Category.Name
FROM Makes INNER JOIN (Category INNER JOIN Models ON
        Category.CategoryID = Models.CategoryID) ON
        Makes.MakeID = Models.MakeID
WHERE (((Makes.MakeID)=2) AND ((Models.Year)=#1/1/2002#));
```

If you try to switch to the Design view for the query, you will see that the option is grayed out and cannot be selected. This is because the Design view doesn't support the creation of union queries.

Now run the query. You will see all of the models for Geord and the Suburbia Monster models for Hevy listed. Figure 4-11 shows the query results.

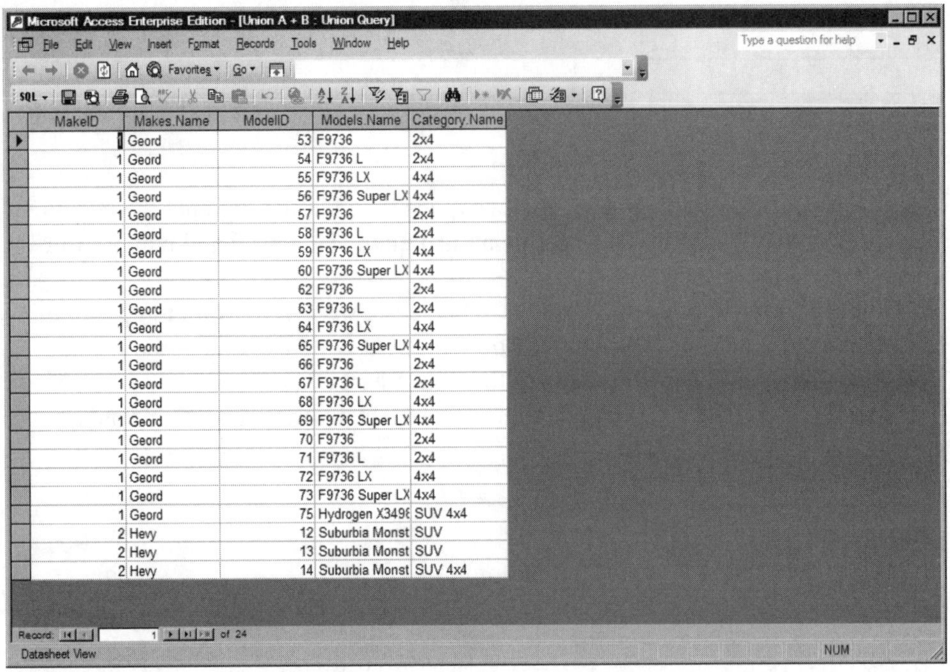

FIGURE 4-11   Union query results

As you can see, union queries and other more complex queries can be created in Access using straight SQL even though they are not supported by the Design view. If you are building Access applications or prototyping in Access, you are not limited to the Design view and wizards, and can utilize more complex SQL queries.

Summary

In this chapter and in the previous one, we have shown how Access can be leveraged for its powerful querying capabilities. Learning and utilizing the Access query tools can have a significant impact on data management, software development, and other data-related tasks.

We will be using many of the techniques demonstrated in Chapters 3 and 4 in later chapters to demonstrate how we can utilize Access' query capabilities quickly and efficiently to achieve professional results in our database work.

In the next two chapters, we are going to explore development applications against Access databases. Access has evolved over the years from a basic self-contained database tool to become the database engine behind sophisticated software applications. We will explore using .NET development tools for developing against Access.

Chapter 5

Programming Microsoft Access with Web Matrix

Have you ever had need of a lightweight web application that doesn't require the full power of an enterprise database? This is often the case for minor department-level applications, temporary applications, prototypes, and other basic needs. Access provides a great database platform for these applications. And, Microsoft has a public web development project that makes developing .NET web applications simple and free.

In this chapter we are going to use the principals used in the previous chapters of the book to build an ASP.NET web application with Access and Web Matrix. The focus of the application will be reporting for a simple employee punch card system.

Introducing the Web Matrix

Web Matrix can be downloaded for free at www.asp.net, which is a Microsoft-supported site. The Microsoft ASP.NET Web Matrix Project is a free, easy-to-use, community-supported web development tool for building ASP.NET web applications quickly.

The tool provides the ability to build ASP.NET web applications without requiring a full copy of Visual Studio .NET. It utilizes ADO.NET for database access. Microsoft's goal for Web Matrix is to make it a test platform for new techniques to develop web applications.

Web Matrix is built on C# entirely using C# and the .NET framework. You will find that the development environment has a similar feel to Visual Studio, but it provides a different set of tools with a specific focus on building web pages.

With Web Matrix, you can build web services, ASP.NET user controls, HTML pages, SQL scripts, and much more. Our focus will be on building ASP.NET ASPX data-driven web pages.

There are two key aspects of Web Matrix to keep in mind. The first is that the data integration tools built into the project are for Microsoft SQL Server, not Access. But, as we will see, this doesn't significantly hinder developing in Web Matrix. It just means that we can't take advantage of some of these tools. The second thing to keep in mind is that you cannot build code behind files like you can with Visual Studio .NET. In this case, all of the code, including the HTML, lives in the same ASPX page.

We will walk through building a Web Matrix project once we have a database to develop against. So, let's develop the employee database to be used in the application. Instead of using Web Matrix, consider using Data Access Pages. See Appendix C for more information.

Designing the Employee Database

Our employee time clock database is going to track several related sets of data so that reports can be developed in our Web Matrix application.

Business Rule Requirements

The business rules for our employee data are pretty simple. We want to record when an employee punches in and punches out. We also want to know the rate history of each employee.

With this data, reports on payroll, payroll history, and salary history can easily be built. Building these reports is the focus of the application in this example. For the examples in this chapter, we are only going to be focusing on building reports. We will not be building data entry functionality. In the next chapter, we will build an extended .NET application where data will be added, updated, and deleted.

Designing the Data

The database will consist of three tables. We will also be building several queries to retrieve the data for the reports.

The first table is for storing the basic employee data. This will include name, address, and other contact data. A primary key ID number must be added to uniquely identify each employee. Table 5-1 shows the fields for the table.

The next table is for the punch card time data. It will store the beginning and ending punch card entries for each shift. Table 5-2 shows the data.

Field	Type	Description
EmployeeID	AutoNumber	Primary key for the employee data.
First_Name	Text	The first name of the employee.
Last_Name	Text	The last name of the employee.
Address	Text	Address of the employee.
City	Text	City of the employee.
State	Text	State of the employee.
Zip	Text	ZIP code of the employee.
Phone	Text	Phone number of the employee.
Email	Text	E-mail address of the employee.

TABLE 5-1   Employees Table

Field	Type	Description
PunchID	AutoNumber	Primary key unique identifier for each entry.
EmployeeID	Number	Foreign key that relates to the Employees table.
Time_In	Date/Time	Date and time of the punch in.
Time_Out	Date/Time	Date and time of the punch out.

TABLE 5-2   PunchTimes Table

The final table in the database stores the rate history for the employee. Each time the employee's salary rate changes, a new entry is stored in the table. Table 5-3 shows the fields for the table.

The next step is to build the table relationships in Access. Click the Relationships icon on the toolbar. In the relationships screen, add all three tables to the view. Build a relationship between the Employees table EmployeeID field and the foreign key EmployeeID fields in the PunchTimes and RateHistory tables.

For referential integrity between the tables, it isn't critical that any properties are set since only reports will be built off of the data. Were this a full data entry database, then at a minimum referential integrity should be enforced. Cascade updates are not relevant given the autonumber primary keys. Cascade deletes could be helpful if indeed employees were ever to be deleted. Figure 5-1 shows the table relationships.

That does it for building our tables. The downloadable database (found at www .osborne.com) includes sample data for demonstrating the application.

Building Queries

The database will consist of three tables. We will also be building several queries to retrieve the data for the reports. The specific queries are shown in Table 5-4.

To build these queries, we are simply going to build select statements with the wizards that return the data regardless of specific where clause parameters.

Field	Type	Description
Rate_ID	Auto Number	Primary key unique identifier for each entry.
EmployeeID	Number	Foreign key that relates to the Employees table.
Hourly_Rate	Currency	The salary rate of the employee.
Date_Set	Date/Time	The date the salary rate was set.

TABLE 5-3   RateHistory Table

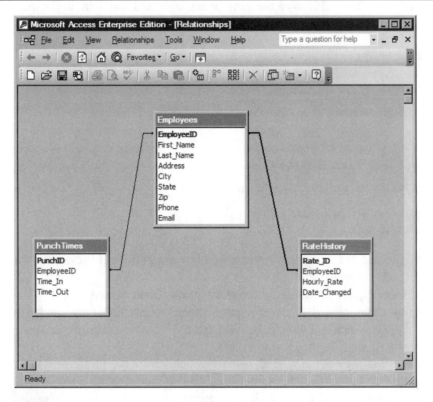

FIGURE 5-1   Table relationships diagram

For example, the PayRoll report needs a date range for the report. We will use the query for this report essentially as a view that can in turn be queried against our web application.

To build the first query, we will use the Simple Query Wizard to build a query that returns all of the employee data. To create the query, start up the wizard.

Query	Description
Employees	Returns all of the employees' data.
PayRoll	Returns payroll data for all employees' for a given set of dates.
Salary History	Returns the salary history for an employee.

TABLE 5-4   Employee Data Queries

Select all of the fields from the Employees table and add them to the query. Click through the next two screens and save the query as vw_Employees.

We will use the vw_ prefix to indicate that the query is being returned as a view that can then be queried against in the application.

The SQL created by the query is shown in Listing 5-1.

Listing 5-1

```
SELECT Employees.EmployeeID, Employees.First_Name, Employees.Last_Name,
Employees.Address, Employees.City, Employees.State, Employees.Zip,
Employees.Phone, Employees.Email
FROM Employees;
```

As expected, the query that is generated is a straightforward select statement against the Employees table.

The second query to build is for the salary history. In this case we need to combine the employee and salary data to provide the history. Once again we are going to return all of the data, which can then be queried against to retrieve records for specific employees. Again start the Query Wizard.

On the first page of the wizard, select the fields from the Employees table. Then select the fields from the RateHistory table. Click through the next two screens and save the query as vw_RateHistory.

Listing 5-2 shows the SQL code generated by the query.

Listing 5-2

```
SELECT RateHistory.RateID,
       RateHistory.EmployeeID AS RateHistory_EmployeeID,
       RateHistory.Hourly_Rate, RateHistory.Effective_StartDate,
       RateHistory.Effective_EndDate, Employees.EmployeeID AS
       Employees_EmployeeID, Employees.First_Name,
       Employees.Last_Name, Employees.Address,
       Employees.City, Employees.State, Employees.Zip,
       Employees.Phone, Employees.Email
FROM Employees INNER JOIN RateHistory ON
    Employees.EmployeeID = RateHistory.EmployeeID;
```

In this case a simple inner join of both tables is created, with all of the fields returned. The next query for payroll is going to get a little more complicated. We need to combine the data from all of the tables and do some calculations.

The first step is to build a query with the Query Wizard that combines the Employees and PunchTimes tables. Do that following the standard steps. The initial query that is created is shown in Listing 5-3.

Listing 5-3

```
SELECT Employees.EmployeeID AS Employees_EmployeeID,
       Employees.First_Name, Employees.Last_Name,
       Employees.Address, Employees.City, Employees.State,
       Employees.Zip, Employees.Phone, Employees.Email,
       PunchTimes.PunchID,
       PunchTimes.EmployeeID AS PunchTimes_EmployeeID,
       PunchTimes.Time_In, PunchTimes.Time_Out,
FROM   Employees INNER JOIN PunchTimes ON
       Employees.EmployeeID = PunchTimes.EmployeeID;
```

At this stage we have a simple join of the punch times and the employee data. But, we need to calculate the amount that the employee should be paid for each day. That is going to require that we pull the hourly rate data from the RateHistory table, as well as calculate the pay amount for each day's work.

In order to do that, we are going to need to use a subquery to pull in the rate data for the date worked. And, we are going to need to calculate the daily pay in minutes since the daily amount worked doesn't break down to clean hours.

Listing 5-4 shows the subquery we will use to pull the rate.

Listing 5-4

```
select hourly_rate/60 from ratehistory where punchtimes.time_in >=
effective_startdate  and punchtimes.time_out <= effective_enddate  and
employees.employeeid = employeeid
```

The rate is returned in minutes by dividing it by 60. The rate that is current for the day's work is pulled. Note that the punch times data is pulled from the top-level query shown in Listing 5-3.

Designing the Employee Database

The final thing we have to do is get the number of minutes that the employee worked. This will be calculated by using the DateDiff SQL function. The amount of minutes between the start and end work times is calculated as shown in Listing 5-5.

Listing 5-5

```
DateDiff("n", PunchTimes.Time_In, PunchTimes.Time_Out) AS PunchMinutes
```

The small "n" indicates the minutes between the two date/time fields that should be calculated. Now let's put it all together in one final query, shown in Listing 5-6.

Listing 5-6

```
SELECT Employees.EmployeeID AS Employees_EmployeeID,
       Employees.First_Name, Employees.Last_Name,
       Employees.Address, Employees.City, Employees.State,
       Employees.Zip, Employees.Phone, Employees.Email,
       PunchTimes.PunchID, PunchTimes.EmployeeID AS PunchTimes_EmployeeID,
       PunchTimes.Time_In, PunchTimes.Time_Out,

       DateDiff( "n" , PunchTimes.Time_In , PunchTimes.Time_Out )
       AS PunchMinutes,

       (select hourly_rate from ratehistory where punchtimes.time_in >=
        effective_startdate and punchtimes.time_out <= effective_enddate
        and employees.employeeid = employeeid) AS HourlyRate,

       (select hourly_rate/60 from ratehistory where
        punchtimes.time_in >= effective_startdate and
        punchtimes.time_out <= effective_enddate and
        employees.employeeid = employeeid) AS MinuteRate,

       DateDiff( "n" , PunchTimes.Time_In , PunchTimes.Time_Out )
       * (select hourly_rate/60 from ratehistory where
        punchtimes.time_in >= effective_startdate  and
        punchtimes.time_out <= effective_enddate  and
        employees.employeeid = employeeid) AS PayAmount

FROM   Employees INNER JOIN PunchTimes ON
       Employees.EmployeeID = PunchTimes.EmployeeID;
```

By using the subquery, we are able to return the applicable hourly rate and minute rate for each record. With the DateDiff function, the minutes worked combined with the rate of pay for the day is calculated.

With this query, the payroll data for any time period can be retrieved with a pay total by day. Then, in our web application, the total pay for the period can also be calculated.

With that, our database is ready to be programmed against. So, let's get started with Web Matrix.

Building the Web Application

First, make sure you have the Web Matrix application downloaded and installed. There are no web projects per se for a Web Matrix application. Basically, you build ASPX web pages one at a time.

Start up Web Matrix. The startup screen is shown in Figure 5-2.

If you click on the Data Pages option, you will get a list of options for building data-based pages. They will automatically add the code and web form controls for building SQL-based data interfaces. For us, it is going to be easier to start with

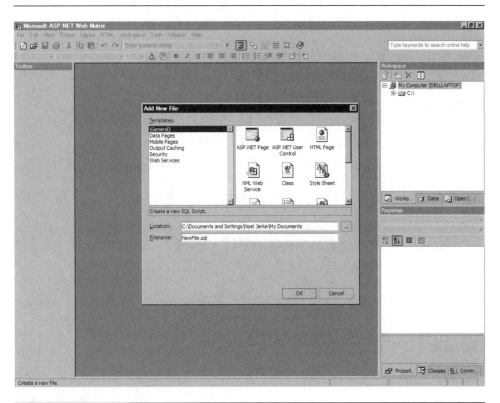

FIGURE 5-2 Web Matrix startup screen

a blank ASPX page and build the functionality we need. So, select ASP.NET page and save the page as employees.aspx.

This page is going to list the employees and provide three options for each employee. The first will be to view the current paycheck. The second will be to see the detail (name, address, etc.) on the employee. The third will be to see the salary history of the employee.

First make sure you are in the Design view by clicking on the appropriate tab at the bottom of the page. On the blank page, we want to add three items. At the top of the page type **Employee Listing** and make the font a large-sized text. Below that, drag a horizontal rule from the HTML Elements toolbar to below the added text.

Next, we need to add a DataGrid control from the Web Controls toolbar below the horizontal rule. We are going to be binding data to the DataGrid control in the VB code for the page. Table 5-5 has the key property settings for the control.

Next we need to define the columns for our grid. For this page, we just want to see the employee's ID, first name, and last name. There are two different ways to build the columns. The first is to go directly into the HTML and create the grid column tags and settings. The second is to use the property builder functionality in the design environment. We will build two of the columns here and then show the HTML for the full data grid.

In the Properties window of the data grid, click the Property Builder link. This will bring up a screen where all of the properties of the data grid can be set. We are concerned with building the columns for the grid. Click the Columns option on the left bar.

There are several different types of columns that can be added to the grid. The first is a standard bound column, which can be bound to a specific column returned from the database. The second is a button column that provides options for editing data in the grid. The third option is a hyperlink column that allows the user to go to another page. We will be using these to build the view options for the employee.

Property	Setting
(ID)	dgEmployee
AutoGenerateColumns	False
HeaderStyle.BackColor	#4A3C8C
ItemStyle.BackColor	#DEDFDE

TABLE 5-5   dgEmployee Data Grid Property Settings

The final option is to create a template column that can be used for the grid template formatting. Figure 5-3 shows the property builder screen.

First, add a bound column to the Selected Columns list. Set the Header Text to Employee ID. That is what will show on the header row of the grid. Next set the Data Field to EmployeeID. That indicates that the field should be bound to the EmployeeID column returned from the database. Your screen should look like Figure 5-4.

Add in bound columns for first and last name as well. Next we will add a hyperlink column to the Selected Columns list. Set the Text field to Current Payroll. That is the text that will show up in the hyperlink. Set the URL field to EmployeeID. The last thing we need to add is the URL format string. This indicates how the URL for the hyperlink should be built. Set it as follows:

```
payroll.aspx?employeeid={0}
```

Building the Web Application

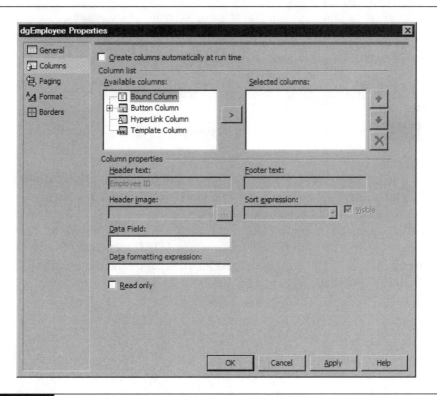

FIGURE 5-3 Data grid columns property builder screen

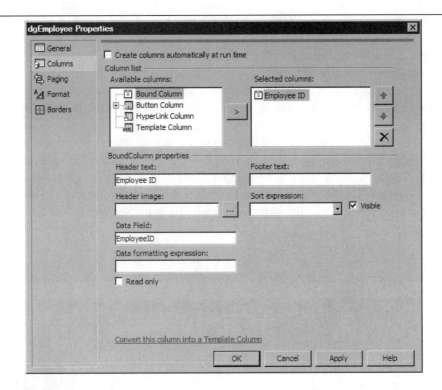

FIGURE 5-4   Settings for the EmployeeID column

The {0} indicates that the first data field should be used to fill in the string, which in this case will be the employee ID that will be passed to the payroll.aspx page. Your screen should now look like Figure 5-5.

Finally, set up the Employee Detail and Salary History hyperlink columns the same way as for the Current Payroll column. The HTML generated for the page is shown in Listing 5-7. The code generated for your page should be similar. You can copy Listing 5-7 onto the page and then explore the DataGrid properties.

Listing 5-7

```
<html>
<head>
</head>
<body style="FONT-FAMILY: arial">
    <h2>Employee Listing
        <hr size="1" />
```

```
    </h2>
    <form runat="server">
        <p>
            <asp:datagrid id="dgEmployee" runat="server"
             CellSpacing="1" GridLines="None" CellPadding="3"
             BackColor="White" ForeColor="Black"
             EnableViewState="False" AutoGenerateColumns="False">
            <HeaderStyle font-bold="True" forecolor="White"
             backcolor="#4A3C8C"></HeaderStyle>
                <ItemStyle backcolor="#DEDFDE"></ItemStyle>
                <Columns>
                    <asp:BoundColumn DataField="EmployeeID"
                        HeaderText="Employee ID"></asp:BoundColumn>
                    <asp:BoundColumn DataField="First_Name"
                        HeaderText="First Name"></asp:BoundColumn>
                    <asp:BoundColumn DataField="Last_Name"
                        HeaderText="Last Name"></asp:BoundColumn>
                    <asp:HyperLinkColumn Text="Current Payroll"
                        DataNavigateUrlField="EmployeeID"
              DataNavigateUrlFormatString="payroll.aspx?employeeid={0}">
                        </asp:HyperLinkColumn>
                    <asp:HyperLinkColumn Text="Employee Detail"
                        DataNavigateUrlField="EmployeeID"
           DataNavigateUrlFormatString="employeedetail.aspx?employeeid={0}">
                        </asp:HyperLinkColumn>
                    <asp:HyperLinkColumn Text="Salary History"
                        DataNavigateUrlField="EmployeeID"
           DataNavigateUrlFormatString="salaryhistory.aspx?employeeid={0}">
                        </asp:HyperLinkColumn>
                </Columns>
            </asp:datagrid>
        </p>
    </form>
</body>
</html>
```

Note the tagging for the data grid columns. Each of the properties set in the property builder is set in the column tags.

Now that the grid is built, we are ready to add the code to the page as well. In the Web Matrix environment, click on the All tab. We have to add a couple of namespace imports to the page for the .NET system.data classes. This allows us to create the connections to the database and query for data. Add the following code near the top of the page, right below the language=VB line:

```
<%@ import Namespace="System.Data" %>
<%@ import Namespace="System.Data.SqlClient" %>
```

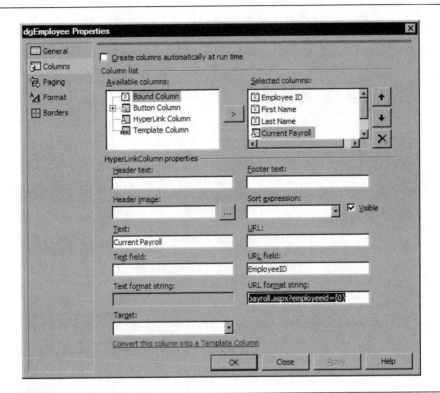

FIGURE 5-5   Current payroll hyperlink column

Next, we are ready to work with the code for the page. Click on the Code tab to switch to viewing only the code section of the page. We need to add an event subroutine to the page that will be fired off when the page is loaded. Within that subroutine, code will be executed to open the database connection and return the list of employees. Listing 5-8 shows the code.

Listing 5-8

```
Sub Page_Load(Sender As Object, E As EventArgs)
        Dim objCMD As New OleDb.OleDbCommand()
        Dim objConn As New OleDb.OleDbConnection()
        Dim strSQL As String
        Dim objDR As OleDb.OleDbDataReader
        Dim strConn as string
```

```
'  First time the page is loaded
If Not IsPostBack Then

    strConn = "PROVIDER=Microsoft.Jet.OLEDB.4.0;" & _
    "DATA SOURCE=c:\inetpub\wwwroot\employee\employee.mdb;"

    ' Open a DB connection
    objConn.ConnectionString = strConn
    objConn.Open()

    '  Set the commad connection
    objCMD.Connection = objConn

    '  Retrieve all of the data from the view
    strSQL = "select * from vw_employees order by last_name"

    '  Set the query
    objCMD.CommandText = strSQL

    '  Set the data to read
    objDR = objCMD.ExecuteReader

    '  Set the grid data source
    dgEmployee.DataSource = objDR

    '  Show the data
    dgEmployee.DataBind()
End If
End Sub
```

The first thing that happens on the page is the creation of our variables and objects. We are going to be using OLE DB provider to do our database connection to the Access database. For that, we need an OLE DB connection, command object, and data reader objects.

> TIP
>
> *To learn more about OLE DB, visit the following link on the Microsoft site: http://msdn.microsoft.com/library/en-us/oledb/htm/oledbstartpage1 .asp?frame=true*

The connection string to the database points to our Access database. Be sure to update this to point appropriately to your Access database. Next, the connection to the database is opened by setting the connection object's connection string property to our connection string and using the open method. Once the connection is open, then the command object's connection is set to the connection object.

Building the Web Application

Next, the query is built to retrieve the employees from the database. In this case we are actually building a query against the employee query that we created. Here, the query acts very much like a SQL view. We can use all of the standard table query keywords with this view. In this case we are ordering the employee listing by last name.

Once the query is created, we set it to the command text of the command object. Then the execute reader method of the command object is called, which will return the data from the query in a suitable format for a data reader object. The result is set to our data reader object.

Finally, we are ready to bind our data to the data grid. The datasource property of our data grid object is set to the reader. Then the bind method of the data grid is called. That method essentially tells the data reader to walk through the data and display it per the setup of the columns.

To view the page, click on the start arrow on the toolbar. That will give you the option of either running the built-in Web Matrix web server or using IIS. Regarding the Web Matrix web server, Microsoft notes in the product documentation:

> *This simple web server is automatically installed with ASP.NET Web Matrix and does not require any other web server to be installed on your machine (ideal for quick development scenarios).*
> *http://www.asp.net/webmatrix/tour/section1/runviamatrixweb.aspx*

Choose either to use the Web Matrix web server or to have Web Matrix create an IIS application virtual root for running your pages. Figure 5-6 shows the page in action once everything is set up and running.

The page is pretty simple. We have the employees listing in alpha order by last name. The Employee ID and first name are also displayed. If you scroll your cursor over the hyperlinks, you will note the links to the pages as we defined them with the employee ID on the query string.

That is it for our first page. Let's next work on the employee detail page, which will show the full data listing for an employee. Create a new ASP.NET file and save it as employeedetail.aspx.

In this page we are going to build an HTML table with a set of rows where the employee data can be displayed. There will be two columns in the table. The left column will have HTML text that describes the data (e.g., First Name:) The second column is where the employee data will be displayed.

The first step to creating the page is to click on the HTML view of the page. Between the form tags, build a two-column table. For the first column, ensure the text is aligned right (align="right"). For each left column, put in the name

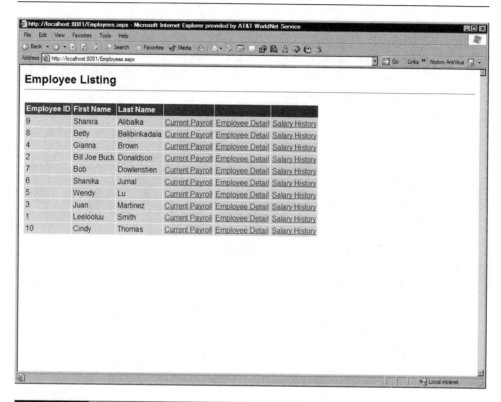

FIGURE 5-6   Employees listing

of the database field to be displayed. Leave the second column blank. When you are done, your HTML table should look like Listing 5-9.

Listing 5-9

```
<table cellspacing="3" cellpadding="3">
        <tbody>
            <tr>
                <td align="right">Employee ID:</td>
                <td></td>
            </tr>
            <tr>
                <td align="right">First Name:</td>
```

```
            <td></td>
        </tr>
        <tr>
            <td align="right">Last Name:</td>
            <td></td>
        </tr>
        <tr>
            <td align="right">Address:</td>
            <td></td>
        </tr>
        <tr>
            <td align="right">City:</td>
            <td></td>
        </tr>
        <tr>
            <td align="right">State:</td>
            <td></td>
        </tr>
        <tr>
            <td align="right">Zip:</td>
            <td></td>
        </tr>
        <tr>
            <td align="right">Phone:</td>
            <td></td>
        </tr>
        <tr>
            <td align="right">Email:</td>
            <td></td>
        </tr>
    </tbody>
  </form>
</table>
```

Now we are ready to fill in that right column. In order to display the data dynamically, we are going to use a Label Web control to display the employee data. With the Web control, we can set the value of the label from our VB code dynamically.

Switch to the Design view. You should see your table displayed. Now click the Label control in the Web Controls toolbar. Drag it to the top-right cell to the right of the Employee ID cell. Change the ID of the label to be EmployeeID. You might also want to set the text value to Employee ID to make it clear what the label is used for. Repeat the same steps and set up the rest of the cells for all of the employee data. The resulting HTML from the page should look like Listing 5-10.

Listing 5-10

```
<html>
<head>
</head>
<body>
    <center>
        <table cellspacing="3" cellpadding="3">
            <form runat="server">
                <tbody>
                    <tr>
                        <td align="right">Employee ID:</td>
                        <td><asp:Label id="lblEmployeeID"
                          runat="server">Employee ID</asp:Label></td>
                    </tr>
                    <tr>
                        <td align="right">First Name:</td>
                        <td><asp:Label id="lblFirstName"
                         runat="server">first name</asp:Label></td>
                    </tr>
                    <tr>
                        <td align="right">Last Name:</td>
                        <td><asp:Label id="lblLastName" runat="server">
                            last name</asp:Label></td>
                    </tr>
                    <tr>
                        <td align="right">
                            Address:</td>
                        <td>
                            <asp:Label id="lblAddress"
                                runat="server">address</asp:Label>
                        </td>
                    </tr>
                    <tr>
                        <td align="right">
                            City:</td>
                        <td>
                            <asp:Label id="lblCity"
                                runat="server">City</asp:Label>
                        </td>
                    </tr>
                    <tr>
```

```
        <td align="right">
            State:</td>
        <td>
            <asp:Label id="lblState"
                runat="server">State</asp:Label>
        </td>
    </tr>
    <tr>
        <td align="right">
            Zip:</td>
        <td>
            <asp:Label id="lblZip"
                runat="server">Zip</asp:Label>
        </td>
    </tr>
    <tr>
        <td align="right">
            Phone:</td>
        <td>
            <asp:Label id="lblPhone"
                runat="server">Phone</asp:Label>
        </td>
    </tr>
    <tr>
        <td align="right">
            Email:</td>
        <td>
            <asp:Label id="lblEmail"
                runat="server">Email</asp:Label>
        </td>
    </tr>
</tbody>
</form>
</table>
</center>
</body>
</html>
```

Note the ASP:Label tagging for each of the data cells in our table. That is it for setting up the HTML interface for this page. Now we are ready to build the VB code to display the data.

> **TIP**   *Using the HTML view and copying and setting up the label controls or other similar web form controls can be faster and easier than using the GUI interface tools.*

Click the All tab in Web Matrix to view the code for the whole page. Once again, we need to import the system.data namespaces for our data access. Add the following lines of code below the language setting:

```
<%@ import Namespace="System.Data" %>
<%@ import Namespace="System.Data.SqlClient" %>
```

Now click the Code tab and switch to the Code view. Listing 5-11 shows the code for the page.

Listing 5-11

```
Sub Page_Load(Sender As Object, E As EventArgs)

        Dim objCMD As New OleDb.OleDbCommand()
        Dim objConn As New OleDb.OleDbConnection()
        Dim objDR As OleDb.OleDbDataReader
        Dim strSQL As String
        Dim strConn as string

        '  First time the page is loaded
        If Not IsPostBack Then

          ' Set the connection to the employee MDB
          strConn = "PROVIDER=Microsoft.Jet.OLEDB.4.0;" & _
             "DATA SOURCE=c:\inetpub\wwwroot\employee\employee.mdb;"

          ' Open a DB connection
          objConn.ConnectionString = strConn
          objConn.Open()

          ' Set the command connection
          objCMD.Connection = objConn

          ' Retrieve the employee information for the specified employee
          strSQL = "select * from vw_employees where employeeid = " & _
                  request.querystring("employeeid")

          ' Set the query
          objCMD.CommandText = strSQL

          ' Set the data to read
          objDR = objCMD.ExecuteReader
```

```
' Read the first record
objDR.read

' Set each label control to the appropriate value
' from the returned data
lblEmployeeID.text = objDR.getvalue(0)
lblFirstName.text = objDR.getvalue(1)
lblLastName.text = objDR.getvalue(2)
lblAddress.text = objDR.getvalue(3)
lblCity.text = objDR.getvalue(4)
lblState.text = objDR.getvalue(5)
lblZip.text = objDR.getvalue(6)
lblPhone.text = objDR.getvalue(7)
lblEmail.text = objDR.getvalue(8)
End If
End Sub
```

Once again, OLE DB objects are created for interfacing with the database. The connection string is the same for the database as utilized on the employees.aspx page, and the command object is set up in the same fashion.

TIP
Consider adding a global.asax page to the project and setting up an application-level variable that contains the connection string. This variable can then be accessed by all pages, and if the database location changes you only have to go to one file to update the connection string.

Next, the query string to retrieve the employee data is built. Once again we are selecting against the vw_Employees Access query. In order to retrieve the specified employee's data, we have to read the EmployeeID variable off of the query string. This is then used to build the where clause on our query.

Next, the command object command text property is set, the execute reader method called, and the data returned to the data reader. We now have the data ready to be displayed to the user.

Displaying the data in the label controls is very straightforward. Each label control contains a Text property that can be set. The data is retrieved from the data reader by using the GetValue method and referencing the ordinal position of the data in the returned string.

TIP
There are many additional methods for retrieving data from the data reader, including referencing the columns by name and using data type–specific get methods. To learn more, review Microsoft's data reader object documentation.

Now our page is ready to be displayed. Start up the employees.aspx page and click on one of the Employee Detail links. The detail data for the employee is displayed. Figure 5-7 shows the page.

Let's next work on the salary history page. For this page we want to retrieve and display the salary history for the employee. Create a new ASP.NET file and save it as salaryhistory.aspx.

To display the salary data, a DataGrid control will be utilized once again. And, at the top of the page we will want to display the employee's name. To get started, from the Design view, drag a DataGrid control from the Web control's tab onto the page. Name it dgHistory. Set the grid properties to those shown in Table 5-5.

In this case, we want to display three columns of data: the start date, end date, and rate. Following the property builder steps outlined earlier in the chapter, add in these three bound columns to the data grid.

At the top of the page, add a label that will be used to display the employee's name dynamically. Name the label lblEmployee. Below the label, add in a horizontal line from the HTML Elements toolbar.

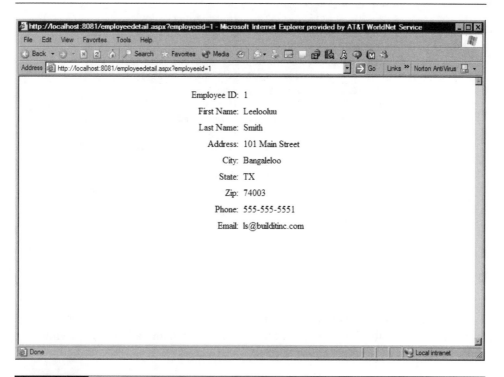

FIGURE 5-7   Employee detail

That is it for designing the HTML interface for the page. Listing 5-12 shows the generated HTML code.

Listing 5-12

```html
<html>
<head>
</head>
<body>
    <form runat="server">
        <p>
            <asp:Label id="lblEmployee" runat="server"
                Font-Bold="True" Font-Size="X-Large">Label</asp:Label>
        </p>
        <h2>
            <hr size="1" />
        </h2>
        <p>
            <asp:datagrid id="dgHistory" runat="server"
                AutoGenerateColumns="False"
                EnableViewState="False" ForeColor="Black"
                BackColor="White" CellPadding="3" GridLines="None"
                CellSpacing="1">
                <HeaderStyle font-bold="True" forecolor="White"
                        backcolor="#4A3C8C"></HeaderStyle>
                <ItemStyle backcolor="#DEDFDE"></ItemStyle>
                <Columns>
                    <asp:BoundColumn DataField="Effective_StartDate"
                        HeaderText="Start Date"></asp:BoundColumn>
                    <asp:BoundColumn DataField="Effective_EndDate"
                        HeaderText="End Date"></asp:BoundColumn>
                    <asp:BoundColumn DataField="Hourly_Rate"
                        HeaderText="Rate"></asp:BoundColumn>
                </Columns>
            </asp:datagrid>
            <!-- Insert content here -->
        </p>
    </form>
</body>
</html>
```

There are no surprises in the HTML code for this page. Next, we are ready to set up the code for the page. First click on the All tab and add the following namespace imports to the top of the page:

```
<%@ import Namespace="System.Data" %>
<%@ import Namespace="System.Data.SqlClient" %>
```

Next, click on the Code tab to switch to the Code view. The technique followed on this page is similar to the employees.aspx page. Listing 5-13 shows the code for the page.

Listing 5-13

```
Sub Page_Load(Sender As Object, E As EventArgs)
    ' Only execute if not a form post back to this page
    If Not Page.IsPostBack Then

        ' Call the subroutine to show the data
        BindGrid()
    End If
End Sub

Sub BindGrid()
    Dim objConn As New OleDb.OleDbConnection()
    Dim objCMDGrid As New OleDb.OleDbCommand()
    Dim objCMDEmp As New OleDb.OleDbCommand()
    Dim objDRGrid As OleDb.OleDbDataReader
    Dim objDREmp As OleDb.OleDbDataReader
    Dim strSQL As String
    Dim strConn as string

    ' Set the connection to the database for OLEDB Access
    strConn = "PROVIDER=Microsoft.Jet.OLEDB.4.0;" & _
        "DATA SOURCE=c:\inetpub\wwwroot\employee\employee.mdb;"

    ' Open a DB connection
    objConn.ConnectionString = strConn
    objConn.Open()

    ' Set the command connection
    objCMDGrid.Connection = objConn

    ' Set the command connection
    objCMDEmp.Connection = objConn
```

```
'  Retrieve the rate history for the specified employee
strSQL = "select * from vw_RateHistory where " & _
          "RateHistory_employeeid = " & _
          request.querystring("employeeid") & _
          " order by Effective_StartDate"

'  Set the query
objCMDGrid.CommandText = strSQL

'  Set the data to read
objDRGrid = objCMDGrid.ExecuteReader

'  Set the grid data source
dgHistory.DataSource = objDRGrid

'  Bind the grid to the data source and show the data
dgHistory.DataBind()

'  Close the data reader
objDRGrid.close

'  Retrieve the employee data
strSQL = "select * from vw_employees where employeeid = " & _
          request.querystring("employeeid")

'  Set the query
objCMDEmp.CommandText = strSQL

'  Set the data to read
objDREmp = objCMDEmp.ExecuteReader

'  Read the first record
objDREmp.read

' Show the employee name in the labels
lblEmployee.text = objDREmp.getvalue(1) & _
                    " " & objDREmp.getvalue(2)


End Sub
```

When the page is loaded the first time, the BindGrid routine is called to display the salary history data. In the BindGrid subroutine, the first thing that happens is the setup of the OLE DB objects. In this case, we are going to need two sets of command and data reader objects. The first will be used for the display of the data in the grid. The second will be used to retrieve the employee's name for display in the label at the top of the page.

The connection string is the same as utilized on the previous pages. The connection is open and both command objects are set to point to the connection.

Next, a query is built to retrieve the rate history for the employee. The vw_RateHistory Access query is utilized. A select query is built against this query that retrieves the data for the specified employee. The employee ID is read from the query string and utilized in the query where clause. The salary data is ordered by the effective start date of the rate.

Once the query is built, the command object is set and executed with the data stored in the data reader. And, like before, the grid data source is set to the data reader and the Bind method is called to display the data. But we aren't quite through yet. We need to display the employee name to make it clear whom the salary history is for. A second query is built that retrieves the specific employee's data. In fact, this query is exactly the same one as utilized on the employeedetail.aspx page.

The command object is set to the query and the data is read and stored in a data reader. The Read method of the data reader is called to retrieve the first record, and the name of the employee is displayed in the lblEmployee label control.

Now we are ready to see the page in action. Start up the employees.aspx page in the browser. Click on the Salary History link for one of the employees. Figure 5-8 shows the page in action.

> **TIP** *You can perform formatting on the data displayed in the columns of the data grid. For example, you might want the rate to show up in a currency format. Or, you might want the date to just show the month, day, and year. The data grid documentation provides details on performing this type of formatting.*

Now we are ready to look at our final page, the display of the payroll data. In this case we are going to make the process simple. We are going to display the daily pay amount over a period of 14 days starting from when the report is run.

To get started, create a new ASP.NET file and save it as payroll.aspx. Once again we are going to utilize the DataGrid for displaying the payroll data. We are also going to utilize two Label controls to display the employee's name and the data range for the payroll data.

Add two Label controls at the top of the page. Name the first lblEmployee. Name the second lblDates. Below the two labels, add a horizontal rule from the HTML Elements toolbar.

Building the Web Application

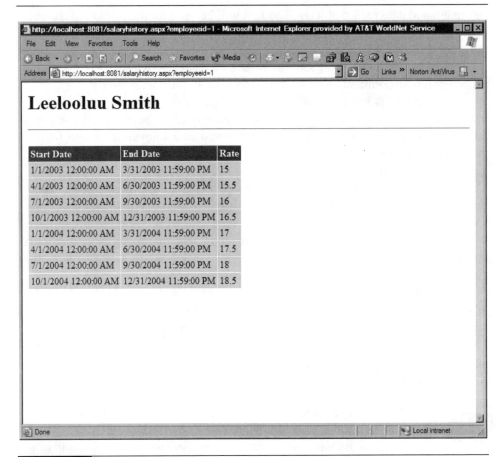

FIGURE 5-8   Salary History page

Next, add a DataGrid to the page, and name it dgPayroll. Set the grid properties the same as shown in Table 5-5. For this grid, we need four data bound columns. Use the Property Builder tool to make columns for Time In, Time Out, Rate, and Pay.

That is it for setting up the design for the page. Listing 5-14 shows the HTML generated by Web Matrix.

Listing 5-14

```
<html>
<head>
```

```
</head>
<body style="FONT-FAMILY: arial">
    <h2>
        <asp:Label id="lblEmployee" Font-Size="X-Large"
            Font-Bold="True" runat="server">Label</asp:Label>
    </h2>
    <h2>
        <asp:Label id="lblDates" runat="server">Label</asp:Label>
        <hr size="1" />
    </h2>
    <form runat="server">
        <asp:datagrid id="dgPayroll" runat="server"
            AutoGenerateColumns="False" width="80%"
            CellSpacing="1" GridLines="None" CellPadding="3"
            BackColor="White" ForeColor="Black">
            <HeaderStyle font-bold="True" forecolor="White"
                backcolor="#4A3C8C"></HeaderStyle>
            <PagerStyle horizontalalign="Right"
                backcolor="#C6C3C6" mode="NumericPages">
                </PagerStyle>
            <ItemStyle backcolor="#DEDFDE"></ItemStyle>
            <Columns>
                <asp:BoundColumn DataField="Time_In"
                    HeaderText="Time In"></asp:BoundColumn>
                <asp:BoundColumn DataField="Time_Out"
                    HeaderText="Time Out"></asp:BoundColumn>
                <asp:BoundColumn DataField="HourlyRate"
                    HeaderText="Rate"></asp:BoundColumn>
                <asp:BoundColumn DataField="PayAmount"
                    HeaderText="Pay"></asp:BoundColumn>
            </Columns>
        </asp:datagrid>
    </form>
</body>
</html>
```

Again, there is nothing unusual in the HTML code for the page, and we are now ready to build the code. Once again, we need to import the data namespace at the top of the page right below the language setting. Click on the All tab to view the code for the page.

```
<%@ import Namespace="System.Data" %>
<%@ import Namespace="System.Data.SqlClient" %>
```

Next, click on the Code tab for the page. Again, we are going to use the PageLoad event to show the data when the page is displayed. The code is shown in Listing 5-15.

Listing 5-15

```
Sub Page_Load(Sender As Object, E As EventArgs)
    ' Only execute when the page is first displayed
    If Not Page.IsPostBack Then

        ' Call the subroutine to show the data
        BindGrid()

    End If
End Sub


Sub BindGrid()
    Dim objConn As New OleDb.OleDbConnection()
    Dim objCMDGrid As New OleDb.OleDbCommand()
    Dim objCMDEmp As New OleDb.OleDbCommand()
    Dim objDRGrid As OleDb.OleDbDataReader
    Dim objDREmp As OleDb.OleDbDataReader
    Dim strSQL As String
    Dim strConn as string

    ' Start and end dates for the payroll period
    Dim startDate as date
    Dim EndDate as date

    ' Instance of the Interval data structure for doing the
    ' date difference
    Dim DI as DateInterval

    ' Set our connection to the MDB
    strConn = "PROVIDER=Microsoft.Jet.OLEDB.4.0;" & _
              "DATA SOURCE=c:\inetpub\wwwroot\employee\employee.mdb;"

    ' Open a DB connection
    objConn.ConnectionString = strConn
    objConn.Open()

    ' Set the command connection
    objCMDGrid.Connection = objConn

    ' Set the command connection
    objCMDEmp.Connection = objConn
```

```
' Set the start date for the payroll period to be two weeks prior
' to today
StartDate = DateAdd(DI.day, -15, now)

'  set the end date of the payroll period to today
EndDate = now

'  Query for the payroll data where the punch times are in the
'  current time period for the specified employee
strSQL = "select * from vw_payroll where punchtimes.time_in >= #" & _
         StartDate & "# and punchtimes.time_out <= #" & _
         EndDate & "# and  punchtimes_employeeid = " & _
         request.querystring("employeeid") & " order by Time_In"

'  Set the query
objCMDGrid.CommandText = strSQL

'  Set the data to read
objDRGrid = objCMDGrid.ExecuteReader

'  Set the grid data source
dgPayroll.DataSource = objDRGrid

'  Bind the data to the grid for display
dgPayroll.DataBind()

'  Close the grid data reader
objDRGrid.close

'  Retrieve the employee data
strSQL = "select * from vw_employees where employeeid = " & _
         request.querystring("employeeid")

'  Set the query
objCMDEmp.CommandText = strSQL

'  Set the data to read
objDREmp = objCMDEmp.ExecuteReader

'  Read the first record
objDREmp.read

'  Set the label control for the employee data and dates
lblEmployee.text = objDREmp.getvalue(1) & " " & objDREmp.getvalue(2)
lblDates.text = StartDate & " to " & EndDate

End Sub
```

When the page is loaded for the first time, the BindGrid subroutine is called to display the data. As we have seen on the previous pages, the OLE DB connection, command, and data reader objects are created. Two sets of command and data reader objects are created; one is for the data grid and the second is for the employee Label control.

In order to display the data for the 14-day period, we need to calculate the date two weeks previous to the current date. A variable, DI, is declared of type DateInterval. The interval is used in the DateAdd function to determine how much time should be added (or subtracted) from the date.

In this case, we want to subtract 15 days from the current date since any current shifts that are in progress should not be included. The start date for the data is calculated using DateAdd with an interval type of Day. The end date for the period is the current day.

Next, the query is built to retrieve data form the vw_Payroll Access query. Remember that the query combines data from all of the tables to calculate the current rate for each work shift. The dates are used in the where clause of the query. Remember that in Access dates are bounded by # signs. In addition, the employee is set and the data is ordered by the Time In for the shift.

The command object commandtext property is set and the ExecuteReader method is called. The results of the query are stored in the data reader. Then the data grid datasource property is set to the data reader. Finally, the DataBind method of the grid is called to display the data.

The last step is to query for the employee's name and display it in the Label lblEmployee control. The calculated start and end dates are also displayed in the second Label control.

That is it for building the page. Start the employees.aspx page to get the employee listing. Click on the Current Payroll link for one of the employees. The payroll history for the employee is displayed as shown in Figure 5-9.

That is it for building our sample Web Matrix application. There have been several books written on Web Matrix, if you are interested in learning more. On the ASP.NET site there are support forums and additional information on using Web Matrix. Keep in mind that the basic coding environment is still .NET with all of the classes, programming environment, etc.

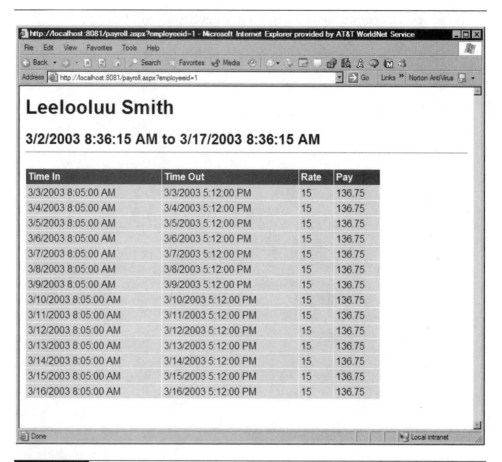

FIGURE 5-9   Employee payroll data

Summary

In this chapter we have shown how Access can be used to build a web application. This included building queries that act like views for our web application. We also introduced the Web Matrix web development tool, which can be downloaded for free. The combination of Access and Web Matrix enable low-cost and easy-to-implement web applications to be deployed. It is also a great combination for building quick and easy prototype applications.

In the next chapter we are going to explore developing full-featured .NET applications based on Microsoft Access. We will take Access-based application development a step further and utilize .NET to build a full-featured application.

Chapter 6

Programming Microsoft Access with .NET

In the last chapter we saw how to do simple ASP.NET Access applications with Web Matrix. Now, in this chapter, we are going to move to Microsoft's enterprise development platform, Visual Studio .NET. With Visual Studio .NET we can build ASP.NET applications with the full power of Visual Basic or C#. In this chapter we are going to build a sample help ticket system for providing customer support. We are going to utilize Visual Basic .NET along with ASP.NET web pages.

We will see how Access can be utilized as the database engine behind more sophisticated applications. This example will also demonstrate how Access can be utilized for prototyping enterprise-wide applications. The database structure, queries, and code created can be migrated to the enterprise platform.

Utilizing .NET

It is not possible to cover all of the issues related to utilizing .NET in this chapter. There have been dozens (if not hundreds) of books written on ASP.NET development using Visual Studio .NET.

For this chapter we will be utilizing Visual Basic .NET for our primary coding platform. All coding will be done using the *code behind* technique, which allows the page interface to be separated from the Visual Basic code. ASP.NET pages will be created and will leverage the controls provided in the Visual Studio design environment.

NOTE   *You might consider reading* ASP.NET: The Complete Reference *or* ASP.NET: A Beginner's Guide *(both McGraw-Hill/Osborne, 2002) to become more familiar with ASP.NET development.*

In addition to .NET, we will be utilizing JavaScript code to implement some of the interface features of our application. There are some interesting techniques we will demonstrate for using a little client-side JavaScripting in the ASP.NET environment.

Designing the Help Ticket System Database

The help ticket system is focused on allowing end users of a particular system or service to be able to log a help ticket and track it. For the support group, it allows them to view and claim tickets. The tickets can then be managed to completion.

Our example in this chapter is the base foundation for the system. This foundation can be easily expanded to provide a number of useful features.

Business Rule Requirements

The business rules for our help ticket data are fairly straightforward. At the core of the system is a ticket that has a creation date, a creator, a support owner, a description of the problem, and a description of the resolution.

A ticket can go through several different stages of support, including being submitted, reviewed, in progress, and closed/completed. Each of these status stages has status notes, a start time, and an owner for that status.

Finally, we will have users for the system. Some of the users are designated as administrators, and they will manage the ticket statuses. Administrator users will be able to claim tickets as they come in and work to resolve them. Standard users can only create tickets and view the status of their tickets. The following shows the logical view of the requirements:

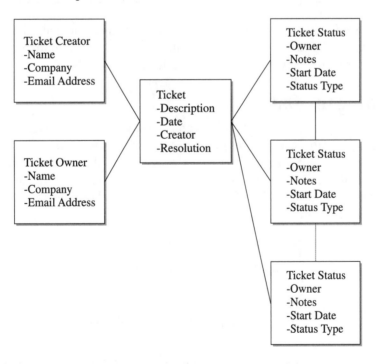

In addition to the capabilities outlined for the users, we also want to be able to search the ticket database for similar tickets to help resolve current open tickets.

As mentioned, we are not attempting to build a complete and fully functional help ticket system. If you would like to leverage this code for your internal use, here are some additional features to consider:

Feature	Description
Email Notifications	When a ticket changes status, emails can be sent to the ticket creator letting them know the status.
Email Requests	Add the ability to receive ticket creation requests via email. This could be done by reading email from a specified email box for tickets and creating the ticket from the body of the email.
Remember Me	Add in a "remember me" capability so users don't have to log in every time.
Password Reminder	Send the user's password to their email address.
Administrative Back End	The example solution does not include any way to update a user's information (such as their password) or set a user to be an admin. These types of tasks would have to be done directly in the database.

As you work with the system you will likely see many additional enhancements, including migrating to SQL Server as an enterprise platform. Importantly, the example code shows how to utilize Access effectively with .NET.

Designing the Data

Our database is going to consist of four tables to store all of the ticket-related data. We are also going to create a series of queries that will be used from our application.

The first table will store the user data. The second will store the primary ticket data. The third is going to store the status history data, and the fourth and final stores the different status types. The following diagram shows the relationship among the tables:

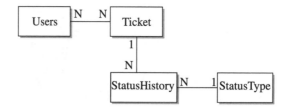

Now let's look at the structure for each table. The following shows the fields for the Users table:

Field	Type	Description
UserID	AutoNumber	Primary key for the users data
UserFirstName	Text	The first name of the user
UserLastName	Text	The last name of the user
UserEmailAddress	Text	Email address of the user
Company	Text	Company the user works for
Admin	Yes/No	Flag indicating if the user is an administrator or not
UserName	Text	Login username for the user
Password	Text	Login password for the user
DateCreated	Date/Time	Date the record was created

This table is pretty straightforward. Note that the Admin field will identify which of the users are administrators of the system. If the flag is not set, a user is just a standard user and can only create and view tickets.

The next table is for storing the ticket data:

Field	Type	Description
TicketID	AutoNumber	Primary key for the ticket data. This will also be used as a ticket identifier for the user.
UserID	Number	Foreign key for the user who created the ticket.
TicketDescription	Memo	The description of the ticket entered by the user.
Archived	Yes/No	Flag indicating if the ticket has been archived or not. A ticket can be closed and not archived. Archived means it will no longer show up on any lists.
TicketResolution	Memo	The resolution description entered when the ticket is closed.
Last_Status	Number	Foreign key to the last status in status history.
OwnerID	Number	Foreign key for the administrative ticket owner/user.

NOTE *Technically, we do not need the Last_Status field in this table. This actually denormalizes the database a little bit because we can get the last status for a ticket by looking in the StatusHistory table directly. But, as we will see in the code, it makes our queries a bit easier to not have to traverse the status history list and get the last status entry. This is a good example of where you may not want to have 100-percent normalization. This type of denormalization will also speed up our application a bit.*

Designing the Help Ticket System Database

Note that in this case our table has two pointers to the Users table. One is to the creator of the ticket and the other is to the administrative owner of the ticket.

Our next table is for storing the StatusHistory data:

Field	Type	Description
StatusHistoryID	AutoNumber	Primary key for the status history data
TicketID	Number	Foreign key to the ticket that this status is for
StatusTypeID	Number	Foreign key to the StatusType table that indicates the type of status
StatusStartDate	Date/Time	Start date when the new status was created
UpdateUserID	Number	Foreign key for the user who set the status
StatusNotes	Memo	Stores the status notes

NOTE   *We do not have a StatusEndDate field. You could add it in the table, and in the application have an explicit feature to indicate when a status step is complete.*

The final table is the StatusType table, which defines the latest status for a ticket:

Field	Type	Description
StatusTypeID	AutoNumber	Primary key for the status type data
StatusName	Text	Name of the status type
StatusDescription	Memo	Description of the status type

The final relationship diagram among the tables is shown in Figure 6-1.

That does it for building our tables. The database provided from the downloadable database site (www.osborne.com) includes sample data for demonstrating the application.

Building Queries

For our application, we are also going to need several queries to pull the data together in appropriate ways. The following table shows the list of queries and the purpose for each.

Query	Description
Claimed_Tickets	Returns the list of tickets that have been claimed by an administrator
End_User_Tickets	Retrieves the list of tickets for end users
Ticket_History	Returns the status history for all tickets
Unclaimed_Tickets	Retrieves the list of tickets not yet claimed by an administrator
Users_List	Returns the list of users

Based on the techniques outlined in the earlier query-focused chapters, you can create these queries. We are not going to step through the process of creating the queries in this chapter. Note that all of the queries were built using the Design view except for the Users_List, which was created using the Query Wizard and modified in the Design view.

The first query, Claimed_Tickets, pulls ticket data where the ticket has an owner. When the data is returned, we want to send back the created user data, the ticket data, and the last status. Figure 6-2 shows the Design view for the query.

Listing 6-1 shows the SQL code for the query.

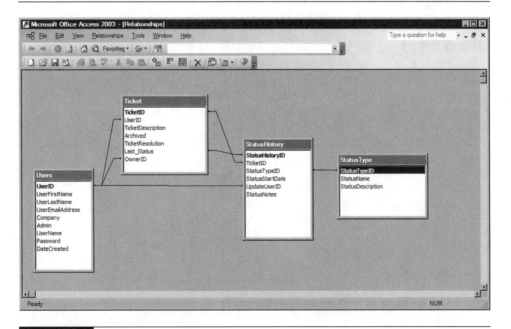

FIGURE 6-1   Table relationships

Designing the Help Ticket System Database

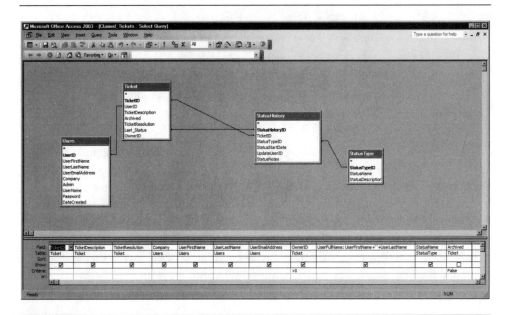

FIGURE 6-2   Claimed_Tickets query Design view

Listing 6-1

```
SELECT Ticket.TicketID, Ticket.TicketDescription,
       Ticket.TicketResolution, Users.Company,
       Users.UserFirstName, Users.UserLastName,
       Users.UserEmailAddress, Ticket.OwnerID,
       UserFirstName+' '+UserLastName AS UserFullName,
       StatusType.StatusName
FROM StatusType INNER JOIN
    ((Users INNER JOIN Ticket ON Users.UserID = Ticket.UserID)
     INNER JOIN StatusHistory ON (Users.UserID =
     StatusHistory.UpdateUserID) AND
     (Ticket.Last_Status = StatusHistory.StatusHistoryID) AND
     (Ticket.TicketID = StatusHistory.TicketID)) ON
     StatusType.StatusTypeID = StatusHistory.StatusTypeID
WHERE (((Ticket.OwnerID)>0) AND ((Ticket.Archived)=False));
```

The query consists of two inner joins, which brings the data together for the three tables. The where clause ensures that archived tickets are not returned, as are tickets that do not have an owner (are unclaimed). Note that we also create a returned field (UserFullName) that combines the user first name and last name.

This will make things a bit easier for utilizing the data in the data grid. Note that all claimed tickets are returned by the query—not just the claimed tickets for a specific user.

The next query, End_User_Tickets, returns all of the tickets created by users. When the tickets are returned, we also want to show the last status. The StatusHistory and StatusType tables are joined with the Ticket table to show the last status. Figure 6-3 shows the Design view for the query.

The SQL generated by the query is shown in Listing 6-2.

Listing 6-2

```
SELECT Ticket.TicketID, Ticket.TicketDescription,
       Ticket.TicketResolution, StatusType.StatusName,
       Ticket.UserID, StatusHistory.StatusStartDate
FROM StatusType INNER JOIN
    (Ticket INNER JOIN StatusHistory ON
    Ticket.Last_Status = StatusHistory.StatusHistoryID)
    ON StatusType.StatusTypeID = StatusHistory.StatusTypeID
WHERE (((Ticket.Archived)=False));
```

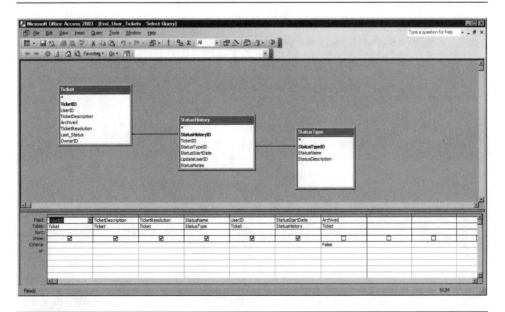

FIGURE 6-3   End_User_Tickets query Design view

Designing the Help Ticket System Database

The SQL for this query is what you would expect. Note that the Ticket.Last_ Status field is joined with the StatusHistoryID. The StatusHistory table is joined with the StatusType table so that the name of the last status for the ticket is retrieved.

The next query, Ticket_History, retrieves the status history for a specific ticket. The user who set the status and the status name are pulled. Figure 6-4 shows the Design view for the query.

The SQL generated for the query is shown in Listing 6-3.

Listing 6-3

```
SELECT Ticket.TicketID, StatusHistory.StatusStartDate,
      StatusHistory.StatusNotes,
      StatusHistory.UpdateUserID, Users.UserFirstName,
      Users.UserLastName, Users.UserEmailAddress,
      StatusType.StatusName, StatusHistory.StatusHistoryID,
      UserFirstName+' '+UserLastName AS UpdateUserFullName
FROM Users INNER JOIN (Ticket INNER JOIN (StatusType
      INNER JOIN StatusHistory ON
      StatusType.StatusTypeID = StatusHistory.StatusTypeID) ON
      Ticket.TicketID = StatusHistory.TicketID) ON
      Users.UserID = StatusHistory.UpdateUserID
ORDER BY StatusHistory.StatusStartDate;
```

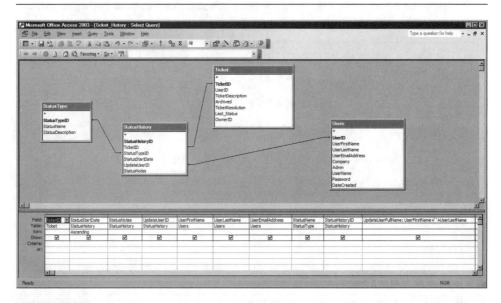

FIGURE 6-4   Ticket_History query Design view

The query contains the three inner joins to pull the tables together. Note that we once again built a field that combines the user's first and last names into one field for easy display.

Our next query, Unclaimed_Tickets, pulls the tickets that have not been claimed by an administrative user. This list will allow administrators to claim tickets to be worked on. The query is similar to the Claimed_Tickets query. But in this case we want tickets where there is no owner, and we do not need to show the last status since it is always Submitted. Figure 6-5 shows the Design view for the query.

The SQL generated for the query is shown in Listing 6-4.

Listing 6-4

```
SELECT Users.Company, Users.UserFirstName,
       Users.UserLastName, Users.UserEmailAddress,
       StatusType.StatusName, StatusHistory.StatusStartDate,
       Ticket.TicketDescription, StatusHistory.TicketID,
       UserFirstName+' '+UserLastName AS EmployeeFullName
FROM Users INNER JOIN (Ticket INNER JOIN (StatusType
     INNER JOIN StatusHistory ON StatusType.StatusTypeID =
     StatusHistory.StatusTypeID) ON Ticket.TicketID =
     StatusHistory.TicketID) ON Users.UserID = Ticket.UserID
WHERE (((Ticket.OwnerID)=0) AND ((Ticket.Archived)=False));
```

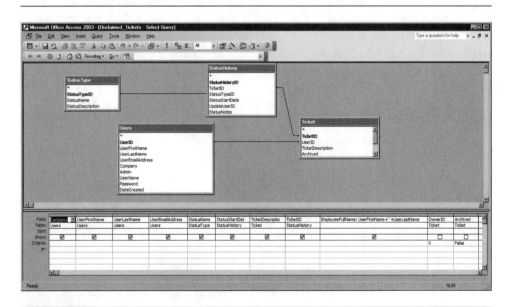

FIGURE 6-5   Unclaimed_Tickets query Design view

Designing the Help Ticket System Database

The query joins together the Users, StatusType, StatusHistory, and Ticket tables. Again, a field is built to combine the user's first and last name.

Our final query returns the list of users from the database. We could get this data using a standard select query from within the application code. But, we also want to have the name combined into one field. Listing 6-5 shows the SQL generated for the query.

Listing 6-5

```
SELECT Users.*,
       UserLastName+', '+UserFirstName AS UserFullName
FROM Users
ORDER BY Users.UserLastName;
```

That does it for setting up the database and the queries. Now we are ready to begin building our .NET application that will utilize the database.

Building the Application

The first step to building the application is to create a new Visual Basic project. The template will be for an ASP.NET web application. Set the location as appropriate for your web server. Save the project as Ticket.

In all, we are going to have 13 web forms for our project. We will be demonstrating different techniques for working with .NET and data as we work through the project.

The first thing we are going to do is create a global application variable that defines the connection string to our database. The database should be placed in a directory called Database at a level below the web location directory of the project.

Now open up the global.asax.vb project file. We are going to add an application-level variable that is created in the Application_Start event. When the Ticket application is started, that event is fired off and we will create our variable. Listing 6-6 shows the code for the event.

Listing 6-6

```
Sub Application_Start(ByVal sender As Object, ByVal e As EventArgs)
    ' Fires when the application is started
    '  Sets the connection string to the database
    Application("strConn") = "PROVIDER=Microsoft.Jet.OLEDB.4.0;" & _
       "DATA SOURCE=" & Server.MapPath("database/ticket.mdb") & ";"
    End Sub
```

Our connection string indicates that a Microsoft Jet OLE DB connection should be utilized. The directory of the database is referenced by using the Server.MapPath function, which returns the hard drive directory location of the Ticket application. We then reference the database subdirectory and the name of the Access database file.

The first page we will build is the login page for the help system. Create a new web form and save it as Default.aspx. We are going to add several items to the page.

First, add a header label that shows the title of the application, Help Ticket System. Next, add a label and name it lblShowError. Change the font to red and bold. This will be used to display login error messages.

Now add a label with instructions indicating the user should enter in their username and password. Add labels for the username and password input fields, then add two text boxes. Name the first txtUserName and the second txtPassword. Add two validator controls for each text box (set the Control.Validate property to the text box). Add appropriate error messages to each validator indicating the user must enter in a username and password.

Finally, add two Submit buttons to the page. The first should be titled "Log In" and named btnLogin. The second should be titled "Register" and named btnRegister. Your page should look similar to Figure 6-6.

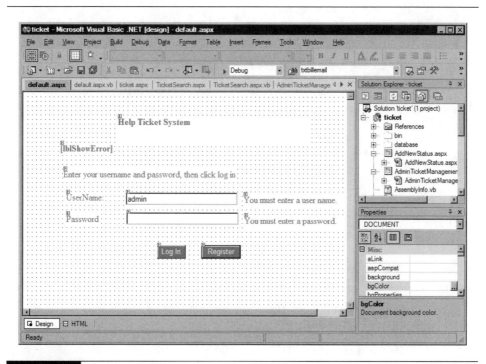

FIGURE 6-6   Login page design

Now we are ready to add the code behind code that will handle the user actions on the page. Listing 6-7 shows the code for the Visual Basic code behind page. Add it to the default.aspx.vb project file.

Listing 6-7

```
Private Sub btnRegister_Click(ByVal sender As System.Object, _
ByVal e As System.EventArgs) Handles btnRegister.Click
    ' Transfer to the registration page
    Server.Transfer("registration.aspx")
End Sub

Private Sub btnLogin_Click(ByVal sender As System.Object, _
ByVal e As System.EventArgs) Handles btnLogin.Click

    Dim objDR As OleDb.OleDbDataReader
    Dim objCMD As New OleDb.OleDbCommand()
    Dim objConn As New OleDb.OleDbConnection()
    Dim blnResult As Boolean
    Dim strSQL As String

    ' Open the DB connection
    objConn.ConnectionString = Application("strConn")
    objConn.Open()

    ' See if the username already exists
    strSQL = "select UserID, Admin from Users where UserName= '" & _
    Replace(txtUserName.Text, "'", "''") & "' and Password = '" & _
    Replace(txtPassword.Text, "'", "''") & "'"

    ' Set the command connection
    objCMD.Connection = objConn

    ' Set the command query
    objCMD.CommandText = strSQL

    ' Set the reader
    objDR = objCMD.ExecuteReader()

    ' Get the result of the read
    blnResult = objDR.Read

    ' If no results, then there is not a match
    If blnResult = False Then
        lblShowError.Text = "Error: User not found."
        lblShowError.Visible = True
```

```
Else
    '  There is a match, track the user id and if they are an admin
    Session("UserID") = objDR.Item("UserID")
    Session("Admin") = objDR.Item("Admin")

    If Session("Admin") = False Then
        '  Transfer to the user tickets page if a user
        Server.Transfer("usertickets.aspx")
    Else
        '  Transfer to the admin ticket management page if an admin
        Server.Transfer("adminticketmanagement.aspx")

    End If

End If

End Sub
```

When the user clicks the Login button, the Click event for the button is fired off. A check is then done to see if the user exists in the database.

> **NOTE** *The database access method we will be using throughout the application uses the OLE DB data access provider. We will be using the various OLE DB objects, including data adaptors, data readers, command objects, etc. To learn more about OLE DB, check out http://msdn.microsoft.com/library/ en-us/dnoledb/html/choosingcomponents.asp?frame=true.*

The first thing that happens in the validation process is that the connection to the database is opened. Note the use of the application-level variable to get the connection string. A SQL statement is created that looks for a matching user with the same username and password. A command object is used to execute the query, with the data returned to a data reader.

A check is done to see if the query returned any results—if not, the error label on our form is displayed with an error message. If a match was returned, we set the UserID session variable to store the user ID. We also check to see if the user is an administrator. If so, that is stored in a session variable.

Depending on if the user is a standard or administrative user, the user is transferred to their corresponding home page. The last thing that happens in the code is that the user is sent to the registration page if they click the Register button.

> **NOTE** *We will be opening and utilizing database access methods on every page. We will not review those steps for the rest of the pages as we discuss them. We will, however, point out new techniques as they are utilized.*

The registration page is a simple form where the user can enter in their first name, last name, username, password, email address, and company. We will also want the user to enter the password twice for verification.

To build the page, add a header label at the top of the page with "Help System" as the text. Below that, add a label called ShowError. Set the font to red and bold.

Next, the form is built. For each of the mentioned fields, create a label, text box, and validator control. The text box names should be prefixed with "txt" and then the field name (e.g., txtUserName, txtFirstName).

Finally, a Submit button needs to be added below the form. Name it SubmitRegistration and set the text to Register. That does it for setting up the page. Figure 6-7 shows the layout of the page.

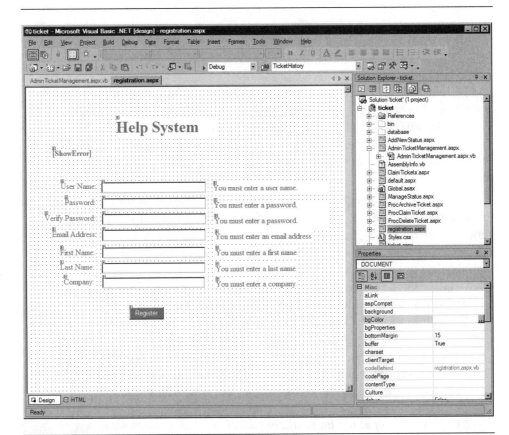

FIGURE 6-7 Registration design layout

Now we are ready to build the code behind page. The form submission will be handled in the Click event of the Submit button. Listing 6-8 shows the code to be added to the Click event.

Listing 6-8

```
Private Sub SubmitRegistration_Click(ByVal sender As _
System.Object, ByVal e As System.EventArgs) Handles _
SubmitRegistration.Click

    Dim objDR As OleDb.OleDbDataReader
    Dim objCMD As New OleDb.OleDbCommand()
    Dim objConn As New OleDb.OleDbConnection()
    Dim strSQL As String
    Dim blnResult As Boolean

    '  Set the connection
    objConn.ConnectionString = Application("strConn")

    '  Open the connection
    objConn.Open()

    '  Set the command connection
    objCMD.Connection = objConn

    '  See if an existing player with the same name exists
    strSQL = "select UserID from Users where UserName= '" & _
    Replace(txtUserName.Text, "'", "''") & "'"

    '  Set the command query
    objCMD.CommandText = strSQL

    '  Set the reader
    objDR = objCMD.ExecuteReader

    '  Get the data and see if anything is returned
    blnResult = objDR.Read

    '  If no data returned
    If (blnResult = False) And _
    (txtPassword.Text = txtVerifyPassword.Text) Then

        '  Build a SQL statement to insert the new user
        strSQL = "insert into Users(UserName, " & _
            "[Password], " & _
            "UserEmailAddress, " & _
```

```
               "UserFirstName, " & _
               "UserLastName, " & _
               "Company, " & _
               "DateCreated) values('" & _
               Replace(txtUserName.Text, "'", "'''") & " ', '" & _
               Replace(txtPassword.Text, "'", "'''") & " ', '" & _
               txtUserEmailAddress.Text & "', '" & _
               Replace(txtUserFirstName.Text, "'", "'''") & "', '" & _
               Replace(txtUserLastName.Text, "'", "'''") & "','" & _
               Replace(txtCompany.Text, "'", "'''") & "', '" & _
               Now() & "')"

        '  Set the command query
        objCMD.CommandText = strSQL

        '  Close the reader
        objDR.Close()

        '  Execute the query
        objCMD.ExecuteNonQuery()

        '  Send the user to the log in page
        Server.Transfer("default.aspx")

    Else

        If blnResult = True Then
            '  Indicate there is a user with the name already
            ShowError.Text = "- The User Name you " & _
            "selected has already been taken.<BR>"
        End If

        If txtPassword.Text <> txtVerifyPassword.Text Then
            '  Indicate the passwords do not match
            ShowError.Text = "- Your password entries do not match."
        End If

        ShowError.Visible = True

        End If
    End Sub
```

When the user clicks Submit, we first have to ensure that another user doesn't have the same username. A select statement is used to see if the same username exists. If so, we will set the error label to indicate that they need to pick another one.

A second check is also done to ensure that the two entered passwords match. If they don't, an error is added to the label control.

If the username is unique and the passwords are correct, the user is set up in the Users table. An insert query is created with the appropriate parameters. Once the registration is complete, the user is sent to the login page.

Next, we are going to review administrative features of the ticket system. These pages will be utilized primarily by users who are administrators.

Add a new web form to the project and save it as AdminTicketManagment .aspx. This page will display the list of tickets that the logged-in administrator currently owns.

The navigation for the application will be a simple series of buttons at the top of the page. We will need options to create a ticket, search tickets, view unclaimed tickets, and log out. Add four buttons with appropriate text at the top of the page. The Click events of each of these buttons will send the user to the appropriate page. For the Logout button, the session variables that store the user ID will need to be cleared. The button names from the sample application can be found in Listing 6-9.

Next, add a label control that says Claimed Tickets. Below that, add a data grid to the page. Name the data grid dgClaimedTickets. The data grid is going to need seven columns set up. The simplest way to set up the columns is to use the property builder feature of the control. Table 6-1 shows the columns for the data grid and settings for the columns.

Column Header Text	Settings	Description
View Ticket Detail	1) URL – ViewStatusHistory.aspx 2) URL Field – TicketID 3) URL Format String – TicketHistory.aspx?ticketid={0}	Hyperlink that will show the ticket history
Archive Ticket	1) URL – ProcArchiveTicket.aspx 2) URL Field – TicketID 3) URL Format String – ProcArchiveTicket.aspx?ticketid={0}	Hyperlink to a page that will archive the ticket
Ticket ID	1) Data Field – TicketID	TicketID data field
Ticket Description	1) Data Field – TicketDescription	TicketDescription data field
Company	1) Data Field – Company	Company data field
User	1) Data Field – UserFullName	The full name of the user, which is created in the query
Last Status	1) Data Field – StatusName	The name of the last status set for the ticket

TABLE 6-1 Data Grid Columns

Note that for the two hyperlink columns the ticket ID is passed on the URL to the target pages. The {0} on the URL format string indicates to the data grid to place the URL field value in that spot of the string. Figure 6-8 shows the layout design of the page.

The code for this page is fairly straightforward. The heavy lifting is done by the Claimed_Tickets query that was created earlier. Listing 6-9 show the code for the page.

Listing 6-9

```
Private Sub Page_Load(ByVal sender As System.Object, _
ByVal e As System.EventArgs) Handles MyBase.Load
    'Put user code to initialize the page here
    Dim objConn As New OleDb.OleDbConnection()
    Dim strSQL As String
    Dim objCMD As New OleDb.OleDbCommand()
    Dim objDa As New OleDb.OleDbDataAdapter()
    Dim objDs As New Data.DataSet()

    '  Open the DB connection
    objConn.ConnectionString = Application("strConn")
    objConn.Open()

    '  Retrieve the claimed tickets
    strSQL = "select * from claimed_tickets where OwnerID=" & _
            Session("UserID")

    '  Set the command connection
    objCMD.Connection = objConn

    '  Set the command query
    objCMD.CommandText = strSQL

    '  Set the command for the data adapter
    objDa.SelectCommand = objCMD

    '  Retrieve the data and set to the data source
    dgClaimedTickets.DataSource = _
        objDa.SelectCommand.ExecuteReader()

    '  Bind the data to the grid
    dgClaimedTickets.DataBind()

End Sub
```

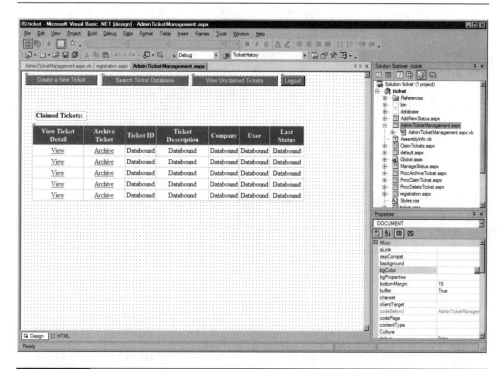

FIGURE 6-8   AdminTicketManagement design layout

The code opens a database connection and uses a data adapter to retrieve the data. The data is then bound to the data grid for display—the data grid takes over and does its thing to display the data.

The following set of code handles the navigation features of the page.

Listing 6-9 *(continued)*

```
Private Sub TicketAgain_Click(ByVal sender As Object, _
ByVal e As System.EventArgs) Handles TicketAgain.Click
    ' Transfer to the ticket page
    Server.Transfer("ticket.aspx")
End Sub

Private Sub Logout_Click(ByVal sender As Object, _
ByVal e As System.EventArgs) Handles Logout.Click
    ' Clear the user and transfer to the log in page
    Session("UserID") = ""
    Server.Transfer("default.aspx")
End Sub
```

```
Private Sub ViewUnclaimed_Click(ByVal sender As System.Object, _
ByVal e As System.EventArgs) Handles ViewUnclaimed.Click
     '  Transfer to the claim tickets
     Server.Transfer("ClaimTickets.aspx")
End Sub

Private Sub GoSearch_Click(ByVal sender As System.Object, _
ByVal e As System.EventArgs) Handles GoSearch.Click
     '  Transfer to the ticket search
     Server.Transfer("TicketSearch.aspx")
End Sub
```

In each of the navigation buttons, the user is sent to the appropriate page. For the Logout button, the session variable is cleared first.

NOTE *The administration navigation buttons are pretty much the same throughout all of the administration pages. We will not be reviewing the subroutines throughout the rest of the text.*

Next, let's take a look at how a ticket is added to the system. Create a new web form for the project and save it as ticket.aspx. This page will allow a new ticket to be created.

Add navigation buttons to the top of the page. In this case, we are going to have buttons that will be seen by both administrators and standard users. Standard users will be able to create tickets as well. For the administrator, buttons are needed for returning to the claimed ticket list, searching for tickets, viewing unclaimed tickets, and logging out. For the end user, a button is needed for returning to their ticket list. Name the buttons as appropriate, and for each have the user sent to the appropriate page. Remember for the logout to clear the UserID session variable.

Next, add a text box on the page and name it TicketBox. Set the TextMode property to MultiLine. Finally, add a Submit button below the text box. Name it submitTicket. Figure 6-9 shows the design layout of the page.

When the page loads, we need to ensure the right navigation buttons are visible based on who the user is. A check is done on the Admin session variable. If the user is an admin, the administrative-related navigation buttons are displayed and the end user buttons are set to invisible. The opposite is true if the user is not an administrator. Listing 6-10 shows the code.

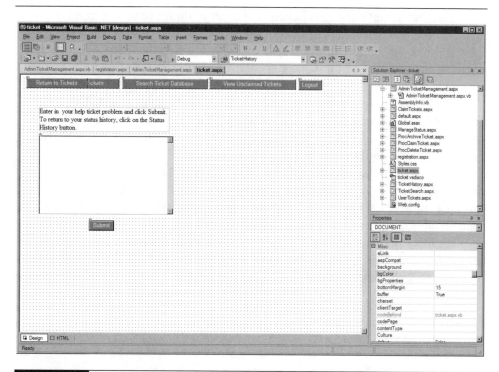

FIGURE 6-9 Ticket design layout

Listing 6-10

```
Private Sub Page_Load(ByVal sender As System.Object, _
ByVal e As System.EventArgs) Handles MyBase.Load
    'Put user code to initialize the page here

    '  Check to see if the user is an administrator
    If Session("admin") = False Then

        '  Show the right navigation buttons
        SearchTickets.Visible = False
        ViewUnclaimed.Visible = False
        ViewTickets.Visible = False
    Else
        '  Show only the option to go back to the ticket list
        UserTickets.Visible = False
    End If
End Sub
```

When the Submit button is clicked, a number of things have to happen to insert the ticket into the database. The ticket data is first inserted into the database. This sets the ticket description, creation date, and user creating the ticket. We also have to check and see if an administrator is creating the ticket. If so, we will automatically set the ticket owner to be the administrative user.

After the insert, we need to get the ID of the newly created ticket. This can be done by requesting a meta variable value from the database. The @@identity variable will return the last incremented autonumber value from our insert. Thus, we retrieve the ticketID value of the newly inserted ticket.

With the ticketID in hand, we can now insert the status of the ticket into the status history. In this case, we will be setting the status to Submitted (value of 1). Once the status history is inserted, we once again need to use the @@identify meta variable to retrieve the ID of the new status history entry.

With that status entry ID, the ticket can be updated to point to the last status record. An update query is executed to update the Last_Status field of our ticket. And with that, the ticket has been created.

Listing 6-10 *(continued)*

```
Private Sub submitTicket_Click(ByVal sender As Object, _
ByVal e As System.EventArgs) Handles submitTicket.Click

    '  See if the form was posted back
    If IsPostBack Then
        Dim objConn As New OleDb.OleDbConnection()
        Dim strSQL As String
        Dim objDa As New OleDb.OleDbDataAdapter()
        Dim TicketID As Integer
        Dim objCMD As New OleDb.OleDbCommand()
        Dim StatusHistoryID As Integer

        '  Open the DB connection
        objConn.ConnectionString = Application("strConn")
        objConn.Open()

        '  Insert the ticket into the database
        strSQL = "insert into Ticket(UserID, " & _
        "TicketDescription, Last_Status)" & _
        " values('" & Session("UserID") & " ', '" & _
        Replace(TicketBox.Text, "'", "''") & "', 1)"

        '  Execute an insert command
        objDa.InsertCommand() = New OleDb.OleDbCommand(strSQL, objConn)
```

```
objDa.InsertCommand.ExecuteNonQuery()

'  Get back the new Ticket ID value
objDa.SelectCommand() = New OleDb.OleDbCommand(_
"Select @@IDENTITY", objConn)

'  Get the ticketid value
TicketID = objDa.SelectCommand.ExecuteScalar()

'  Check to see if the user is an administrator or not
If Session("Admin") = True Then

    '  Insert the ticket and indicate the administrator who
    '  created the ticket is the owner
    strSQL = "insert into StatusHistory(TicketID, " & _
    "StatusTypeID, StatusStartDate, UpdateUserID)" & _
    " values('" & TicketID & "','1','" & Now() & "', " & _
    Session("UserID") & ")"

Else

    '  Insert an unclaimed ticket
    strSQL = "insert into StatusHistory(TicketID, " & _
    " StatusTypeID, StatusStartDate, UpdateUserID)" & _
    " values('" & TicketID & "','1','" & Now() & "', " & _
    Session("UserID") & ")"
End If

'  Execute the insert
objDa.InsertCommand.CommandText = strSQL
objDa.InsertCommand.Connection = objConn
objDa.InsertCommand.ExecuteNonQuery()

'  Get back the new status history ID value
objDa.SelectCommand() = New OleDb.OleDbCommand(_
"Select @@IDENTITY", objConn)

'  Get the statushistoryid value
StatusHistoryID = objDa.SelectCommand.ExecuteScalar()

'  Update the last status for the ticket
strSQL = "update ticket set " & _
        "last_status = " & StatusHistoryID & _
        " where ticketid = " & TicketID

'  Set the command connection
objCMD.Connection = objConn
```

```
        '  Set the command query
        objCMD.CommandText = strSQL

        '  Execute for no returned data
        objCMD.ExecuteScalar()

        '  Close the connection
        objConn.Close()

        '  Send the user to the right page depending on who they are
        If Session("Admin") = True Then
            Server.Transfer("adminticketmanagement.aspx")
        Else
            Server.Transfer("usertickets.aspx")
        End If
    End If
End Sub
```

The following code handles the navigation buttons of the page. Note that the ViewTickets_Click routine checks to see which page to send the user to based on if they are an administrator or not.

```
'  *******  Navigate to the appropriate page
Private Sub ViewUnclaimed_Click(ByVal sender As System.Object, _
ByVal e As System.EventArgs) Handles ViewUnclaimed.Click
    Server.Transfer("claimtickets.aspx")
End Sub

Private Sub ViewTickets_Click(ByVal sender As System.Object, _
ByVal e As System.EventArgs) Handles ViewTickets.Click
    If Session("admin") = True Then
        Server.Transfer("adminticketmanagement.aspx")
    Else
        Server.Transfer("UserTickets.aspx")
    End If
End Sub

Private Sub Logout_Click(ByVal sender As System.Object, _
ByVal e As System.EventArgs) Handles Logout.Click
    Session("userid") = ""
    Server.Transfer("default.aspx")
End Sub

Private Sub SearchTickets_Click(ByVal sender As System.Object, _
ByVal e As System.EventArgs) Handles SearchTickets.Click
```

```
    Server.Transfer("TicketSearch.aspx")
End Sub

Private Sub UserTickets_Click(ByVal sender As System.Object, _
ByVal e As System.EventArgs) Handles UserTickets.Click
    Server.Transfer("UserTickets.aspx")
End Sub
```

Next, let's look at how unclaimed tickets are displayed and selected by administrators to work on. Create a new web form and save it as ClaimTickets.aspx. Add navigation buttons for returning to the claimed tickets list, searching for tickets, creating a new ticket, and logging out. Name the buttons as appropriate and add in the appropriate redirect code.

Next, add a label control to the page and set the text to "Unclaimed Tickets:". Finally, add a data grid control to the page and name it dgUnclaimedTickets. Table 6-2 shows the columns for the grid.

That is it for setting up the page. Figure 6-10 shows the design layout for the page.

Listing 6-11 shows the code for the page. Note that the navigation button code is not included in the listing.

Building the Application

Column Header Text	Settings	Description
Claim Ticket	1) URL - ProcClaimTicket.aspx 2) URL Field – TicketID 3) URL Format String – ProcClaimTicket.aspx?TicketID={0}	Hyperlink that will allow the user to claim the ticket
Delete Ticket	1) URL – ProcDeleteTicket 2) URL Field – TicketID 3) URL Format String – ProcDeleteTicket.aspx?ticketid={0}	Hyperlink to delete the ticket
Ticket ID	1) Data Field – TicketID	TicketID data field
Ticket Description	1) Data Field – TicketDescription	TicketDescription data field
Company	1) Data Field – Company	Company data field
User	1) Data Field – EmployeeFullName	The full name of the user, which is created in the query
Date/Time Submitted	1) Data Field – StatusStartDate	The date/time the ticket was created

TABLE 6-2   Data Grid Columns

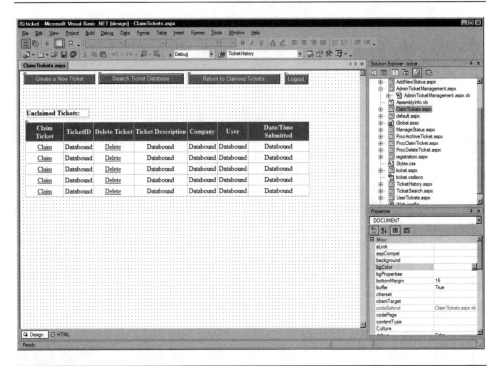

FIGURE 6-10   ClaimTicket.aspx design layout

Listing 6-11

```
Private Sub Page_Load(ByVal sender As System.Object, _
ByVal e As System.EventArgs) Handles MyBase.Load
    'Put user code to initialize the page here
    '  Check to see if this is the first time the page is displayed
    If Not IsPostBack Then

        Dim objConn As New OleDb.OleDbConnection()
        Dim strSQL As String
        Dim objCMD As New OleDb.OleDbCommand()
        Dim objDa As New OleDb.OleDbDataAdapter()
        Dim objDs As New Data.DataSet()

        '  Open the DB connection
        objConn.ConnectionString = Application("strConn")
        objConn.Open()

        '  Retrieve the unclaimed tickets
        strSQL = " SELECT * from unclaimed_tickets"
```

```
        '  Set the command connection
        objCMD.Connection = objConn

        '  Set the command query
        objCMD.CommandText = strSQL

        '  Set the select command
        objDa.SelectCommand = objCMD

        '  Set the data source
        dgUnclaimedTickets.DataSource = _
            objDa.SelectCommand.ExecuteReader()

        '  Bind the data to the data grid
        dgUnclaimedTickets.DataBind()

        '  Close the connection
        objCMD.Connection.Close()

    End If

  End Sub
```

Most of the work for the page is done by the Unclaimed_Tickets query in the Access database. All of the data from that query is retrieved and then bound to the data grid. That is it.

Let's now look at how the tickets are claimed and deleted. Add a new web form to the project and save it as ProcClaimTicket.aspx, the page of which is shown in Listing 6-12. The design of the page has the same navigation buttons as the claim tickets page. In addition, there is a label control that indicates the ticket was claimed successfully.

Listing 6-12

```
    Private Sub Page_Load(ByVal sender As System.Object, _
        ByVal e As System.EventArgs) Handles MyBase.Load
      'Put user code to initialize the page here

      Dim objConn As New OleDb.OleDbConnection()
      Dim strSQL As String
      Dim objCMD As New OleDb.OleDbCommand()
      Dim objDa As New OleDb.OleDbDataAdapter()
      Dim objDs As New Data.DataSet()

      '  Open the DB connection
```

Building the Application

```
objConn.ConnectionString = Application("strConn")
objConn.Open()

' Update the ticket and change the owner to the claimed owner
strSQL = "Update Ticket set " & _
         "OwnerID = " & Session("UserID") & _
         " where ticketid = " & Request.QueryString("ticketid")

' Set the command connection
objCMD.Connection = objConn

' Set the command query
objCMD.CommandText = strSQL

' Execute the query
objCMD.ExecuteScalar()

End Sub
```

To claim the ticket, the OwnerID field of the ticket is set to the current user ID of the administrator.

The next page handles deleting an unclaimed ticket. Add a new web form to the project and save it as ProcDeleteTicket.aspx. Note that the delete logic is only available on the unclaimed ticket listing. Active tickets can only be archived. Listing 6-13 shows the code for deleting a ticket. The page has the same navigation buttons as the unclaimed tickets page.

Listing 6-13

```
Private Sub Page_Load(ByVal sender As System.Object, _
       ByVal e As System.EventArgs) Handles MyBase.Load
    'Put user code to initialize the page here
    Dim objConn As New OleDb.OleDbConnection()
    Dim strSQL As String
    Dim objCMD As New OleDb.OleDbCommand()
    Dim objDa As New OleDb.OleDbDataAdapter()
    Dim objDs As New Data.DataSet()

    ' Open the DB connection
    objConn.ConnectionString = Application("strConn")
```

```
    objConn.Open()

    ' Delete the status history entries for the ticket
    strSQL = "delete from StatusHistory where ticketid = " & _
            Request.QueryString("ticketid")

    ' Set the command connection
    objCMD.Connection = objConn

    ' Set the command query
    objCMD.CommandText = strSQL

    ' Execute the query
    objCMD.ExecuteScalar()

    ' Open and close the connection
    objConn.Close()
    objConn.Open()

    ' Delete the ticket
    strSQL = "delete from Ticket where ticketid = " & _
            Request.QueryString("ticketid")

    ' Set the command connection
    objCMD.Connection = objConn

    ' Set the command query
    objCMD.CommandText = strSQL

    ' Execute the query
    objCMD.ExecuteScalar()
End Sub
```

When the ticket is deleted, note that any related status history records need to be deleted as well. Note that only status record should be for the Submitted status.

The processing for archiving a ticket works the same as claiming and deleting tickets. Note that the archive link is shown on the claimed ticket listing. Add a new web form to the project and save it as ProcArchiveTicket.aspx. Listing 6-14 shows the code for the page.

Listing 6-14

```
Private Sub Page_Load(ByVal sender As System.Object, _
ByVal e As System.EventArgs) Handles MyBase.Load
    'Put user code to initialize the page here
    Dim objConn As New OleDb.OleDbConnection()
    Dim strSQL As String
    Dim objCMD As New OleDb.OleDbCommand()
    Dim objDa As New OleDb.OleDbDataAdapter()
    Dim objDs As New Data.DataSet()

    '  Open the DB connection
    objConn.ConnectionString = Application("strConn")
    objConn.Open()

    '  Update the ticket and set the archived field
    strSQL = "Update ticket set archived = True where ticketid = " & _
             Request.QueryString("ticketid")

    '  Set the command connection
    objCMD.Connection = objConn

    '  Execute the query
    objCMD.CommandText = strSQL

    objCMD.ExecuteScalar()

End Sub
```

On this page, a query is executed that sets the archive flag on the ticket. All of the listing queries return only tickets that are not archived.

Now we are ready to look at the administrative pages that handle the status for a ticket. Add a new web form to the project and save it as TicketHistory.aspx. This page handles listing the ticket history for the page.

Add four navigation buttons to the page—one for creating a new ticket, the second for searching the tickets database, the third for viewing the claimed tickets, and the last for logging out. Name the buttons appropriately and add the appropriate code logic.

There are two sections to the page. The first is a form for managing the core ticket data, including the ticket description, owner, and ticket resolution. First, add a label control to the form and name it lblTicketCreator. Next to it, add a label with the text set to "Customer:".

Next, add a text box and set its TextMode to MultiLine. Name the control txtDescription. Add a label control next to it with the text set as "Ticket Description". Add a drop-down list control to the page and name it ddlUsers. Add a label control next to it with the text set as "Owner:". Add a second text box and set its TextMode property to MultiLine. Name the control txtResolution. Add a label control next to it with the text set as "Ticket Resolution". Finally, add a Submit button and name it btnUpdate. Set the text for the button to "Update".

The next section of the page lists the status entries for the ticket and a link is shown for adding a new status. Add a HyperLink web control to the page and name it AddNewStatus. Set the Text property to "Add New Status". Next, add a data grid control to the page and name it dgTicketHistory. Table 6-3 shows the column properties for the control.

The design layout for the page is shown in Figure 6-11.

For this page, we are going to use a little bit of JavaScript magic to pop up the status management pages for adding a new status and managing an existing status. In order to do this, we want the window to pop up without any toolbars or menus. A JavaScript function needs to be added to the HTML of the TicketHistory.aspx page. Listing 6-15 shows a partial listing for the page. Add the JavaScript section to your page.

This pop-up function essentially takes in the URL and pop-up window width and height. It then opens up a new window with the URL, with the specified width and height. The window.open function specifies the settings for the window. The scroll bar and toolbar options are not set.

Column Header Text	Settings	Description
Manage Status		This is a template column—see the template code in Listing 6-15.
Status History ID	1) Data Field – StatusHistoryID	StatusHistoryID data field
Start Date	1) Data Field – StatusStartDate	StatusStartDate data field
Status	1) Data Field – StatusName	Status data field
Status Notes	1) Data Field – StatusNotes	StatusNotes data field
Status Admin	1) Data Field – UpdateUserFullName	The status admin user

TABLE 6-3   Data Grid Columns

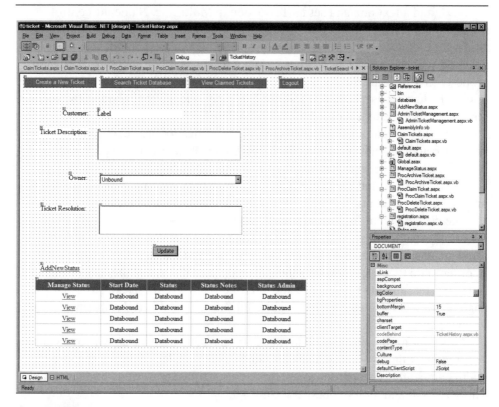

FIGURE 6-11   TicketHistory.aspx design layout

Listing 6-15

```javascript
<script language="javascript">
    function popUp(url, width, height) {
        var intWidth=340;
        var intHeight=100;
        if(width > 0) intWidth = width;
        if(height > 0) intHeight = height;

        var winPopUp = window.open(url,'popup','width=' +
         intWidth + ',height=' + intHeight + ',
        resizable,left=30,top=45');

        if(typeof window.focus != 'undefined') javascript:
            winPopUp.focus();
    }
```

```
            </script>
      </HEAD>
. . . . . . .
. . . . . . .
          <asp:datagrid id="dgTicketHistory" style="Z-INDEX: 100; ⤶
          LEFT: 38px; POSITION: absolute; TOP: 480px" runat="server" ⤶
          BackColor="White"
              Width="656px" AutoGenerateColumns="False" CellPadding="3"
              BorderWidth="1px" BorderStyle="None" BorderColor="#CCCCCC">
          <SelectedItemStyle Font-Bold="True" HorizontalAlign="Center"
              ForeColor="White" BackColor="#669999"></SelectedItemStyle>
          <EditItemStyle HorizontalAlign="Center"></EditItemStyle>
          <AlternatingItemStyle HorizontalAlign="Center">
            </AlternatingItemStyle>
          <ItemStyle HorizontalAlign="Center" ForeColor="#000066"></ItemStyle>
          <HeaderStyle Font-Bold="True" HorizontalAlign="Center"
              ForeColor="White" BackColor="#006699"></HeaderStyle>
          <FooterStyle ForeColor="#000066" BackColor="White"></FooterStyle>
              <Columns>
                  <asp:TemplateColumn HeaderText="Manage Status">
                      <ItemTemplate>
                          <asp:Hyperlink runat="server" Text="View" ⤶
    NavigateUrl='<%# "javascript:popUp(""ManageStatus.aspx? ⤶
    statushistoryid=" & Container.DataItem("StatusHistoryID")& ⤶
"&ticketid=" & Container.DataItem("ticketid") & """)"  %>' ⤶
    ID="Hyperlink1"/>
                      </ItemTemplate>
                  </asp:TemplateColumn>
                  <asp:BoundColumn Visible="False" DataField="StatusHistoryID"
                      ReadOnly="True"></asp:BoundColumn>
                  <asp:BoundColumn DataField="StatusStartDate"
                      HeaderText="Start Date"></asp:BoundColumn>
                  <asp:BoundColumn DataField="StatusName"
                      HeaderText="Status"></asp:BoundColumn>
                  <asp:BoundColumn DataField="StatusNotes"
                      HeaderText="Status Notes"></asp:BoundColumn>
                  <asp:BoundColumn DataField="UpdateUserFullName"
                      HeaderText="Status Admin"></asp:BoundColumn>
              </Columns>
              <PagerStyle Visible="False" HorizontalAlign="Left"
                  ForeColor="#000066" Position="TopAndBottom"
                  BackColor="White"></PagerStyle>
          </asp:datagrid>
```

Things get a little tricky when trying to use the datagrid control with JavaScript. When the View links for the Manage Status columns are clicked on, we need to invoke the popUp function and pass in the URL. The URL also needs to contain a query string parameter indicating what status record for what ticket is being managed.

The View hyperlink was set up as an item template. That allows us to go into the HTML code for the data grid and modify it. We are then able to use the Container object, which contains the data to be shown in the data grid. The NavigateUrl property for the hyperlink column can then be set up to have the two query string parameters (statushistoryID and ticketID) that need to be passed to the pop-up window. From Listing 6-15, the following is the NavigateUrl property for the HyperLink.

```
NavigateUrl='<%# "javascript:popUp(""ManageStatus.aspx? ⤸
   statushistoryid=" & Container.DataItem("StatusHistoryID")& ⤸
   "&ticketid=" & Container.DataItem("ticketid") & """)"  %>' ⤸
   ID="Hyperlink1"/>
```

Note the javascript:popUp code that calls the popUp function. Then the container object is used to insert the right data values into the URL call for the ManageStatus .aspx page. The end result is a call to the popUp function with a URL that contains the right query string.

Now let's look at the code for the TicketHistory.aspx page. Listing 6-16 shows the code for the page (except for the navigation buttons). Three things happen when the page is loaded for the first time. First, the Add New Status link is set to pop up the AddNewStatus.aspx page. It follows the same logic as was used in the data grid. The ticketID is passed on the query string so the status can be associated with the right ticket. Second, the data grid is bound to the TicketHistory query results where the status history records are for the current ticket. Note that the ticketID is read off of the query string. Third, the core ticket data is read and displayed in the fields of our page. The drop-down list of users is filled with all of the current users of the system. Note that for the drop-down list of users, we loop through the list and default the current owner.

Listing 6-16

```
Private Sub Page_Load(ByVal sender As System.Object, _
ByVal e As System.EventArgs) Handles MyBase.Load

    Dim objConn As New OleDb.OleDbConnection()
    Dim strSQL As String
    Dim objCMD As New OleDb.OleDbCommand()
```

```
Dim objDa As New OleDb.OleDbDataAdapter()
Dim objDs As New Data.DataSet()
Dim objDR As OleDb.OleDbDataReader
Dim OwnerID As Integer
Dim intCnt As Integer
'  Check to see if this is the first time the page is displayed
If Not IsPostBack Then

'  Build the navigation URL to execute JavaScript to
'  pop up the page
   AddNewStatus.NavigateUrl = _
      "javascript:popUp('addnewstatus.aspx?ticketid=" & _
      Request.QueryString("ticketid") & "');"

      '  Open the DB connection
      objConn.ConnectionString = Application("strConn")
      objConn.Open()

'  Retrieve the ticket history
strSQL = "select * from Ticket_History where " & _
         "Ticket.ticketid = " & _
         Request.QueryString("ticketid")

      '  Set the command connection
      objCMD.Connection = objConn

      '  Set the command query
      objCMD.CommandText = strSQL

      '  Set the select command
      objDa.SelectCommand = objCMD

      '  Set the data source and retrieve the data
      dgTicketHistory.DataSource = _
            objDa.SelectCommand.ExecuteReader()

      ' Display the grid data
      dgTicketHistory.DataBind()

      '  Close and open the connection
      objConn.Close()
      objConn.Open()

      '  Retrieve the claimed ticket data
      strSQL = "Select * from Claimed_Tickets where " & _
        "ticket.ticketid = " & Request.QueryString("ticketid")

      '  Set the command query
```

```
objCMD.CommandText = strSQL

' Retrieve the data
objDR = objCMD.ExecuteReader()

' Get the result of the read
objDR.Read()

' Show the ticket originator
lblTicketCreator.Text = objDR.Item("UserFirstName") & " " & _
  objDR.Item("UserLastName") & " - " & objDR.Item("Company")

' Show the ticket description
txtDescription.Text = objDR.Item("TicketDescription")

' If there is a resolution, display it
If Not IsDBNull(objDR.Item("TicketResolution")) Then
    txtResolution.Text = objDR.Item("TicketResolution")
End If

' Get the owner id
OwnerID = objDR.Item("OwnerID")

' Open and close the data connection
objConn.Close()
objConn.Open()

' Retrieve the list of users
strSQL = "Select * from Users_List"

' Set the command query
objCMD.CommandText = strSQL

' Send the data to the grid
ddlUsers.DataSource = objCMD.ExecuteReader

' Indicate the table/view to retrieve the data from
ddlUsers.DataMember = "Claimed_Tickets"

' Set the field to use for display
ddlUsers.DataTextField = "UserFullName"

' Set the field for the option value
ddlUsers.DataValueField = "UserID"

' Bind the list of users to the data grid
ddlUsers.DataBind()
```

```vb
        '  Loop through the rows in the drop down list
        For intCnt = 0 To ddlUsers.Items.Count - 1

            '  Check to see if the user matches the current owner
            If ddlUsers.Items(intCnt).Value = OwnerID Then

                '  Set the current owner as the default and exit
                ddlUsers.SelectedIndex = intCnt
                Exit For
            End If

        Next
    End If
End Sub

Private Sub btnUpdate_Click(ByVal sender As System.Object, _
ByVal e As System.EventArgs) Handles btnUpdate.Click

    Dim objConn As New OleDb.OleDbConnection()
    Dim strSQL As String
    Dim objCMD As New OleDb.OleDbCommand()

    '  Open the DB connection
    objConn.ConnectionString = Application("strConn")
    objConn.Open()

'  Update the ticket data
strSQL = "update ticket set " & _
"TicketResolution = '" & Replace(txtResolution.Text, "'", "''") & _
"', TicketDescription = '" & _
Replace(txtDescription.Text, "'", "''") & _
"', ownerid = " & ddlUsers.SelectedItem.Value & _
"  where ticket.ticketid = " & Request.QueryString("ticketid")

    '  Set the command connection
    objCMD.Connection = objConn

    '  Set the command query
    objCMD.CommandText = strSQL

    '  Execute the query
    objCMD.ExecuteScalar()

    objConn.Close()

End Sub
```

The Click event for the Update button is called when the user is ready to update the core ticket data. When the event is fired, a SQL update statement is created that updates the ticket data.

Next, let's look at how current status settings are managed. Add a new web form to the project and save it as ManageStatus.aspx. Remember that this page is a pop-up from the View links in the ticket history page data grid. It does not need any navigation buttons.

Four items need to be added to the page. The first is a multiline text box named txtStatusNotes. Add a label next to it with the text set as "Status Notes:". A drop-down box needs to be added for displaying the status types. Name the drop-down box ddlStatusTypes. Add a label next to it with the text set as "Status Type:".

Add a Submit button to the page and name it btnUpdate. Set the text to "Update". Finally, add a hyperlink web control to the page. Set the text to "Status Added – Click to Continue". The design layout for the page is shown in Figure 6-12.

A JavaScript function also needs to be added to the HTML of the page. The following shows the code for the function.

```
<script language="JavaScript">
<!--
//  Link to the program page to show the program -
//  the link is stored as the select box value
function RefreshTopParent()
{
window.opener.location="tickethistory.aspx?ticketid=↵
<%=request.querystring("ticketid")%>"
window.close();
}
-->
```

This function will update the parent page so that the change in status is displayed. Note the use of a bit of ASP VBScript to insert the ticketID on the query string call to TicketHistory.aspx. Add this code to the HTML of the ManageStatus.aspx page.

Listing 6-17 shows the code for the page. When the page is loaded, a couple of things happen. If the page is being displayed for the first time, the navigate URL is set for returning to the ticket history page. Note the call to the RefreshTopParent JavaScript function.

The status data is also retrieved from the database based on the StatusHistoryID on the query string URL. The current StatusTypeID is retrieved. The ddlStatusType drop-down list is populated from the database. The current status type is defaulted as the selection in the list box.

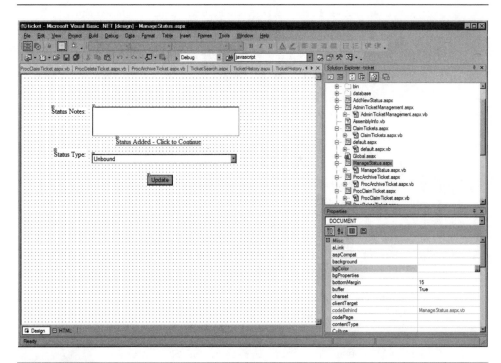

FIGURE 6-12 ManageStatus.aspx design layout

Listing 6-17

```
Private Sub Page_Load(ByVal sender As System.Object, _
ByVal e As System.EventArgs) Handles MyBase.Load

    'Put user code to initialize the page here
    Dim objConn As New OleDb.OleDbConnection()
    Dim strSQL As String
    Dim objCMD As New OleDb.OleDbCommand()
    Dim objDa As New OleDb.OleDbDataAdapter()
    Dim objDs As New Data.DataSet()
    Dim objDR As OleDb.OleDbDataReader
    Dim intCnt As Integer
    Dim StatusTypeID As Integer

    If Not IsPostBack Then

        '   Set the navigation to the javascript to
        '   refresh the parent and close the window
```

```
StatusAdded.NavigateUrl = "javascript: RefreshTopParent( );"

' Open the DB connection
objConn.ConnectionString = Application("strConn")
objConn.Open()

' Set the command connection
objCMD.Connection = objConn

' Retrieve the status history data for the status
strSQL = "Select * from statushistory where " & _
        "statushistoryid = " & _
            Request.QueryString("statushistoryid")

' Set the command query
objCMD.CommandText = strSQL

' Execute the query and get the results
objDR = objCMD.ExecuteReader()

' Get the result of the read
objDR.Read()

' Ensure data is in the field
If Not IsDBNull(objDR.Item("StatusNotes")) Then
    ' Show the status
    txtStatusNotes.Text = objDR.Item("StatusNotes")
End If

' Ensure data is in the field
If Not IsDBNull(objDR.Item("StatusTypeID")) Then
    ' Get the ID
    StatusTypeID = objDR.Item("StatusTypeID")
End If

' Close and reopen the connection
objConn.Close()
objConn.Open()

' Set the command connection
objCMD.Connection = objConn

' Get all of the status types
strSQL = "Select * from StatusType"

' Set the command query
objCMD.CommandText = strSQL
```

```
'  Set the drop down list data source
ddlStatusTypes.DataSource = objCMD.ExecuteReader

'  Indicate the table
ddlStatusTypes.DataMember = "StatusType"

'  Indicate the display text as the status name
ddlStatusTypes.DataTextField = "StatusName"

'  Set the value field to the type id
ddlStatusTypes.DataValueField = "StatusTypeID"

'  Bind the data to the drop down list
ddlStatusTypes.DataBind()

'  Loop through the drop down list options
For intCnt = 0 To ddlStatusTypes.Items.Count - 1

'  Find the status type that matches the currently set type id
    If ddlStatusTypes.Items(intCnt).Value = StatusTypeID Then
        '  If found then select it and exit the loop
        ddlStatusTypes.SelectedIndex = intCnt
        Exit For
    End If

Next

Else

'  Open the DB connection
objConn.ConnectionString = Application("strConn")
objConn.Open()

'  Update the status history based on the data entered by the user
strSQL = "update statushistory set " & _
  "StatusTypeID = " & ddlStatusTypes.SelectedItem.Value & _
  ", statusnotes='" & _
  Replace(txtStatusNotes.Text, "'", "''") & _
  "' where statushistoryid = " & _
  Request.QueryString("statushistoryid")

'  Set the command connection
objCMD.Connection = objConn

'  Set the command query
objCMD.CommandText = strSQL

'  Execute the query with no returned results
```

Building the Application

```
objCMD.ExecuteScalar()

objConn.Close()

'  Show the message
StatusAdded.Visible = True

'  Hide the rest of the page elements
btnUpdate.Visible = False
ddlStatusTypes.Visible = False
lblStatusType.Visible = False
txtStatusNotes.Visible = False
lblStatusNotes.Visible = False

    End If

End Sub
```

When the user clicks the Update button, the status history data is updated with the new notes and with any status type change. When that happens, the data entry elements of the page are hidden. The hyperlink is then displayed. The user can then click on the link to close the window and see the ticket history updated.

Our next page handles adding a new status to the ticket. Add a new web form to the project and save it as AddNewStatus.aspx. Add the same elements and JavaScript code from the ManageStatus.aspx to this page. There are two minor differences. The first is that the text on the hyperlink should be "Status Added – Click to Continue". The second is that the Submit button should be named btnAdd and the text should be "Add". Figure 6-13 shows the design layout for the page.

When the page is first displayed, the drop-down list of status types is populated. Note that no status is defaulted. Also, the hyperlink is set to call the RefreshTopParent JavaScript function. Listing 6-18 shows the code for the page.

Listing 6-18

```
Private Sub Page_Load(ByVal sender As System.Object, _
ByVal e As System.EventArgs) Handles MyBase.Load
    Dim objConn As New OleDb.OleDbConnection()
    Dim strSQL As String
    Dim objCMD As New OleDb.OleDbCommand()
    Dim objDa As New OleDb.OleDbDataAdapter()
    Dim StatusHistoryID As Integer

    If Not IsPostBack Then

        '  Build the navigation URL to execute the javascript
```

```
'  and refresh the parent and close the window
StatusAdded.NavigateUrl = "javascript: RefreshTopParent( );"

'  Open the DB connection
objConn.ConnectionString = Application("strConn")
objConn.Open()

'  Set the command connection
objCMD.Connection = objConn

'  Get all of the status types
strSQL = "Select * from StatusType"

'  Set the command query
objCMD.CommandText = strSQL

'  Set the drop down list data source to the returned data
ddlStatusTypes.DataSource = objCMD.ExecuteReader

'  Specify the table
ddlStatusTypes.DataMember = "StatusType"

'  The display text field is the status name
ddlStatusTypes.DataTextField = "StatusName"

'  The Value of each option is set to the ID for status type
ddlStatusTypes.DataValueField = "StatusTypeID"

'  Bind the data
ddlStatusTypes.DataBind()

Else

'  Open the DB connection
objConn.ConnectionString = Application("strConn")
objConn.Open()

'  insert the new status
strSQL = "insert into statushistory(TicketID, " & _
         "StatusTypeID, " & _
         "StatusStartDate, " & _
         "UpdateUserID, " & _
         "StatusNotes) " & _
         "values(" & _
         Request.QueryString("ticketid") & ", " & _
         ddlStatusTypes.SelectedItem.Value & ", '" & _
         Now & "', " & _
         Session("userid") & ", '" & _
         Replace(txtStatusNotes.Text, "'", "''") & _
```

```
                     "')"

         ' Execute an insert command
         objDa.InsertCommand() = New OleDb.OleDbCommand(strSQL, objConn)
         objDa.InsertCommand.ExecuteNonQuery()

         ' Get back the new status history id value
         objDa.SelectCommand() = New OleDb.OleDbCommand(_
           "Select @@IDENTITY", objConn)

         ' Get the statushistoryid value
         StatusHistoryID = objDa.SelectCommand.ExecuteScalar()

         ' Close the connection
         objConn.Close()

         ' Reopen the connection
         objConn.Open()

         ' Update the last status for the ticket
         strSQL = "update ticket set " & _
                 "last_status = " & StatusHistoryID & _
                 " where ticketid = " & Request.QueryString("ticketid")

         ' Set the command connection
         objCMD.Connection = objConn

         ' Set the command query
         objCMD.CommandText = strSQL

         ' Execute for no returned data
         objCMD.ExecuteScalar()

         ' Close the connection
         objConn.Close()

         ' Show the message
         StatusAdded.Visible = True

         ' Hide the other page elements
         btnAdd.Visible = False
         ddlStatusTypes.Visible = False
         lblStatusType.Visible = False
         txtStatusNotes.Visible = False
         lblStatusNotes.Visible = False

     End If

  End Sub
```

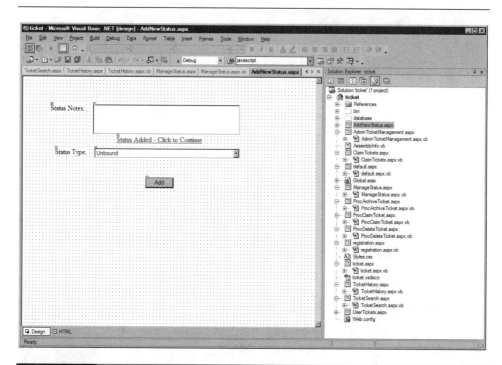

FIGURE 6-13   AddNewStatus.aspx design layout

When the page is posted, the new status is inserted into the StatusHistory table. Once again we run into a situation where we need to retrieve the autonumber for the last inserted record so we can update another set of data. In this case, we need to update the Last_Update field of the ticket to point to the newly inserted status. The @@Identity meta variable is retrieved to get the new StatusHistoryID and the Ticket record is updated.

Now, we are ready to look at the ticket listing page for the nonadministrative users. This page is very similar to the AdminTicketManagement.aspx page. Create a new web form for the project and save it as UserTickets.aspx.

Add two navigation buttons to the page. The first button links to the ticket creation page and the second handles logging out. Set the server transfer code as appropriate.

Next, add a data grid to the page and name it dgTickets. This will show the status of all the tickets created by the user. For this data grid, only data fields are shown. There are no hyperlinks for the grid. Add the data bound columns shown in Table 6-4 to the grid.

Column Header Text	Settings	Description
Ticket #	1) Data Field – TicketID	TicketID data field
TicketDescription	1) Data Field – TicketDescription	TicketDescription data field
TicketResolution	1) Data Field - TicketResolution	TicketResolution data field
Status	1) Data Field – StatusName	StatusName data field
Status Date	1) Data Field – StatusStartDate	The date the last status was set

TABLE 6-4 Data Grid Columns

Figure 6-14 shows the design layout of the page.

Listing 6-19 shows the code for the page. The heavy lifting for the page is done in the end_user_tickets query in our Access database. The records for the current user are queried from the data.

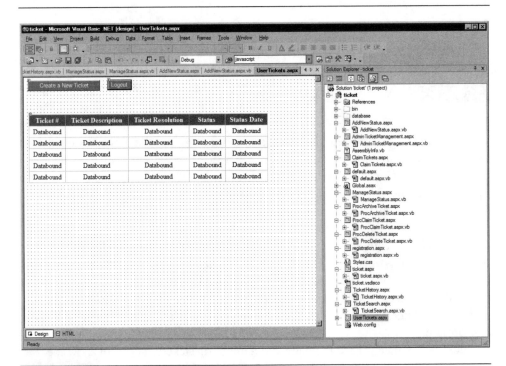

FIGURE 6-14 UserTickets.aspx design layout

Listing 6-19

```
Private Sub Page_Load(ByVal sender As System.Object, _
        ByVal e As System.EventArgs) Handles MyBase.Load
    'Put user code to initialize the page here

    Dim objConn As New OleDb.OleDbConnection()
    Dim strSQL As String
    Dim objCMD As New OleDb.OleDbCommand()
    Dim objDa As New OleDb.OleDbDataAdapter()
    Dim objDs As New Data.DataSet()

    '  Open the DB connection
    objConn.ConnectionString = Application("strConn")
    objConn.Open()

    '  Retrieve the tickets for the user
    strSQL = " select * from end_user_tickets where userid =" & _
      Session("userid")

    '  Set the command connection
    objCMD.Connection = objConn

    '  Set the command query
    objCMD.CommandText = strSQL

    '  Set the select command
    objDa.SelectCommand = objCMD

    '  Set the data source and retrieve the data
    dgTickets.DataSource = objDa.SelectCommand.ExecuteReader()

    '  Bind the data to the grid
    dgTickets.DataBind()

End Sub

'  *******  Navigate to the appropriate page
Private Sub TicketAgain_Click(ByVal sender As Object, _
ByVal e As System.EventArgs) Handles TicketAgain.Click
    Server.Transfer("ticket.aspx")
End Sub

Private Sub Logout_Click(ByVal sender As Object, _
ByVal e As System.EventArgs) Handles Logout.Click
    If IsPostBack Then
        Session("UserID") = ""
```

```
            Server.Transfer("default.aspx")
        End If
    End Sub
```

That is it for the page and all that the user sees. Each time a ticket is updated, the status will be updated as well.

Our final feature is for searching tickets. This feature allows the administrative user to search for a ticket description or resolution by keyword. Create a new web form and save it as TicketSearch.aspx.

Add standard navigation buttons to the page. Next add a text box to the page and name it txtSearchText. Add a label control next to it and set the text as "Search Text:". Add a button to the page and name it btnSearch. Set the text to "Search".

Finally, add a data grid to the page and name it dgTicketSearch. Table 6-5 shows the columns set up for the data grid.

Figure 6-15 shows the design layout of the page.

Listing 6-20 shows the code for the page. When the search is posted a query is executed to retrieve the matching tickets. Along with the core ticket data, the last status and user who created the matching tickets are returned.

> **NOTE** *The like statement in the query uses the % wildcard character to wrap the search term. The same query in Access would use the * character. This difference is because the query is being processed by the OLE DB provider before being sent to Access.*

Column Header Text	Settings	Description
View	1) Url- ViewStatusHistory.aspx 2) URL Field – TicketID 3) URL Format String – TicketHistory.aspx?ticketid={0}	Hyperlink to view the status history of the ticket
TicketID	1) Data Field – TicketID	TicketID data field
Ticket Description	1) Data Field – TicketDescription	TicketDescription data field
Ticket Resolution	1) Data Field – TicketResolution	TicketResolution data field
Company	1) Data Field – Company	Company data field
User	1) Data Field – UserFullName	UserFullName data field (combination of first and last name)
Last Status	1) Data Field – StatusName	StatusName for the last status

TABLE 6-5 Data Grid Columns

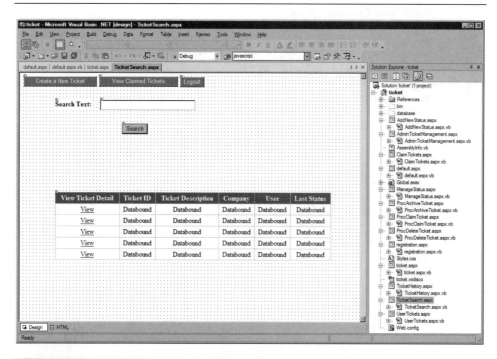

FIGURE 6-15 TicketSearch.aspx design layout

Listing 6-20

```
Private Sub btnSearch_Click(ByVal sender As System.Object, _
ByVal e As System.EventArgs) Handles btnSearch.Click

Dim objConn As New OleDb.OleDbConnection()
Dim strSQL As String
Dim objCMD As New OleDb.OleDbCommand()
Dim objDa As New OleDb.OleDbDataAdapter()
Dim objDs As New Data.DataSet()

If IsPostBack then
   ' Open the DB connection
   objConn.ConnectionString = Application("strConn")
   objConn.Open()

   ' Search for matching ticket records
   strSQL = "SELECT Ticket.TicketID, " & _
   "Users.UserFirstName, " & _
```

```
"Users.UserLastName, " & _
"Users.Company, " & _
"Users.UserEmailAddress, " & _
"Ticket.TicketDescription, " & _
"Ticket.TicketResolution, " & _
"UserFirstName+' '+UserLastName AS UserFullName, " & _
"StatusType.StatusName " & _
"FROM (Users INNER JOIN Ticket " & _
"ON Users.UserID = Ticket.UserID) " & _
"INNER JOIN (StatusType INNER JOIN StatusHistory ON " & _
"StatusType.StatusTypeID = StatusHistory.StatusTypeID) " & _
"ON (Ticket.Last_Status = StatusHistory.StatusHistoryID) " & _
"AND (Ticket.TicketID = StatusHistory.TicketID) " & _
"WHERE Ticket.TicketDescription Like '%" & _
    txtSearchText.Text & "%' " & _
"ORDER BY Ticket.TicketID"

'   Set the command connection
objCMD.Connection = objConn

'   Set the command query
objCMD.CommandText = strSQL

'   Set the command
objDa.SelectCommand = objCMD

'   Set the data grid source
dgTicketSearch.DataSource = objDa.SelectCommand.ExecuteReader

'   Bind the grid
dgTicketSearch.DataBind()
end if
End Sub
```

That is it for building the code. Now we are ready to see the help ticket system in action.

Utilizing the Ticket System

Now we are ready to walk through the use of the system. We will approach it from two perspectives, the administrator and the end user. We will start with the end user opening up a new ticket.

You will need to set up a user to be an administrator manually by setting the admin flag on their user account.

End User

To begin, start up the browser and navigate to the default.aspx login page for the application. The page is shown in Figure 6-16.

We first need to create a user account. Click the Register button. On the registration page, fill in the appropriate information for the user. Figure 6-17 shows the registration page.

Note that if you do not enter all of the data and try to submit the registration, the error validators will stop the page and show the error messages. Once the registration is complete, go ahead and log in. The ticket page for the user is displayed once the login is complete. In this case, there are no tickets in the system yet. Click the Create New Ticket button. The ticket creation page is shown in Figure 6-18.

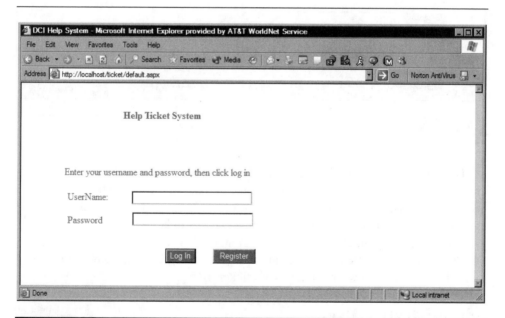

FIGURE 6-16   User login

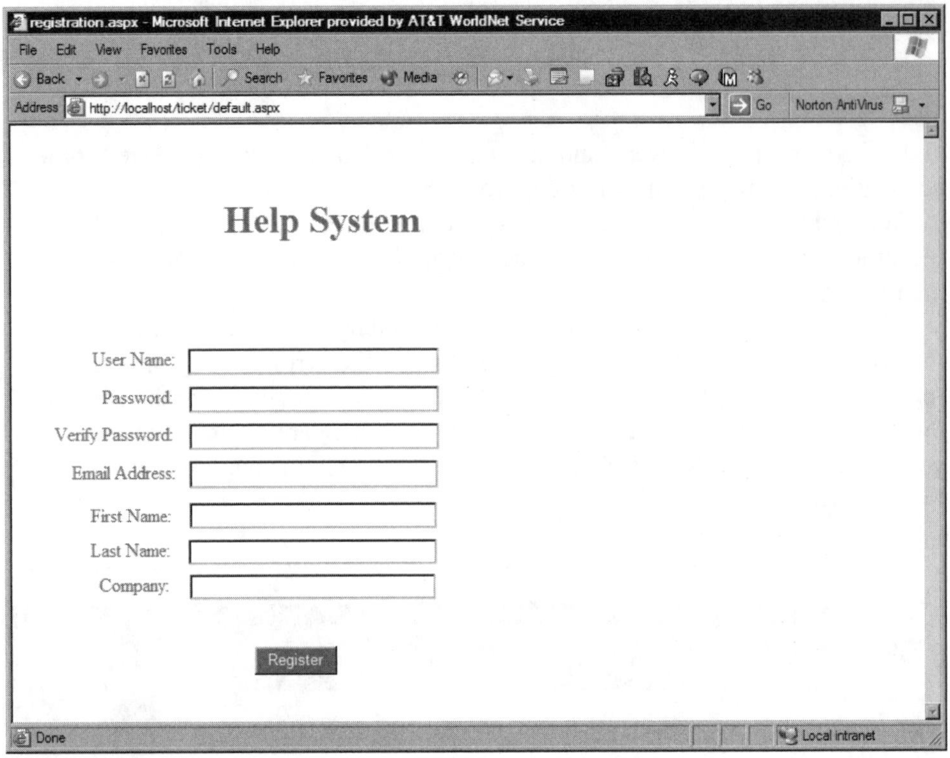

FIGURE 6-17   Registration

The ticket page allows for the entry of the support issue into the text field. Go ahead and enter sample ticket text and then click Submit. Once the ticket is created, the user is taken back to their list of tickets. Now the new ticket is shown with the current status. Figure 6-19 shows the ticket list.

Those are pretty much the only tasks for an end user. As tickets are worked on by administrators, the ticket statuses are updated. Once tickets have been archived, they will no longer show up on the user's ticket list.

Administrative User

Now we are ready to look at the administrative features. Log in as an administrative user. The ticket listing page will show currently claimed tickets. For our example, there are no claimed tickets. Click the View Unclaimed Tickets navigation button. Figure 6-20 shows the ticket list.

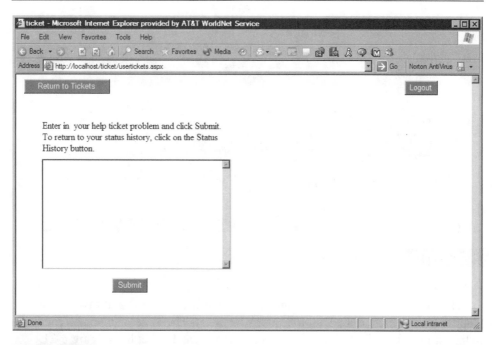

FIGURE 6-18   Create new ticket

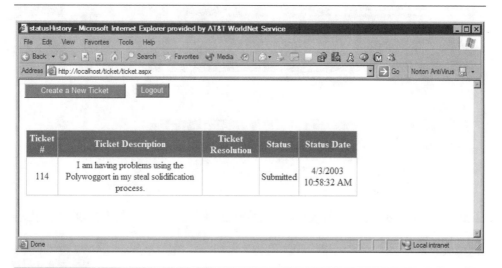

FIGURE 6-19   Ticket listing

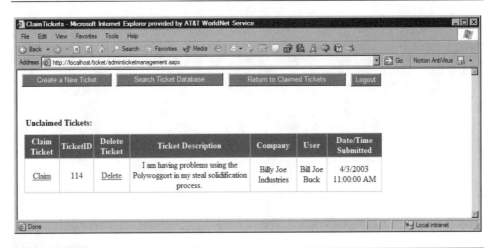

FIGURE 6-20   Unclaimed tickets

The ticket created by the user shows up in the list. Now the administrator can claim it by clicking on the Claim link for the ticket. The ticket is then assigned to the administrator and will show up on their assigned ticket list. Figure 6-21 shows the ticket list for the admin after claiming the ticket.

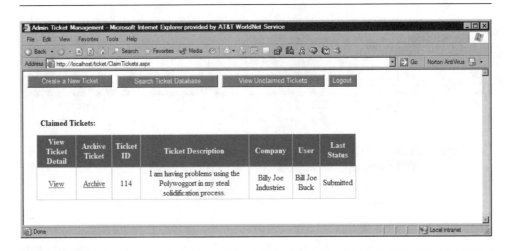

FIGURE 6-21   Claimed tickets

Now the ticket status can be managed for the ticket. Note that the current status is submitted. Also note that the user who created the ticket is also listed. Click on the View link for the ticket. The ticket status history is listed along with fields to update the ticket description, owner, and resolution.

There is also a link for adding a new status for the ticket. Let's add a status of Reviewed to the ticket. Click on the Add New Status link. A pop-up window is displayed with no menus or toolbars. The status notes and status type can be selected. Figure 6-22 shows the page.

Note that when the status is added, a link is displayed. Click on the link to continue. When the link is clicked on, the ticket history page is automatically refreshed and the new status is displayed. Now we see that the ticket was reviewed by the admin and the time of the review. Figure 6-23 shows the ticket history.

Any of the status items for a ticket can also be updated by clicking on the View link for the status. There the notes and the status type can be updated.

The last feature to explore is the ticket search feature. This will allow the database of tickets to be researched. This can be very helpful in resolving new tickets. Click the Search Ticket Database navigation button. The ticket search page is shown.

Now, enter some search text that you know is used in either a ticket description or resolution and click on the search. The results are shown in a data grid on the page. Figure 6-24 shows the sample search.

That does it for testing our application.

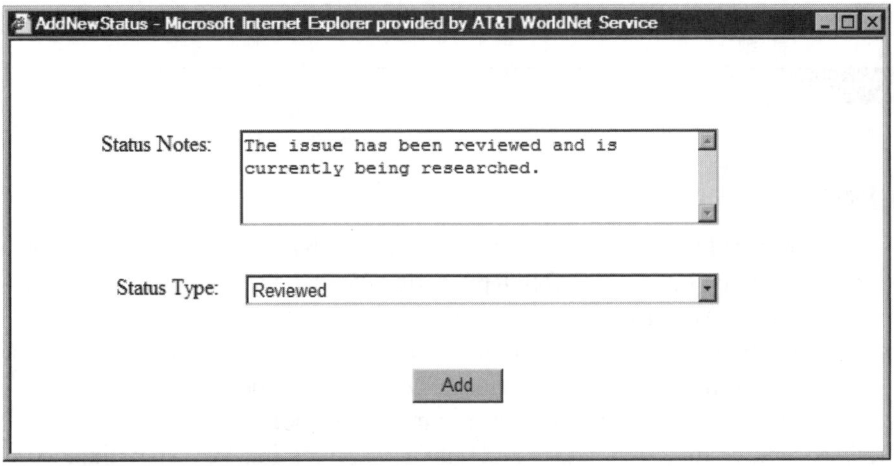

FIGURE 6-22   Add new status

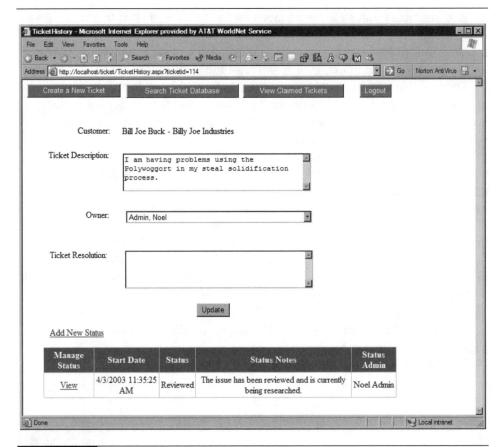

FIGURE 6-23 Ticket history

Summary

In this chapter we learned how to utilize Access with .NET. As we have seen, robust applications can be built on the .NET platform. We also learned some techniques for working with Access data from our applications that are not all that different from working with an enterprise database. This sample help ticket application can be easily upsized to an enterprise database. Much of the code can be utilized as well. One might also want to consider migrating the code-based queries to true stored procedures for performance and data and application-tier separation.

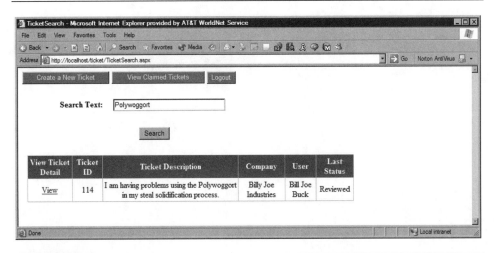

In the next chapter we are going to move in a new direction and focus on how Access can be utilized as a great data manipulation tool—Access is kind of like the Swiss Army Knife for importing, exporting, and manipulating data.

Summary

Chapter 7

Importing and
Exporting Data

Access is a great tool that can act as a type of Swiss army knife for data imports and exports. Its graphical interface, fast query building, and import/export tools make it a great tool for manipulating and transforming data.

In this chapter, we are going to explore an example of importing denormalized data into a normalized database. How many times have you been given data in a spreadsheet or word document, or from a legacy system, that you need to manipulate and import into your relational data structure? We will demonstrate techniques for utilizing Access to make this task easier. We will also look at how to utilize the export tools to make data available for external systems and in other office applications such as Excel.

> **NOTE**   *In the next chapter, we will explore the XML import and export capabilities of Access.*

Import and Export Overview

Microsoft Access provides two options off of the File menu for importing and exporting data. For import, the option is a suboption of Get External Data. Export is a main option off of the File menu.

For the import options, data in a number of file formats can be imported, including other Access data, dBase, Excel, Exchange, HTML, Outlook, Paradox, Text (csv, tab, etc.), and Lotus. In addition, data can be imported via ODBC from ODBC-compliant data sources, including SQL Server.

During import, a number of options are provided to determine how the data will be imported. Field types can be specified, primary keys set, and index settings applied. The Import Wizard will even help to provide some analyses on the imported data and recommend a more normalized structure.

> **TIP**   *The Access data analysis tool should be used with caution. The example shown later in the chapter is actually not properly analyzed by the data analyzer.*

The export capability is very straightforward to utilize. It will provide options based on the export format (e.g., excel, delimited, etc.). A single table or query can be exported at a time. As we will see later in the chapter, if you want to export data from more than one table or query, a query that combines and formats the data can be created.

Normalizing Denormalized Data

Now let's look at how the different capabilities of Access can be utilized to import and manipulate data. Specifically, we want to look at an example of how denormalized data can be imported and placed into a relational structure.

For our example, we are going to be importing test, question, and answer data that has been entered into a spreadsheet. That data has been entered in a fairly logical fashion for a spreadsheet, but not for a relational data structure. The goal will be to import the spreadsheet and normalize the data.

Let's first take a look at the spreadsheet data provided. The spreadsheet has 14 columns of data. Table 7-1 shows the columns.

This structure is enforced no matter what. For example, if a question only has three answers, there is of course a column for answers 4 and 5. If a question has two or more correct responses, then the answer numbers are separated by commas. Table 7-2 shows two sample rows of the data.

Column	Description
Test	Name of the test
Question	Test question
# of Answers	Number of answers for the question
Answer 1	First answer
Answer 2	Second answer
Answer 3	Third answer
Answer 4	Fourth answer
Answer 5	Fifth answer
Correct Answer(s)	Numbers indicating the correct answers
Answer 1 Rational	Rationale for why the first answer is correct or incorrect
Answer 2 Rational	Rationale for why the second answer is correct or incorrect
Answer 3 Rational	Rationale for why the third answer is correct or incorrect
Answer 4 Rational	Rationale for why the fourth answer is correct or incorrect
Answer 5 Rational	Rationale for why the fifth answer is correct or incorrect

TABLE 7-1   Test Data Spreadsheet Columns

Column	Sample Data
Test	Exotic Animals
Question	What animal only lives in the yellow sap tree of Madagascar?
# of Answers	3
Answer 1	Pot belly pig
Answer 2	The wild warbler
Answer 3	Sneegel varmint
Answer 4	
Answer 5	
Correct Answer(s)	3
Answer 1 Rational	This animal can be found around the world.
Answer 2 Rational	The wild warbler is found in green sap trees of Madagascar.
Answer 3 Rational	This is the correct answer.
Answer 4 Rational	
Answer 5 Rational	
Test	Little known TV Shows
Question	Gumby starred in which of these three shows at the same time?
# of Answers	5
Answer 1	Gumby – Look at Me
Answer 2	Gumby Does Opera
Answer 3	Gumby and His Gal
Answer 4	Little Dude Gumby
Answer 5	Gumby Cools
Correct Answer(s)	1, 3, 5
Answer 1 Rational	This was Gumby's attempt at fashion modeling.
Answer 2 Rational	Incorrect
Answer 3 Rational	A romance show starring Gumby and his girlfriend Betty
Answer 4 Rational	Incorrect
Answer 5 Rational	Gumby's cooking show featuring favorite family recipes.

TABLE 7-2   Sample Data Rows

As can be seen, there are a number of problems with the data. First off, the test name is repeated for each question for the test. That is duplicate data. The answers are named for each column and the correct answer data is stored in one field. This data will have to be broken up in order to place it in a relational structure.

Next, let's look at the relational structure for the data. Our database will have three tables, one each for tests, questions, and answers. The following diagram shows the relationship between the tables.

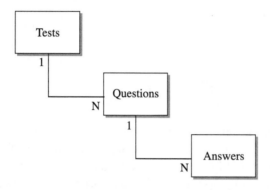

As the illustration shows, tests can have multiple questions, and questions can have multiple answers. The structure is pretty simple. Let's quickly review the table structure.

The Tests table is pretty simple with two fields:

Field	Data Type	Description
TestID	AutoNumber	Primary key of the table
TestName	Text	Name of the test

Our second table defines the question data:

Field	Data Type	Description
QuestionID	AutoNumber	Primary key of the table
QuestionText	Memo	Text of the question
NumAnswers	Number	Number of answers for the question
TestID	Number	Foreign key pointer to the test for the question

The final table contains the answers data:

Field	Data Type	Description
AnswerID	AutoNumber	Primary key of the table
AnswerText	Memo	Text of the answer
AnswerRational	Memo	Rationale for the correctness of the answer
CorrectAnswer	Yes/No	Indicates if the answer is a correct response
QuestionID	Number	Foreign key pointer to the question for the answer

Finally, the relationships between the tables need to be set up. For our example, we just need simple relationships set up between the tables. Enforcing referential integrity isn't important. Figure 7-1 shows the table relationships.

That does it for setting up the data. Now we are ready to move the Excel data into the Access data structure.

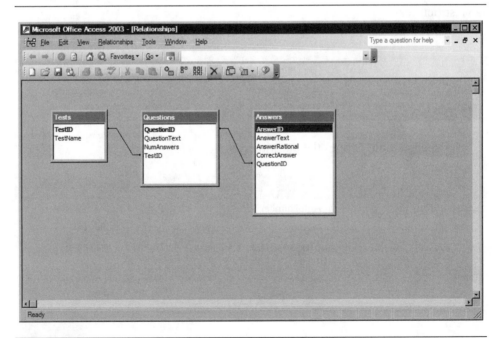

FIGURE 7-1   Table relationships

Normalizing the Data

We are going to follow a three-step process for importing the data. First, the raw data will be imported into a new table. Next, a series of queries will be built to transform and move the data into the relational data structure. Finally, a query will be built to view the imported data and verify it against the original data. Make sure that you have both the import file and database set up for this process.

Importing the Excel Data

Importing the data is the easiest step. On the File menu, select the Import function from the Get External Data option. From the File dialog box, select your spreadsheet with the test data. Ensure that Import File Type is set to Excel.

On the first screen of the wizard, ensure that the worksheet with the test data is selected, and then click the Next button. On the second screen of the wizard, select the check box if you have a header row in the spreadsheet. Click the Next button to continue, and then indicate that the data should be imported into a new table.

The next wizard screen shows the fields to be imported. For each field, you can determine if it should be indexed. Since we are importing from Excel, the data types for import are set for us. You can also indicate if you want a particular field to not be imported. Figure 7-2 shows the dialog box.

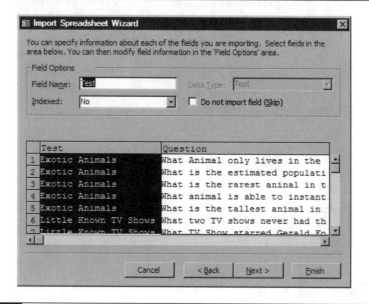

FIGURE 7-2   Field setup

Click the Next button to go to the next screen. This screen allows us to determine if we want a primary key in our table. Three options are provided. The first is to let Access add a primary key. This just means an autonumber field will be added to the table. The second is to select an existing field as a primary key. The last is to not have a primary key. In our case, we don't need a primary key for the imported data since the table the data is imported into is only temporary. Figure 7-3 shows the dialog box.

Finally, the last screen allows us to set the import table name. We can also choose to have the data analyzed by Access. We do not want that option. Save the table as Tests_Import. Your imported data table should look similar to Figure 7-4.

That does it for getting the raw data into the database. Now we need to start building queries to pull the data from our imported table and into the relational structure.

Transforming the Data

The data is going to be transformed from the top down in the structure, starting with test data. An insert query will be built that retrieves the unique test names from the import table and inserts them into the Tests table.

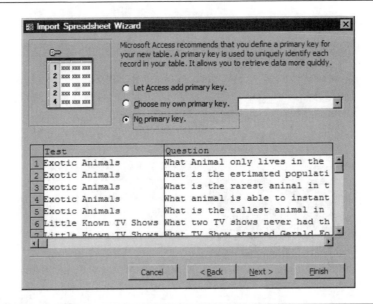

FIGURE 7-3   Primary key setup

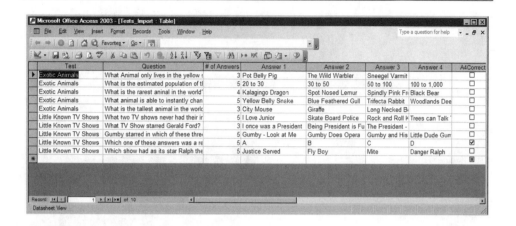

FIGURE 7-4   Imported Tests data

Start up a new query in the Design view. Add in the Tests_Import table to the query. Next, click the Query menu and select Append Query. Select the Tests table for appending the data. Add the Test field to the query grid, and set the Append To field to TestName. If we run the query now, all of the test names will be entered into the table. We don't want that—we want only one unique entry for each test name.

Go to the SQL view and insert the Distinct keyword after the select clause. This will ensure that only one test name will be returned for each test. Figure 7-5 shows the Design view for the query. Listing 7-1 shows the SQL code for the query. Save the query as Setup_Tests.

Listing 7-1

```
INSERT INTO Tests ( TestName )
SELECT DISTINCT Tests_Import.Test
FROM Tests_Import;
```

This query is pretty simple and does the job. When you run it, a unique record for each test is inserted into the Tests table. Next, we need to set up the test questions. But, we also need to make sure that the test ID for each question is set up.

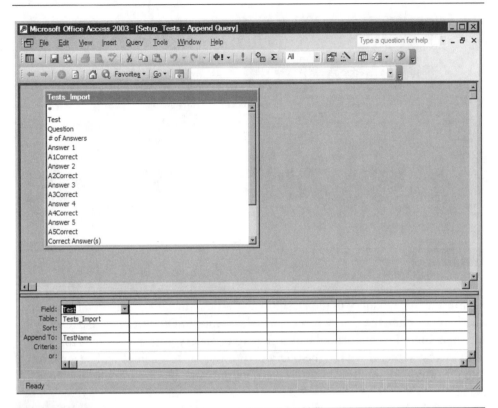

FIGURE 7-5 Setup_Tests query

Create a new query in the Design view. Add in the Tests_Import table and the Tests table. On the Query menu, select Append Query to make the query append data. Select the Questions table as the target append table. For the query, we need to make a relationship link between the Tests_Import and Tests tables. The only link is between the name fields. Drag the TestName field to the Test field to make the link. This link allows us to get to the TestID for the question.

In this case, we need to insert three pieces of data into the questions table: the question text, number of answers, and TestID. From the Tests_Import table, select the Question and # of Answers fields and drag them to the query grid. Select the QuestionText and NumAnswers fields for the Append To settings.

Next, drag the TestID field from the Tests table to the query grid. Set the Append To setting to the TestID field of the Questions table. That will set up the insert of the question data into the Questions table with the appropriate links to the appropriate test. Save the query as Setup_Questions. Figure 7-6 shows the Design view for the query and Listing 7-2 shows the generated SQL.

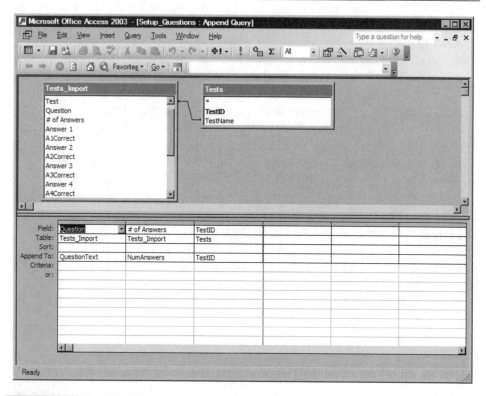

FIGURE 7-6   Setup_Questions query Design view

Listing 7-2

```
INSERT INTO Questions ( QuestionText, NumAnswers, TestID )
SELECT Tests_Import.Question,
       Tests_Import.[# of Answers], Tests.TestID
FROM Tests_Import INNER JOIN Tests ON
    Tests_Import.Test = Tests.TestName;
```

Note the inner join created on the name field. Normally, joins are done on identity fields or some type of numerical data. In this case, the link back to the imported data is the test name. Now we can get the test ID for the newly imported test name and assign it to the questions being imported.

Things are going to get a little more difficult when it comes to the answers. We have a couple of issues to deal with. First, we need to somehow split out the correct answer data from the current single-field, comma-delimited format. We are also going to run into a couple of issues in building our queries to insert the answer data.

Let's first start with breaking out the correct answers. The approach we are going to take is to set up a correct answer field for each answer in our import table. That field will be Yes/No, indicating if the corresponding answer is correct or not.

Insert five new fields into the Tests_Import table and name them A1Correct, A2Correct, A3Correct, A4Correct, and A5Correct. Save the table.

Now we are going to build a series of queries that will set the new fields to True where the answer is a correct response for the question. Create a new query and add in the Tests_Import table. Select the Query menu and select the Update Query option. Add the A1Correct field and Correct Answer(s) field to the query grid.

For the A1Correct field, set the Update To setting to True. For the Correct Answer(s) field, set the criteria to '*1*'. This builds a query that will update the A1Correct field to true where the Correct Answer(s) field has a 1 in the field, which means the first answer is correct. When this query is run, all questions that have a correct answer of 1 will have the A1Correct field updated to True. Save the query as NormA1.

Figure 7-7 shows the Design view of the query and Listing 7-3 shows the SQL code that is generated by the query.

Listing 7-3

```
UPDATE Tests_Import SET Tests_Import.A1Correct = True
WHERE (((Tests_Import.[Correct Answer(s)])
        Like '*1*'));
```

The SQL is pretty straightforward. Now we need to copy this query four times to handle answers 2, 3, 4, and 5. For example, the next query would set A2Correct = True, where the correct answer is Like '*2*'. Once all of these queries are run, we will have successfully broken out the correct answers into a structure we can work with.

Now we are ready to pull the answer data into the Answers table. We need to be sure and pull the associated QuestionID values for each answer to make the relationship links for the data.

To get the answer data, we essentially need to query the answer text, answer rationale, and correct answer. To get the QuestionID, we will have to join the Questions table with the Tests_Import table on the question text.

When we go to make that link, we will find that joins can't be done on memo fields. That presents a problem since we need that QuestionID to make the

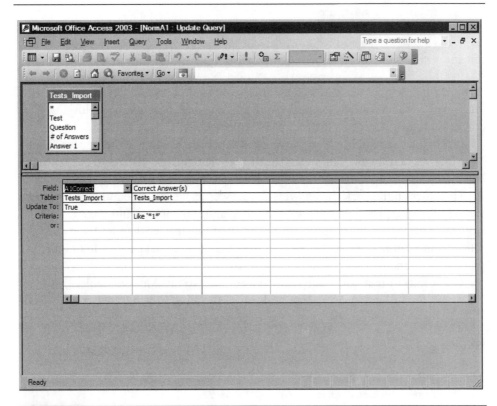

FIGURE 7-7   NormA1 query Design view

relationships work. Fortunately, we can use a little Access SQL formatting to convert the data from memo to a standard text string.

The function that is used is CSTR, which converts the text to a string. In the SQL, the memo field is passed to CSTR. The downside of this is that the Access Design view complains that it can't show the query with the CSTR function on the join. So, in the end we are left with just working in the SQL view.

Listing 7-4 shows the SQL code that returns the proper data.

Listing 7-4

```
SELECT Questions.QuestionID,
       Tests_Import.[Answer 5] as AnswerText,
       Tests_Import.[Answer 5 Rational] as AnswerRational,
```

```
       A5Correct as Correct
FROM Tests_Import INNER JOIN Questions ON
     cstr(Tests_Import.Question)=cstr(Questions.QuestionText)
WHERE Tests_Import.[Answer 5]<>""
```

In the query, note the join statement. The Tests_Import and Questions tables are joined on the question text data. And, as discussed, both memo fields are converted to text strings so the join can take place.

In this query, we are pulling the answer data for answer 5 in the import data. Note that we don't want blank records, so the where clause checks to ensure that blank records are not returned.

That query pulls back the answers for answer 5. We still need to pull back the answers for 1, 2, 3, and 4. And, we need that entire list pulled into the Answers table. To make this happen, union together all of the answer data into one query. Then, create similar queries for each of the other answer data sets, and union each set together. Finally, save the query as All_Answers.

The results of that query can then be inserted into the Answers table. Listing 7-5 shows the full union query that pulls all of the answer data together.

Listing 7-5

```
SELECT Questions.QuestionID,
       Tests_Import.[Answer 5] as AnswerText,
       Tests_Import.[Answer 5 Rational] as AnswerRational,
       A5Correct as Correct
FROM Tests_Import INNER JOIN Questions ON
     cstr(Tests_Import.Question)=cstr(Questions.QuestionText)

WHERE Tests_Import.[Answer 5]<>""

union
SELECT Questions.QuestionID,
       Tests_Import.[Answer 4] as AnswerText,
       Tests_Import.[Answer 4 Rational] as AnswerRational,
       A4Correct as Correct
FROM Tests_Import INNER JOIN Questions ON
     cstr(Tests_Import.Question) = cstr(Questions.QuestionText)
WHERE Tests_Import.[Answer 4] <> ""

union
```

```
SELECT Questions.QuestionID,
       Tests_Import.[Answer 3] as AnswerText,
       Tests_Import.[Answer 3 Rational] as AnswerRational,
       A3Correct as Correct
FROM Tests_Import INNER JOIN Questions ON
     cstr(Tests_Import.Question) = cstr(Questions.QuestionText)
WHERE Tests_Import.[Answer 3] <> ""

union

SELECT Questions.QuestionID,
       Tests_Import.[Answer 2] as AnswerText,
       Tests_Import.[Answer 2 Rational] as AnswerRational,
       A2Correct as Correct
FROM Tests_Import INNER JOIN Questions ON
     cstr(Tests_Import.Question) = cstr(Questions.QuestionText)
WHERE Tests_Import.[Answer 2] <> ""

union

SELECT Questions.QuestionID,
       Tests_Import.[Answer 1] as AnswerText,
       Tests_Import.[Answer 1 Rational] as AnswerRational,
       A1Correct as Correct
FROM Tests_Import INNER JOIN Questions ON
       cstr(Tests_Import.Question) = cstr(Questions.QuestionText)
WHERE Tests_Import.[Answer 1] <> "";
```

Note that the return field names for each of the queries are the same. And, in each case, the CSTR function is used on the joins.

Now we are ready to actually import the answer data. A new query will need to be built that will use the All_Answers query results to insert the Answers data. Create a new query in the Design view and add the All_Answers query to the query.

On the Query menu, select Append Query to change the query to append data. From the All_Answers query, drag all of the fields to the query grid. For each field, select the corresponding Answers field to match the All_Answers query fields. Save the query as Setup_Answers.

Figure 7-8 shows the Design view of the query. Listing 7-6 shows the SQL generated by the query.

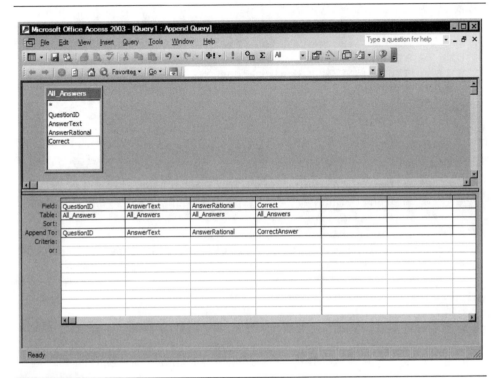

FIGURE 7-8   Setup_Answers query Design view

Listing 7-6

```
INSERT INTO Answers (QuestionID, AnswerText,
                     AnswerRational, CorrectAnswer )
SELECT All_Answers.QuestionID,
      All_Answers.AnswerText,
      All_Answers.AnswerRational,
      All_Answers.Correct
FROM All_Answers;
```

This query is pretty standard. It basically selects the fields that need to be inserted into the Answers table. This is a great example of how multiple queries can be easily stacked in Access to achieve a final result.

That completes all of the queries we need for transforming the data from our imported table into the new relational structure. Once all have been run in order, the data will be converted, and the process is repeatable.

Validating the Data Import

Now that we have the data imported, how can we easily validate it without doing it by hand and checking each table? The next step is to build a query that will give us a view of the data that closely mimics the spreadsheet structure.

The best option is to create a PivotTable that shows the hierarchical structure of the data. Create a new query and add in the Tests, Questions, and Answers tables. See Appendix B for an introduction to PivotTables and PivotCharts.

From the Tests table, add the TestName field to the query grid. From the Questions table, add the QuestionText and NumAnswers fields to the grid. Finally, from the Answers table, add the AnswerText, AnswerRational, and CorrectAnswer fields. Save the query as Validate_Import_Pivot.

This combination of fields will provide a mirror of the data in the spreadsheet. Figure 7-9 shows the query design setup.

The SQL generated by the query is shown in Listing 7-7.

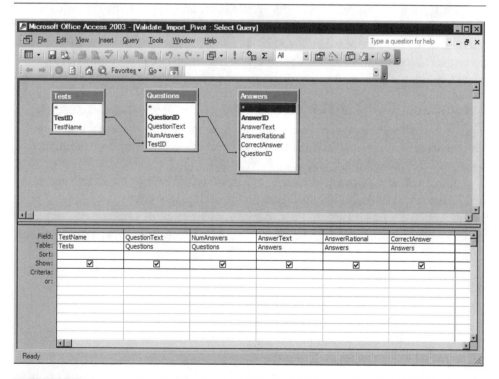

FIGURE 7-9   Validate_Import_Pivot query Design view

Listing 7-7

```
SELECT Tests.TestName, Questions.QuestionText,
       Questions.NumAnswers, Answers.AnswerText,
       Answers.AnswerRational, Answers.CorrectAnswer
FROM (Answers INNER JOIN Questions ON
      Answers.QuestionID = Questions.QuestionID)
      INNER JOIN Tests ON Questions.TestID = Tests.TestID;
```

The query joins together the three tables to build the structure. If all is imported properly, the data should display properly. If you run the query, you get a row for every answer listed in the result. That is close to what we need, but a Pivot view will more closely resemble what we need. Click the PivotTable View for the query.

In setting up the pivot, we want to see questions by test and then the answers for each question along with the correct flag. From the Field List window, drag the TestName field to the Column Fields section of the page. Next, drop the QuestionText field to the Columns Fields section.

Finally, drag the AnswerText, AnswerRational, and CorrectAnswer fields to the Row Fields portion of the page layout. The final result shows the tests and questions, and then answer data listed by question. This can then be easily compared to the spreadsheet to see if the data matches. The PivotTable view is shown in Figure 7-10.

Automating the Import with a Macro

Finally, there is one more step we can take to make the import process a little easier. We can set up a macro that will run the import process step by step and automate it for us.

Click the Macros Objects option on the database. Create a new macro and save it as SetupTests. Table 7-3 shows the setup for each macro entry.

Action	Query Name
OpenQuery	Query Name: Setup_Tests
OpenQuery	Setup_Questions
OpenQuery	NormA1
OpenQuery	NormA2
OpenQuery	NormA3
OpenQuery	NormA4
OpenQuery	NormA5
OpenQuery	Setup_Answers
OpenQuery	Validate_Import_Pivot

TABLE 7-3   SetupTests Macro

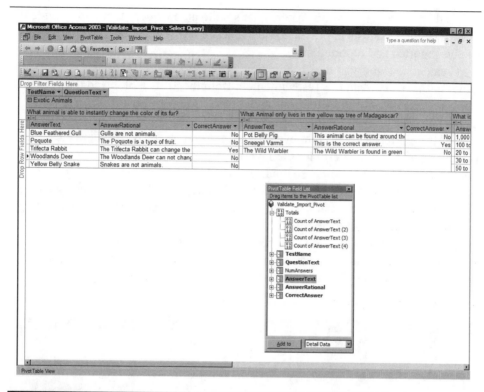

FIGURE 7-10 PivotTable view

Note that the macro assumes that the data has been imported and that the A#Correct fields have been added to the import table.

When the Macro is run, all of the query confirmations pop up for the inserts and updates. The final result is the data is inserted in one fell swoop.

There are a couple of things to keep in mind for the import and transformation process. The relational tables can be linked tables to an ODBC-compliant server. For example, if our relational test structure resided in SQL Server, we could still utilize the Access import and query capabilities to import and transform the data right into an enterprise database server.

Exporting Data

Exporting data obviously provides the opposite process from the import process. In this case, we want to be sure the data is transformed before we export it. We also have a couple of different ways we can export data. There is the standard export where data is written to a file such as Excel, Delimited, dBase, etc. In addition, data can be exported in a formatted style to Word and Excel via reports.

To demonstrate the export features, let's build a new query that will provide the answer key for the tests in our database. Once we have that query, then the results can be exported and reported on.

Create a new query in the Design view. Add the Tests, Questions, and Answers tables to the query. Add the TestName field from the Tests table. Add the QuestionText field for the Questions table. And finally, add the AnswerText and CorrectAnswer fields from the Answers table.

For the CorrectAnswer field, we only want to return answers where the field is set to True. Set the criteria for the field to True. In addition, we don't need this field to show up in the results, so uncheck the Show setting. We also need to do a couple of other formatting changes for use in a report. The memo field needs to be converted to string format. Use the CSTR function to convert the data on the QuestionText and AnswerText fields. In addition, to make the field names a little more friendly, set the QuestionText field to be returned as Question and the AnswerText field to be returned as Answer. Save the query as Answer_Key. Figure 7-11 shows the Design view for the query.

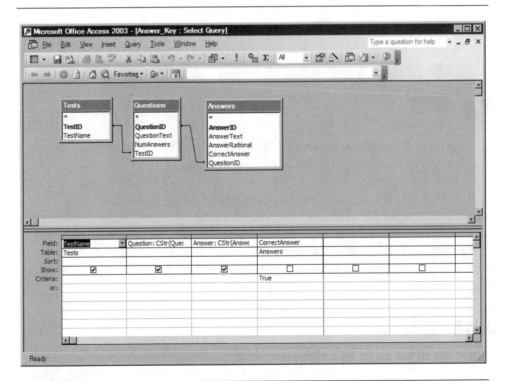

FIGURE 7-11   Answer_Key query Design view

Listing 7-8 shows the SQL generated by the query.

```
SELECT Tests.TestName,
       CStr(Questions.QuestionText) AS Question,
       CStr(Answers.AnswerText) AS Answer
FROM (Questions INNER JOIN Answers ON
       Questions.QuestionID = Answers.QuestionID) INNER JOIN
       Tests ON Questions.TestID = Tests.TestID
WHERE (((Answers.CorrectAnswer)=True));
```

Note the use of the CSTR function to convert the memo fields and the check to make sure the correct answer field is set. The results of the query return an answer key for the tests in the database.

That key can now be exported to Excel. Select the Answer_Key query in the Objects view and then select the Export option from the File menu. Choose the Excel 97-2002 export option. Then, export the file with an appropriate file name. Finally, open the Excel file and view the exported data. Figure 7-12 shows the exported data.

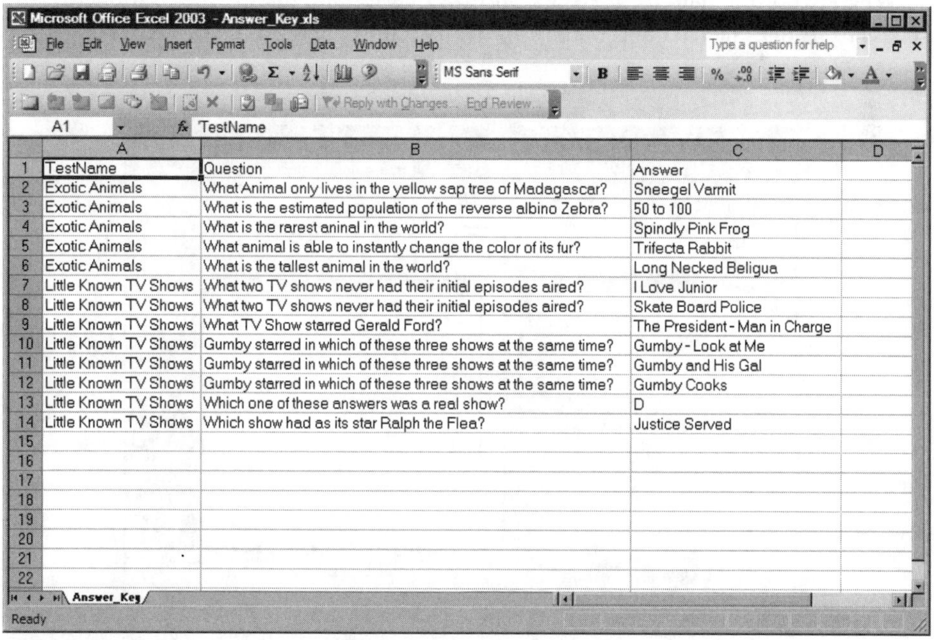

	A	B	C	D
1	TestName	Question	Answer	
2	Exotic Animals	What Animal only lives in the yellow sap tree of Madagascar?	Sneegel Varmit	
3	Exotic Animals	What is the estimated population of the reverse albino Zebra?	50 to 100	
4	Exotic Animals	What is the rarest aninal in the world?	Spindly Pink Frog	
5	Exotic Animals	What animal is able to instantly change the color of its fur?	Trifecta Rabbit	
6	Exotic Animals	What is the tallest animal in the world?	Long Necked Beligua	
7	Little Known TV Shows	What two TV shows never had their initial episodes aired?	I Love Junior	
8	Little Known TV Shows	What two TV shows never had their initial episodes aired?	Skate Board Police	
9	Little Known TV Shows	What TV Show starred Gerald Ford?	The President - Man in Charge	
10	Little Known TV Shows	Gumby starred in which of these three shows at the same time?	Gumby - Look at Me	
11	Little Known TV Shows	Gumby starred in which of these three shows at the same time?	Gumby and His Gal	
12	Little Known TV Shows	Gumby starred in which of these three shows at the same time?	Gumby Cooks	
13	Little Known TV Shows	Which one of these answers was a real show?	D	
14	Little Known TV Shows	Which show had as its star Ralph the Flea?	Justice Served	

FIGURE 7-12   Answer key exported Data

Note that the data is unformatted and has no hierarchical structure. It would be nice to see the questions listed by test and the answers by question. We can achieve this fairly easily with a report, which can then be exported to Excel.

Click the Reports option on the Access database. Click the Create Report by Using Wizard option. In the first dialog box, select the Answer_Key query from the drop-down list. From that query, select all of the fields. Click the Next button to continue.

On the next screen, make sure the structure is by TestName, Question, and Answer. Figure 7-13 shows the dialog box. Click the Next button to continue.

We don't need any sorting per se for our report since everything is grouped by Test and Question. Click the Next button to continue.

On the next screen, select either the Outline1 or Outline2 layout, and then click the Next button to continue. Pick a report style that suits your fancy and click the Next button to continue. Finally, on the last page, save the report as Answer_Key. Now run the report. Figure 7-14 shows the report.

On the report, there is an option to export the report to Word (Publish it to Word) and export it to Excel (Analyze it with Excel). Choose the option to export to Excel. Now the report in Excel has some formatting and structure. Figure 7-15 shows the Excel report.

When exporting data from Access, utilize queries and the full set of tools in Access to format the data and transform the data into the required target format.

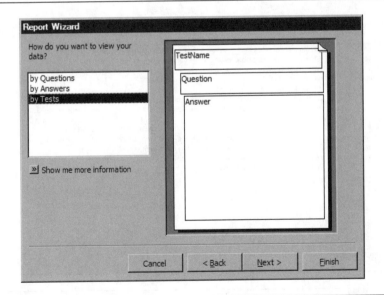

FIGURE 7-13   Report structure setup

TestName	Question	Answer
Exotic Animals		
	What animal is able to instantly change the color of its fur?	
		Trifecta Rabbit
	What Animal only lives in the yellow sap tree of Madagascar?	
		Sneegel Varmit
	What is the estimated population of the reverse albino Zebra?	
		50 to 100
	What is the rarest animal in the world?	
		Spindly Pink Frog
	What is the tallest animal in the world?	
		Long Necked Beligua
Little Known TV Shows		
	Gumby starred in which of these three shows at the same time?	
		Gumby Cooks
		Gumby and His Gal
		Gumby - Look at Me
	What TV Show starred Gerald Ford?	
		The President - Man in Charge
	What two TV shows never had their initial episodes aired?	
		Skate Board Police
		I Love Junior
	Which one of these answers was a real show?	
		D
	Which show had as its star Ralph the Flea?	
		Justice Served

FIGURE 7-14   Answer key report

Other Tips and Tricks

Utilizing advanced queries is a very common technique for transforming imported and exported data. There are other options. If your data is very simple and is relatively manageable in size, then (in many cases) simple cutting and pasting of data between tables can provide the necessary structure and formatting. This is especially true when building denormalized exports.

There are times where SQL will not be able to perform all of the necessary data transformation tasks. Access also has its built-in Visual Basic for Applications (VBA) programming language. Code can be written to manipulate and transform data and then perform updates, inserts, or deletes as appropriate. For example, if you need to significantly denormalize or "flatten" relational data for export to a legacy system, use in a spreadsheet, etc., VBA can be utilized for more advanced data manipulation.

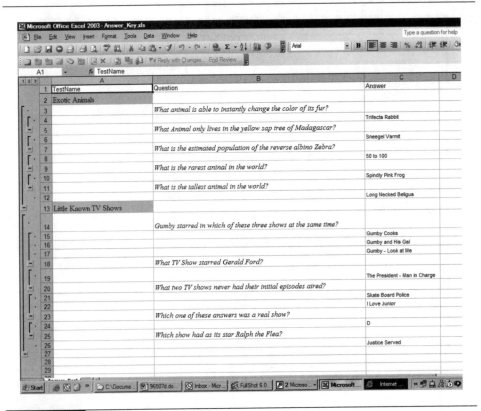

FIGURE 7-15   Answer key Excel report

Summary

Access can be an invaluable tool to manipulate and transform data for import and export between systems. In this chapter, we only explored the querying capabilities for manipulating data. This capability can be expanded by using the VBA programming capabilities.

In the next chapter, we will see how XML import and export capabilities are greatly enhanced in Access 2003, and make Access a great tool for working with XML data as well.

Chapter 8

Working with Access XML

As we saw in the last chapter, Access is a great tool for importing and exporting data. With Office 2003, Microsoft has added extended XML capabilities. Office XP provides basic XML import and export capabilities.

There are quite a number of enhancements in the XML support in Access 2003, including the ability to export related tables, import or export the published XSD namespace, and apply an XSL transformation on export and import. In addition, there are improved export presentation XSLs as well as object model enhancements— all these enhancements are discussed in this chapter.

XML Overview

XML is a markup language that is used to identify structure within a document. The XML standard is published and maintained by the World Wide Web Consortium (W3C), the consortium that maintains many of the standards for the World Wide Web. More information can be found at www.w3.org.

Like other markup languages such as HTML, XML uses tags to define specific elements within a document. XML tags define the document's structural elements and the meaning of those elements. Unlike HTML tags, which specify how a document looks or is formatted, XML can be used to define the document structure and content—not just the look and feel. The separation of data from presentation is a key aspect of XML.

Unlike HTML, the XML specification does not specify the mark-up tags themselves. Instead, it provides a standard way to define tags and relationships and to add the markup to documents. This provides a flexible methodology for modeling and representing data.

The tags that can be used for a particular document type or information type are contained in XML schemas, XSDs, which define the set of tags and the rules for applying them. Schemas define the structure and type of data that each data element in a document can contain and can be created. XML schemas can be created to define and qualify content in the XML document. Note that schemas are not required for an XML document, but having schemas helps to ensure the XML document meets its required intent.

Because XML files are text-based, the data can be easily read and manipulated. For presenting data, style sheets can be utilized. An XSLT (Extensible Stylesheet Language Transformation) defines how information is displayed in a particular instance. In addition to defining the formatting for a particular instance of a document, XSLTs can also translate XML documents into the format required by the application that is consuming the information. In these cases, an XSLT translates the original XML into another XML schema that is required by the target system.

Because an XML document is structured, platform-independent, and text-based, XML documents can be opened and operated on by a range of editing programs (such as Microsoft Office System programs) or integrated into automated business processes.

> NOTE   *For this chapter, we will be using the test, question, and answer data structure from Chapter 7.*

Exporting Data to XML

The Access interface provides for XML export and import capabilities that are very powerful and allows us to move fairly easily between highly structured relational data and the marked-up XML structure.

Let's first work on exporting the data from our test questions into XML. Our first goal is to export all of the test data in a logical XML structure that represents the relationships between the data. We will also export a presentation XLST document and a definition schema.

Single Table Exports

To get started, open up the database with the test data. Select the Tests table for export. Click the File menu and select the Export menu item. In the pop-up dialog box, select the XML type as the Save As format. Also, select the directory where you would like the exported files to be created. Finally, set the file name to Saved As Tests.

The dialog box shown next appears with options on how we want the data to be exported. We have the option of exporting data, the XML schema, and an XSL presentation file.

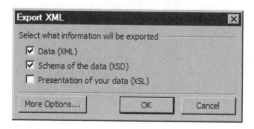

For this first run-through, in addition to the default options, select the Presentation of Your Data (XSL) option and then click OK. We will explore the More Options settings next.

When the export is complete, four files are created—Tests.xml, Tests.htm, Tests.xsd, and Tests.xsl. Note that we check three options but four files are exported. In addition to the core XML file, an XML schema file for the XML file is always created. Let's first look at the XML file. Listing 8-1 shows the generated code.

Listing 8-1

```
<?xml version="1.0" encoding="UTF-8" ?>
 <dataroot xmlns:od="urn:schemas-microsoft-com:officedata"
     xmlns:xsi="http://www.w3.org/2001/XMLSchema-instance"
     xsi:noNamespaceSchemaLocation="Tests.xsd"
     generated="2003-04-23T00:38:55">
  <Tests>
  <TestID>29</TestID>
  <TestName>Exotic Animals</TestName>
  </Tests>
   <Tests>
  <TestID>30</TestID>
  <TestName>Little Known TV Shows</TestName>
  </Tests>
  </dataroot>
```

The structure of this file is pretty straightforward. An appropriate document header is created with a data root, and the data root attribute defines the namespace, location of the data schema, and data generated.

Within the data root we have the structure of the test data and we see our two test entries. The IDs for the tests and test names are represented in the markup.

Next, let's look at the generated XSD file. Listing 8-2 shows the generated code.

Listing 8-2

```
<?xml version="1.0" encoding="UTF-8" ?>
<xsd:schema xmlns:xsd="http://www.w3.org/2001/XMLSchema"
     xmlns:od="urn:schemas-microsoft-com:officedata">

 <xsd:element name="dataroot">

  <xsd:complexType>
```

```
    <xsd:sequence>
        <xsd:element ref="Tests" minOccurs="0" maxOccurs="unbounded" />
    </xsd:sequence>
    <xsd:attribute name="generated" type="xsd:dateTime" />
  </xsd:complexType>

</xsd:element>

<xsd:element name="Tests">

  <xsd:annotation>
    <xsd:appinfo>
    <od:index index-name="PrimaryKey" index-key="TestID " primary="yes"
            unique="yes" clustered="no" />
      <od:index index-name="IDTest" index-key="TestID " primary="no"
            unique="no" clustered="no" />
    </xsd:appinfo>
  </xsd:annotation>

  <xsd:complexType>
   <xsd:sequence>
      <xsd:element name="TestID" minOccurs="1" od:jetType="autonumber"
                od:sqlSType="int" od:autoUnique="yes"
                od:nonNullable="yes" type="xsd:int" />
          <xsd:element name="TestName" minOccurs="0" od:jetType="text"
                od:sqlSType="nvarchar">
          <xsd:simpleType>
          <xsd:restriction base="xsd:string">
             <xsd:maxLength value="50" />
           </xsd:restriction>
          </xsd:simpleType>
       </xsd:element>
    </xsd:sequence>
  </xsd:complexType>

</xsd:element>

</xsd:schema>
```

When the XSD is broken down, there are two primary sections. The first is the definition for the data root element, which shows that it references the Tests element in the structure.

The Tests element structure defines the Test ID and Test name data fields. Note that the data types redefined for Jet, SQL, and the XSD type. The test name type has a restriction that reflects the fact we have a limit of 50 characters for the data in our Access database. The XSD is fairly straightforward.

Now, let's look at the presentation files created, Tests.htm and Tests.xsl. Listing 8-3 shows the generated code for Tests.htm.

Listing 8-3

```
<HTML xmlns:signature="urn:schemas-microsoft-com:office:access">
    <HEAD>
        <META HTTP-EQUIV="Content-Type"
              CONTENT="text/html;charset=UTF-8" />
        </HEAD>
    <BODY ONLOAD="ApplyTransform()">
    </BODY>
    <SCRIPT LANGUAGE="VBScript">
    Option Explicit

    Function ApplyTransform()
        Dim objData, objStyle

        Set objData = CreateDOM
        LoadDOM objData, "Tests.xml"

        Set objStyle = CreateDOM
        LoadDOM objStyle, "Tests.xsl"

        Document.Open "text/html","replace"
        Document.Write objData.TransformNode(objStyle)
    End Function

    Function CreateDOM()
        On Error Resume Next
        Dim tmpDOM

        Set tmpDOM = Nothing
        Set tmpDOM = CreateObject("MSXML2.DOMDocument.5.0")
        If tmpDOM Is Nothing Then
            Set tmpDOM = CreateObject("MSXML2.DOMDocument.4.0")
        End If
        If tmpDOM Is Nothing Then
            Set tmpDOM = CreateObject("MSXML.DOMDocument")
        End If

        Set CreateDOM = tmpDOM
```

```
      End Function

      Function LoadDOM(objDOM, strXMLFile)
           objDOM.Async = False
           objDOM.Load strXMLFile
           If (objDOM.ParseError.ErrorCode <> 0) Then
                MsgBox objDOM.ParseError.Reason
           End If
      End Function

      </SCRIPT>
</HTML>
```

If you pick carefully through this code, you will see that the VBScript executed in Internet Explorer uses the Document Object Model (DOM) to apply the style sheet transformation to display the data in the browser. The key is that the script refers to the Tests.xml and Tests.xls files to get the data and the transformation.

The generated XLS file provides the transformation data for displaying the data in HTML in a browser. Listing 8-4 shows the part of the code generated by the export.

Listing 8-4

```
<?xml version="1.0"?>
<xsl:stylesheet version="1.0"
  xmlns:xsl="http://www.w3.org/1999/XSL/Transform"
  xmlns:msxsl="urn:schemas-microsoft-com:xslt" xmlns:fx="#fx-functions"
  exclude-result-prefixes="msxsl fx">
     <xsl:output method="html" version="4.0" indent="yes"
          xmlns:xsl="http://www.w3.org/1999/XSL/Transform"/>
     <xsl:template match="//dataroot"
          xmlns:xsl="http://www.w3.org/1999/XSL/Transform">
          <html>
               <head>
                    <META HTTP-EQUIV="Content-Type"
                         CONTENT="text/html;charset=UTF-8"/>
                    <title>Tests</title>
                    <style type="text/css">
                    </style>
               </head>
               <body link="#0000ff" vlink="#800080">
                    <table border="1" bgcolor="#ffffff"
                         cellspacing="0" cellpadding="0" id="CTRL1">
                         <colgroup>
                              <col style="WIDTH: 0.9375in"/>
```

```
                    <col style="WIDTH: 0.9375in"/>
                </colgroup>
                <tbody>
                    <tr>
                        <td>
                        <div align="center">
                            <strong>TestID</strong>
                        </div>
                        </td>
                        <td>
                         <div align="center">
                            <strong>TestName</strong>
                         </div>
                        </td>
                    </tr>
                </tbody>
                <tbody id="CTRL2">
                    <xsl:for-each select="Tests">
                    <tr>
                        <td style="VERTICAL-ALIGN: top">
                        <span class="" style="WIDTH: 100%;
                                    HEIGHT: auto; WIDTH: 100%;
                                    WHITE-SPACE: nowrap;
                                    TEXT-ALIGN: left">
                        <xsl:value-of select="TestID"/>
                        </span>
                        </td>
                        <td style="VERTICAL-ALIGN: top">
                        <span class="" style="WIDTH: 100%;
                                HEIGHT: auto; WIDTH: 100%;
                                WHITE-SPACE: nowrap;
                                TEXT-ALIGN: left">
                        <xsl:value-of select="TestName"/>
                        </span>
                        </td>
                    </tr>
                    </xsl:for-each>
                </tbody>
            </table>
        </body>
    </html>
</xsl:template>
<msxsl:script language="VBScript" implements-prefix="fx"
    xmlns:msxsl="urn:schemas-microsoft-com:xslt"><![CDATA[
```

The code continues with a series of VBScript functions that are encoded in the CDATA field. These functions are used in the formatting of the data. The first part of the file is fairly straightforward and defines how the data should be displayed in HTML.

That does it for the export review. It is pretty straightforward, although the XLS transformation is heavily dependent upon VBScript and the browser for displaying the HTML. But, it is all generated on the fly for us with the export.

Multiple Table Exports

Now, let's explore the additional export options when we export data. Select the Tests table again and choose the export option and XML. This time, save the export as Tests2. Select the presentation layer option and then click More Options. A new dialog box is presented. Figure 8-1 shows the dialog box.

Now we have the options to export data from more than one table. Note that the hierarchical structure of our tests, questions, and answers is displayed, and each can be selected for export. Select all three tables for export.

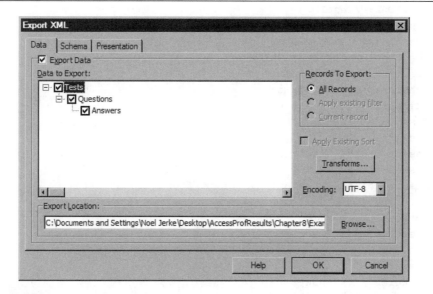

FIGURE 8-1   Additional XML export options

The Schema tab provides options on how the schema should be exported. It includes options for exporting IDs, and how the schema will be created. For this example, accept the default values.

Finally, the Presentation tab provides options for creating the presentation export of the data. Presentation styles can also be created in ASP. If there are images in the data, export options can also be set.

Now, go ahead and export the data. This time, the full set of test data is exported. The XML file is generated that includes the structure of tests, questions, and answers. Listing 8-5 shows a section of the generated markup.

Listing 8-5

```xml
<?xml version="1.0" encoding="UTF-8" ?>
<dataroot xmlns:od="urn:schemas-microsoft-com:officedata"
  xmlns:xsi="http://www.w3.org/2001/XMLSchema-instance"
  xsi:noNamespaceSchemaLocation="Tests2.xsd"
  generated="2003-04-23T02:05:18">
<Tests>
  <TestID>29</TestID>
  <TestName>Exotic Animals</TestName>
  <Questions>
  <QuestionID>41</QuestionID>
  <QuestionText>What Animal only lives in the yellow sap tree of
Madagascar?</QuestionText>
  <NumAnswers>3</NumAnswers>
  <TestID>29</TestID>
  <Answers>
  <AnswerID>215</AnswerID>
  <AnswerText>Pot Belly Pig</AnswerText>
  <AnswerRational>This animal can be found around the
world.</AnswerRational>
  <CorrectAnswer>0</CorrectAnswer>
  <QuestionID>41</QuestionID>
  </Answers>
  <Answers>
  <AnswerID>216</AnswerID>
  <AnswerText>Sneegel Varmit</AnswerText>
  <AnswerRational>This is the correct answer.</AnswerRational>
  <CorrectAnswer>1</CorrectAnswer>
```

```
<QuestionID>41</QuestionID>
</Answers>
<Answers>
<AnswerID>217</AnswerID>
<AnswerText>The Wild Warbler</AnswerText>
<AnswerRational>The Wild Warbler is found in green sap trees of
Madagascar</AnswerRational>
<CorrectAnswer>0</CorrectAnswer>
<QuestionID>41</QuestionID>
</Answers>
</Questions>
```

The structure of the markup is very straightforward and is the expected set of data based on our selections. The corresponding schema, XLS, and HTM files will include the appropriate data related to the HTML.

Transformation Exports

The last export technique to explore is the transformation process. The transformation process allows us to shape the data into a new format. We have seen this already for displaying the exports in HTML with the previous exports, but we can also build our own XSL transformations and apply them.

Listing 8-6 shows the code for an XLS transformation that reformats our test data into a simpler HTML structure for display.

Listing 8-6

```
<?xml version="1.0"?>
<xsl:stylesheet xmlns:xsl="http://www.w3.org/1999/XSL/Transform"
version="1.0">

<xsl:template match="dataroot">
    <html><body>
    <table border="1">
    <xsl:apply-templates/>
    </table>
</body></html>
</xsl:template>
```

```
<xsl:template match="Tests">
  <tr><td>
  <b><xsl:value-of select="TestName"/></b>
  </td><td></td><td></td></tr>
  <xsl:apply-templates select="Questions"/>
</xsl:template>

<xsl:template match="Questions">
  <tr><td></td><td><xsl:value-of select="QuestionText"/>
  </td><td></td></tr>
  <xsl:apply-templates select="Answers"/>
</xsl:template>

<xsl:template match="Answers">
  <tr><td></td><td></td><td><xsl:value-of select="AnswerText"/>
  </td></tr>
</xsl:template>


</xsl:stylesheet>
```

This style sheet is pretty simple. It builds a three-column table that displays the test, questions, and answers in hierarchical order. The rest of the fields in the data are not transformed into the new file. In the first section, we get the data root top-level node. We know to grab this because Access exports the top node as data root (look at the previous XML export of the data).

Within the data root, we have the structure of our exported document set up. In this case, it is essentially HTML tags for setting up the page and wrapping a three-column table around the data. Note that the page and table opening and closing tags are in the data root since that is the top of the tree hierarchy.

Next, the test name of the test data is retrieved. This explicitly defines the data we want to export. Then the <xsl:apply-templates> tag specifies the next level of data to retrieve, which is the question data. The question text is pulled from the source.

Finally, the answer text data is retrieved. Around each of these sets of data are appropriate table row tags that place the test name in the leftmost column, the question in the middle column, and the answers in the rightmost column.

Now, let's utilize the export. Start up the export process as outlined earlier and save the export as Tests3. Do not select a presentation file to be created since our transformation is essentially creating one for us (in HTML). In the More Options settings, select all three tables (Tests, Questions, Answers).

Since we are essentially creating an HTML transformation out of our exported data, we will want to give the exported file an .HTM extension. Change the Export Location so the exported file is Tests3.htm.

Now, click the Transforms button. Add the transformation file created above to the list and then highlight the transformation and click OK. Figure 8-2 shows the Export Transforms dialog box.

Now, we are ready to export the data. Click OK. When the export is complete, two files are created. The first is test3.htm. If you open it, you will see a table created that presents the data hierarchically. Figure 8-3 shows the browser with the page loaded.

The XML generated is in fact a well-formed HTML document. The transformation essentially builds a simple HTML document for us. Unlike the presentation export

FIGURE 8-2   Export Transforms dialog box

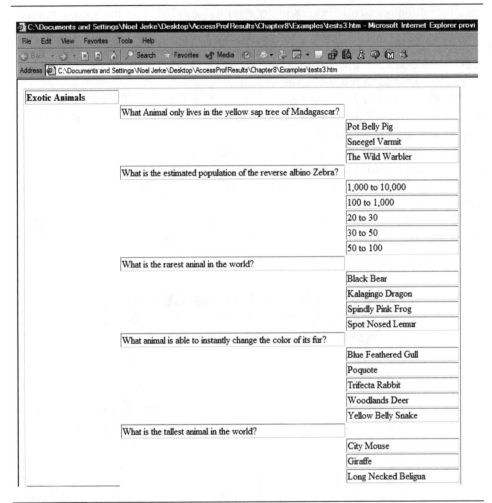

FIGURE 8-3   Transformed test data

that Access automatically builds (which we saw earlier), this HTML presentation document is much simpler and more straightforward (of course, we had to build the XLS by hand). Listing 8-7 shows the generated HTML.

Listing 8-7

```
<html><body>
    <table border="1">
```

```
<tr><td><b>Exotic Animals</b></td><td></td><td></td></tr>
<tr><td></td><td>What Animal only lives in the yellow sap tree
of Madagascar?</td><td></td></tr>
<tr><td></td><td></td><td>Pot Belly Pig</td></tr>
<tr><td></td><td></td><td>Sneegel Varmit</td></tr>
<tr><td></td><td></td><td>The Wild Warbler</td></tr>
<tr><td></td><td>What is the estimated population of the
reverse albino Zebra?</td><td></td></tr>
<tr><td></td><td></td><td>1,000 to 10,000</td></tr>
<tr><td></td><td></td><td>100 to 1,000</td></tr>
<tr><td></td><td></td><td>20 to 30</td></tr>
<tr><td></td><td></td><td>30 to 50</td></tr>
<tr><td></td><td></td><td>50 to 100</td></tr>
<tr><td></td><td>What is the rarest animal in the
world?</td><td></td></tr>
<tr><td></td><td></td><td>Black Bear</td></tr>
<tr><td></td><td></td><td>Kalagingo Dragon</td></tr>
<tr><td></td><td></td><td>Spindly Pink Frog</td></tr>
<tr><td></td><td></td><td>Spot Nosed Lemur</td></tr>
<tr><td></td><td>What animal is able to instantly change the
color of its fur?</td><td></td></tr>
<tr><td></td><td></td><td>Blue Feathered Gull</td></tr>
<tr><td></td><td></td><td>Poquote</td></tr>
<tr><td></td><td></td><td>Trifecta Rabbit</td></tr>
<tr><td></td><td></td><td>Woodlands Deer</td></tr>
<tr><td></td><td></td><td>Yellow Belly Snake</td></tr>
<tr><td></td><td>What is the tallest animal in the
world?</td><td></td></tr>
<tr><td></td><td></td><td>City Mouse</td></tr>
<tr><td></td><td></td><td>Giraffe</td></tr>
<tr><td></td><td></td><td>Long Necked Beligua</td></tr>
<tr><td>
   <b>Little Known TV Shows</b></td><td></td><td>
  </td></tr>
<tr><td></td><td>What two TV shows never had their initial
episodes aired?</td><td></td></tr>
<tr><td></td><td></td><td>I Love Junior</td></tr>
<tr><td></td><td></td><td>My Mother was a Staple</td></tr>
<tr><td></td><td></td><td>Rock and Roll Kindergarten</td></tr>
<tr><td></td><td></td><td>Skate Board Police</td></tr>
<tr><td></td><td></td><td>Trees can Talk Too</td></tr>
<tr><td></td><td>What TV Show starred Gerald
Ford?</td><td></td></tr>
<tr><td></td><td></td><td>Being President is Fun</td></tr>
<tr><td></td><td></td><td>I once was a President</td></tr>
<tr><td></td><td></td><td>The President - Man in Charge</td></tr>
<tr><td></td><td>Gumby starred in which of these three shows at
```

```
the same time?</td><td></td></tr>
         <tr><td></td><td></td><td>Gumby - Look at Me</td></tr>
         <tr><td></td><td></td><td>Gumby and His Gal</td></tr>
         <tr><td></td><td></td><td>Gumby Cooks</td></tr>
         <tr><td></td><td></td><td>Gumby Does Opera</td></tr>
         <tr><td></td><td></td><td>Little Dude Gumby</td></tr>
         <tr><td></td><td>Which one of these answers was a real
show?</td><td></td></tr>
         <tr><td></td><td></td><td>A</td></tr>
         <tr><td></td><td></td><td>B</td></tr>
         <tr><td></td><td></td><td>C</td></tr>
         <tr><td></td><td></td><td>D</td></tr>
         <tr><td></td><td></td><td>E</td></tr>
         <tr><td></td><td>Which show had as its star Ralph the
Flea?</td><td></td></tr>
         <tr><td></td><td></td><td>Danger Ralph</td></tr>
         <tr><td></td><td></td><td>Echo Chamber</td></tr>
         <tr><td></td><td></td><td>Fly Boy</td></tr>
         <tr><td></td><td></td><td>Justice Served</td></tr>
         <tr><td></td><td></td><td>Mite</td></tr>
    </table>
</body></html>
```

There is nothing spectacular in our export file other than very simple HTML tagging, but the beauty is that this was all created for us on the fly in a very simple fashion using the XSL transformation, and Access automated the transformation for us. Apply this to complex data and exports, and the power of XML within Access becomes apparent. We have a little bonus as well—one that you don't get with ordinary HTML exports. An XML schema file was also created for us. This describes the schema and structure of the data in our HTML document. Figure 8-4 shows a graphic representation of the schema in Visual Studio .NET.

With this schema, we know more about the data in our HTML document. All of the fields are typed and the structure of the data is represented. We can use this schema down the road to enforce the integrity of our data.

Programmatically Exporting XML Data

We also have options for exporting data from within VBA code. Office 2003 has an updated version of the ExportXML method that supports exporting related tables and new options for persisting sorts and filters. In addition, the AdditionalData object has been added, which provides the structure for defining what related data should be exported, and the TransformXML method has been added, which allows for transformations of XML data using XLS transforms.

Let's create a new module and save it as XMLExport. Listing 8-8 shows the VBA code to be added to the module.

Listing 8-8

```
Private Sub ExportTestsData()
    Dim objad As AdditionalData

    Set objad = Application.CreateAdditionalData

    objad.Add "Questions"

    objad(Item = "Questions").Add "Answers"

    Application.ExportXML acExportTable, "Tests", _
            "c:\tests4.xml", "c:\tests4.xsd", AdditionalData:=objad

End Sub
```

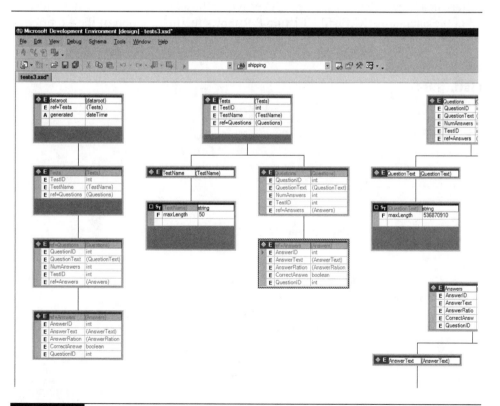

FIGURE 8-4   Test3 XSD schema

NOTE *Appendix A has the definitions for ExportXML, ImportXML, TransformXML, and AdditionalData.*

The first thing that happens in the module is that an AdditionalData object is created. We will utilize this for defining the related data to the Tests table that we want to have exported. Next, the Questions table is added to the AdditionalData object.

We then need to indicate that the Answers data relates to the Questions data. This is done by indicating that the Answers table needs to be connected to the Questions table in the AdditionalData object.

Next, we are ready to use the ExportXML method to export the data into an XML file. The ExportXML method is utilized. The primary table, Tests, is indicated first. Following that, the XML and XSD files are specified. Finally, the additional data is passed in as well.

When the subroutine is run, the two files are created. The XML file has the hierarchical tree of test data. The XSD provides the schema data definitions for all of the data in the XML file. Listing 8-9 shows the first section of the exported XML data.

Listing 8-9

```
<?xml version="1.0" encoding="UTF-8" ?>
<dataroot xmlns:od="urn:schemas-m_u99 ?rosoft-com:officedata"
    xmlns:xsi="http://www.w3.org/2001/X_LSchema-instance"
    xsi:noNamespaceSchemaLocation="tests4.xsd"
    generated="2003-04-23T10:51:14">
    <Tests>
        <TestID>29</TestID>
        <TestName>Exotic Animals</TestName>
        <Questions>
            <QuestionID>41</QuestionID>
            <QuestionText>What Animal only lives in the yellow sap
tree of Madagascar?</QuestionText>
            <NumAnswers>3</NumAnswers>
            <TestID>29</TestID>
            <Answers>
                <AnswerID>215</AnswerID>
                <AnswerText>Pot Belly Pig</AnswerText>
                <AnswerRational>This animal can be found around
the world.</AnswerRational>
                <CorrectAnswer>0</CorrectAnswer>
```

```xml
                    <QuestionID>41</QuestionID>
            </Answers>
            <Answers>
                    <AnswerID>216</AnswerID>
                    <AnswerText>Sneegel Varmit</AnswerText>
                    <AnswerRational>This is the correct
answer.</AnswerRational>
                    <CorrectAnswer>1</CorrectAnswer>
                    <QuestionID>41</QuestionID>
            </Answers>
            <Answers>
                    <AnswerID>217</AnswerID>
                    <AnswerText>The Wild Warbler</AnswerText>
                    <AnswerRational>The Wild Warbler is found in
green sap trees of Madagascar</AnswerRational>
                    <CorrectAnswer>0</CorrectAnswer>
                    <QuestionID>41</QuestionID>
            </Answers>
        </Questions>
        <Questions>
            <QuestionID>42</QuestionID>
            <QuestionText>What is the estimated population of
the reverse albino Zebra?</QuestionText>
            <NumAnswers>5</NumAnswers>
            <TestID>29</TestID>
            <Answers>
                    <AnswerID>218</AnswerID>
                    <AnswerText>1,000 to 10,000</AnswerText>
                    <AnswerRational>Incorrect</AnswerRational>
                    <CorrectAnswer>0</CorrectAnswer>
                    <QuestionID>42</QuestionID>
            </Answers>
            <Answers>
                    <AnswerID>219</AnswerID>
                    <AnswerText>100 to 1,000</AnswerText>
                    <AnswerRational>Incorrect</AnswerRational>
                    <CorrectAnswer>0</CorrectAnswer>
                    <QuestionID>42</QuestionID>
            </Answers>
            <Answers>
                    <AnswerID>220</AnswerID>
                    <AnswerText>20 to 30</AnswerText>
                    <AnswerRational>Incorrect</AnswerRational>
```

```
                    <CorrectAnswer>0</CorrectAnswer>
                    <QuestionID>42</QuestionID>
            </Answers>
            <Answers>
                    <AnswerID>221</AnswerID>
                    <AnswerText>30 to 50</AnswerText>
                    <AnswerRational>Incorrect</AnswerRational>
                    <CorrectAnswer>0</CorrectAnswer>
                    <QuestionID>42</QuestionID>
            </Answers>
            <Answers>
                    <AnswerID>222</AnswerID>
                    <AnswerText>50 to 100</AnswerText>
                    <AnswerRational><![CDATA[The International
Zebra Foundation's 1999 estimate shows a population of 50 to
100.]]></AnswerRational>
                    <CorrectAnswer>1</CorrectAnswer>
                    <QuestionID>42</QuestionID>
            </Answers>
        </Questions>
```

We can also programmatically apply transformations to existing XML files to create new transformed data. This is done with the new TransformXML method. To demonstrate this method, create a new module and subroutine (or create the subroutine in the same module) and save the module as TransformXML. Listing 8-10 shows the code for the module.

Listing 8-10

```
Private Sub TransformData()

    Application.TransformXML _
        "c:\tests2.xml", "c:\transform.xsl", "c:\tests5.htm"

End Sub
```

The code here is pretty straightforward. The TransformXML method takes several parameters. In this case, we are indicating the existing XML file, the XSL transformation file, and the target output file for the transformation.

The result we get is the same as when we applied the transformation using the export functionality from the File menu. In this case, we can make it happen programmatically.

With Access 2003, Microsoft is stepping up to the plate and adding significant XML export support. The key is that they are supporting W3C standards for creating the exported XML.

Importing XML Data

Now we can dig into importing XML data into our relational Access data structure. The XML import requires that an XSD schema be present to define the structure of the data. This is critical for a relational database import.

Multiple Table Import

Let's now reverse the process and import our Tests data from an XML structure and build the relational structure. Create a blank database and save it as XMLImport.mdb.

On the File menu, select the Get External Data option and Import. From the dialog box, select the XML (*.xml, *.xsd) file type option. Navigate to the test2.xml file that was exported previously in the chapter. Click the Import button.

The dialog box that is presented shows the tree structure of the data to be imported. We don't have any options to transform the data directly in the dialog box. In Options, a transform XSL file can be selected (we will demonstrate that in the next section). Figure 8-5 shows the dialog box.

Note the Tests, Questions, and Answers data. When you click OK, the tables are created with the data. If you look at the table structures, you will see the fields

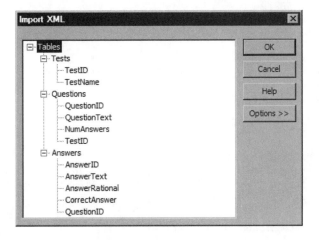

FIGURE 8-5   Import XML dialog box

are set up with the proper data types and so forth. All of this information comes from the XSD file associated with the XML file.

 When importing XML data, it is important that you understand the structure of the data. XML isn't a magic elixir that will just do the "right thing" with the data.

Importing Transformed XML Data

If you need the XML data to be reworked in order for it to be imported into your database, an XSL transformation can also be performed during the import. Let's assume we wanted to import the test data but we had no need for the answer rational data, so we don't want that imported. The way to handle that is to perform an XSL transform on the data as it is imported. The XSL in Listing 8-11 will import everything but the AnswerRational field.

Listing 8-11

```xml
<?xml version="1.0"?>
<xsl:stylesheet xmlns:xsl="http://www.w3.org/1999/XSL/Transform"
version="1.0">

<xsl:template match="dataroot">
    <Tests>
        <xsl:apply-templates/>
    </Tests>
</xsl:template>

  <xsl:template match="Tests">
    <TestID><xsl:value-of select="TestID"/></TestID>
    <TestName><xsl:value-of select="TestName"/></TestName>
    <Questions>
    <xsl:apply-templates select="Questions"/>
    </Questions>
  </xsl:template>

  <xsl:template match="Questions">
    <QuestionID><xsl:value-of select="QuestionID"/></QuestionID>
    <QuestionText><xsl:value-of select="QuestionText"/></QuestionText>
    <TestID><xsl:value-of select="TestID"/></TestID>
    <Answers>
    <xsl:apply-templates select="Answers"/>
    </Answers>
  </xsl:template>
```

```
<xsl:template match="Answers">
    <AnswerID><xsl:value-of select="AnswerID"/></AnswerID>
  <AnswerText><xsl:value-of select="AnswerText"/></AnswerText>
  <CorrectAnswer><xsl:value-of select="CorrectAnswer"/></CorrectAnswer>
  <QuestionID><xsl:value-of select="QuestionID"/></QuestionID>
</xsl:template>

</xsl:stylesheet>
```

Basically, all of the data fields are named in the transformation except the AnswerRational field. The iterative transformation will pull in all of the data in the tree hierarchy.

Now run the import again (delete the tables from the original import) with the same data. In the Import dialog box, click the Options button. Then, click the Transform button and add in the new transformation. Expand the tree view of the data in the import window. The AnswerRational is not in the import list. Figure 8-6 shows the dialog screen.

Now click the OK button to import the data. When you look at the Answer table structure, the AnswerRational field is not listed.

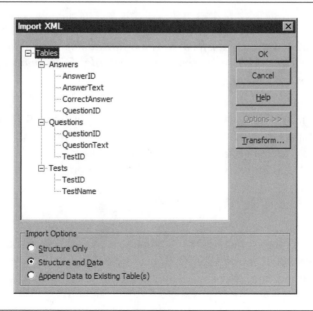

FIGURE 8-6   Test data transformation import

Programmatically Importing XML Data

As with exporting data, XML data can be programmatically imported. The ImportXML VBA function provides support for importing XML data.

Create a new VBA module and save it as ImportXML. Add the code shown in Listing 8-12 to the module.

Listing 8-12

```
Private Sub ImportTestData()

    Application.ImportXML DataSource:="C:\Tests2.xml", _
        IMportOptions:=acStructureAndData

End Sub
```

The coding here is pretty simple. We point to the location of the XML file and then indicate we want the structure and the data to be imported. Keep in mind that once again we need to make sure the corresponding XSD is in the right reference point.

When the subroutine is run, the data is imported automatically and the tables are created. This makes imports fairly simple to automate with VBA programming from Access.

> TIP
>
> *If you also want to transform the data for the import, the first step is to transform the data and create a new XML file. Then, import the newly transformed XML data.*

There are many other capabilities in XML for importing and exporting data. For example, reports can be exported as well, with appropriate XSL presentation data. Advanced features of XML such as XPath, XQuery, and other capabilities can be used in Access for working with the XML imports and exports.

Summary

XML is becoming the de facto data interchange standard between applications, and with Access 2003, support for XML has been expanded. As demonstrated in the chapter, importing, exporting, and transforming are all integral features of Access 2003.

In the next chapter, we will explore the world of Access Data Projects and how we can leverage Access to work directly with our SQL Server enterprise databases.

Chapter 9

Introducing Access Data Projects

Access Data Projects (ADP) provides an Access interface to the Enterprise database level. The environment of Access conforms to the SQL Server database structure, and the power of the projects is the ability to integrate all of the benefits of Access with the powerful back end of the enterprise database.

In this chapter, we will explore how ADPs work and the differences between working with standard Access databases. In the next chapter, we will explore building and working with an ADP database.

Why ADPs?

One of the primary purposes of ADPs is to allow Access developers to migrate existing Access applications to a more robust enterprise database architecture. By upsizing the database to SQL Server, the developer gains all of the benefits on the architecture. With the ADP, though, they can still utilize their investment in Access forms, reports, VBA modules, etc.

A second key focus is the ability to prototype applications in Access, yet actually have the data structure in the enterprise database. This makes reuse and/or migration of the prototype to the enterprise environment less painful.

The final option is to be able to leverage the graphical interface and easy-to-use features of Access against the SQL Server database. For example, Access has always had great reporting capabilities that can be easily leveraged in the ADP interface.

ADPs Overview

The most important thing to understand about working with ADPs is that while the environment is similar to working with standard Access databases, many of the fundamentals of the tables and queries are different.

For ADPs, all of the data is stored on the enterprise server, as well as the queries and database diagrams. The forms, reports, pages, macros, and modules are all stored in the ADP. Figure 9-1 provides a high-level overview of the ADP-to-SQL Server relationship.

NOTE   *We are assuming that the reader has a basic familiarity with SQL Server databases.*

To start with, we (of course) have standard tables that hold data. The concepts are the same, but the data types for the data are based on SQL Server data types.

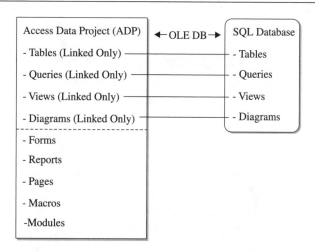

FIGURE 9-1   High-level overview of the ADP-to-SQL Server relationship

For example, there is no AutoNumber field. Instead, the SQL Server Identity column is utilized, but we can still utilize the table design techniques for working with the table structures.

For queries, we have new capabilities that go beyond the standard select, update, and append (insert). With ADPs, we can take full advantage of the SQL Server database and create functions and stored procedures. The standard select queries are now views, and all of the query building techniques demonstrated throughout the book can be utilized.

For data relationships, the functionality relies on the Diagrams capability of SQL Server. Now, diagrams can be created in the Access interface. In fact, Diagrams is an Object type similar to Tables, Queries, Reports, etc.

We still have the ability to create forms, reports, macros, and VBA modules. The beauty is that these can now work against the enterprise SQL Server database.

Setting Up an ADP

The first step to setting up an ADP for an existing database is to create a new project using existing data. You will be prompted to save the database, and you should save it as ADPNW.ADP.

Next, the Data Link Properties dialog box pops up. The information about the SQL Server database needs to be entered. Enter the appropriate data to connect to your server, and then select the database to link. In this case, we are connecting to the Northwind sample database. The dialog box is shown here:

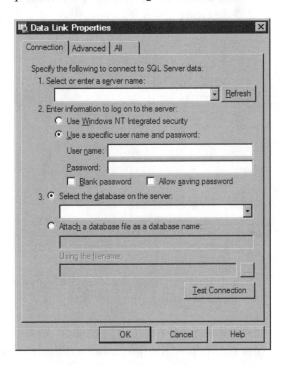

For the Northwind database, there are 13 tables linked and 23 queries. The queries are a mix of stored procedures and views for the database. If you explore the Northwind ADP database against the SQL Enterprise database structure, you will see that they match.

Exploring Tables and Queries

Now let's explore the new interfaces for queries and tables. We will take a look at how the Northwind database can be managed from the ADP environment.

Tables

As mentioned earlier, the table interfaces are reworked to interface with the SQL Enterprise environment. The data types and settings of the tables match the requirements for SQL Server.

Select the Customers table and go to the Design view. Figure 9-2 shows the design interface for the table.

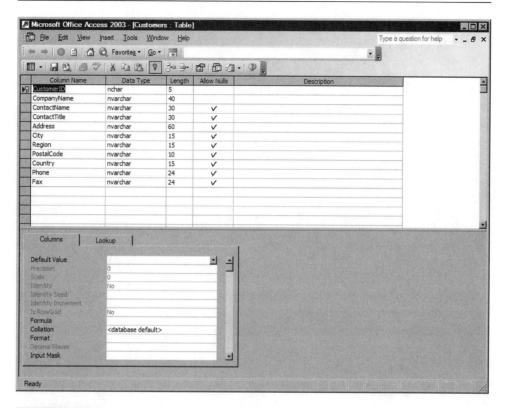

FIGURE 9-2   Customers table Design view

Exploring Tables and Queries

Note the data types for the different fields—most of them are nvarchar. The sizes of the fields are set with a new column, Length. Finally, if the field can have Nulls, this is checked in an additional new column.

For this table, the CustomerID field is the primary key. In this case, it is a standard nchar field with a length of 5.

Now open the Orders table in the Design view. Figure 9-3 shows the table in the Design view.

In this case, our primary key is an integer value. The value is to be autoincremented with each new insert. Note the properties setting for the primary key. The Identity property is set to Yes, the Identity Seed is set to 1, and the Identity Increment is also set to 1. These are all the settings you would expect when setting the table up in SQL Enterprise Manager. Note that these values can all be managed right in the Access Design view.

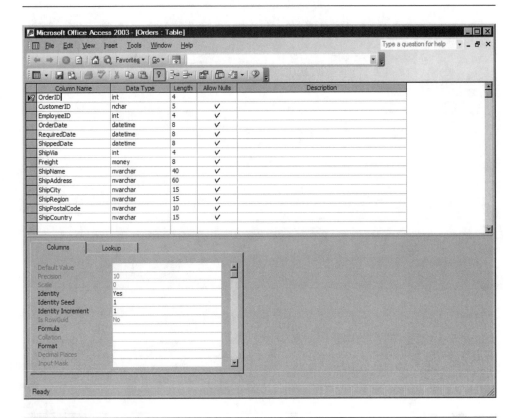

FIGURE 9-3   Orders table Design view

Next, we can also manage triggers for the tables. If you right-click on any table, an option in the pop-up menu is listed for Triggers. Select the Triggers option, and the dialog box shown here is displayed:

For this database, there are no preexisting triggers for any of the tables. If you click on the New button, a new screen pops up that allows for the trigger to be coded.

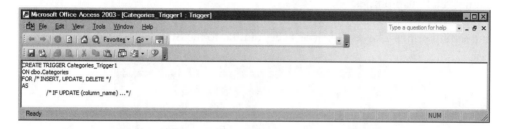

As you can see, the template for writing the trigger is created. Unfortunately, there is no slick GUI for designing the trigger, so it will take standard SQL coding.

We can also manage a table's properties. With a table open in Design view, click on the View menu and select Properties. We have five options to work with: Tables, Relationships, Indexes/Keys, Check Constraints, and Data. The Tables tab is shown here:

Exploring Tables and Queries

The Tables tab allows different tables to be selected, along with other settings. The Relationships tab is used for setting up relationships with the table, including setting relationship rules.

The Indexes/Keys tab, shown next, supports setting up the indexes for the table and setting primary keys. This looks very similar to the SQL Enterprise dialog box.

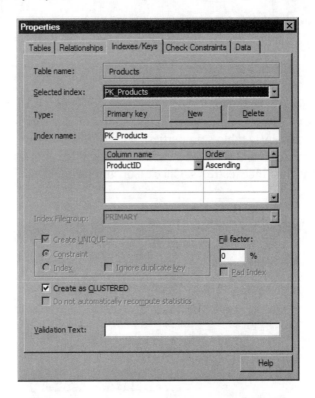

Note that for this table, the primary key is set as an ascending sorted index. The Check Constraints tab, shown next, allows for constraints on the data to be set.

When working with the tables of the enterprise database, we have access to the full set of options for managing our data and data structure.

The standard Data Sheet view is the same as it is in standard projects. The data is updated directly in the enterprise database. That is about it for the major feature changes for tables in ADPs.

Queries and Functions

The query interface changes quite a bit for ADP projects over standard Access projects. We are now working with three different object types—views, stored procedures, and user functions. Access implements all three interfaces.

Exploring Tables and Queries

Let's first take a look at the views. These will be familiar since they are just like the queries we are used to working with in standard Access projects. However, even though these are similar to Access queries, we will find that the design interface is different.

Open up the Sales by Category query of the Northwind database in the Design view. Figure 9-4 shows the design screen. Note that we still have the table Design view and the query grid for setting up the query.

The relationship screen shows the primary key and foreign key relationships between the tables that will create the joins of the tables.

The query grid looks totally different from what we are used to seeing. It is flipped from a left-to-right column listing to a top-down listing. Each field (column) is selected in the first column. The column can be aliased with a new name in the second column.

The third column indicates the table the field is coming from. The output flag indicates if the field should be returned from the query, and the two sort columns determine the type of sort and the order of the sorts.

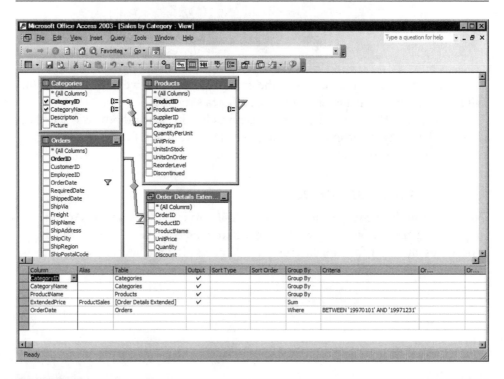

FIGURE 9-4   Query Design view

The Group By column provides options for how the data will be filtered by criteria. In fact, the column is a bit of a misnomer. This column allows options for setting where clauses and aggregates, as well as group by. The criteria column is set for any where clause settings, and several OR options can be added to the where clause. Note that AND options are contained in the same criteria clause.

If you are wondering where the SQL option is for the query, there is a SQL button on the toolbar. When clicked, the SQL is displayed for the query all in the same screen. The SQL for this particular query is as follows:

```
SELECT dbo.Categories.CategoryID, dbo.Categories.CategoryName,
       dbo.Products.ProductName,
       SUM(dbo.[Order Details Extended].ExtendedPrice)
         AS ProductSales
   FROM dbo.Categories INNER JOIN
        dbo.Products INNER JOIN
        dbo.Orders INNER JOIN
        dbo.[Order Details Extended] ON
        dbo.Orders.OrderID = dbo.[Order Details Extended].OrderID ON
        dbo.Products.ProductID = dbo.[Order Details Extended].ProductID ON
        dbo.Categories.CategoryID = dbo.Products.CategoryID
WHERE   (dbo.Orders.OrderDate BETWEEN '19970101' AND '19971231')
GROUP BY dbo.Categories.CategoryID, dbo.Categories.CategoryName,
         dbo.Products.ProductName
```

All of the query grid settings can be seen in the SQL. The mix of the SQL and graphical design capabilities makes the ADP environment very powerful for building SQL views.

Next, let's look at building stored procedures in the ADP environment. As a quick refresher, stored procedures are compiled SQL code that runs on the server. The main difference between stored procedures and views is that stored procedures can take in parameter values and return parameter values (in addition to standard data).

To explore the stored procedure interface, let's review the CustOrdersDetail stored procedure. Select the stored procedure and go into the Design view. Figure 9-5 shows the design.

We have the same three sections of the query Design view—graphic view of the tables, query design grid, and the SQL screen. The first changes we will notice are on the query design grid. We have a new column—Alias—for aliasing table names to another name. This is used to simplify the inner join SQL syntax. In this case, the Product table is aliased as P and the Order Details table is Od.

For this stored procedure, the Criteria setting for the OrderID column is set to the input parameter for the stored procedure, @OrderID. Here, we see an interesting aspect of ADPs. When building input parameters for stored procedures, the ADP

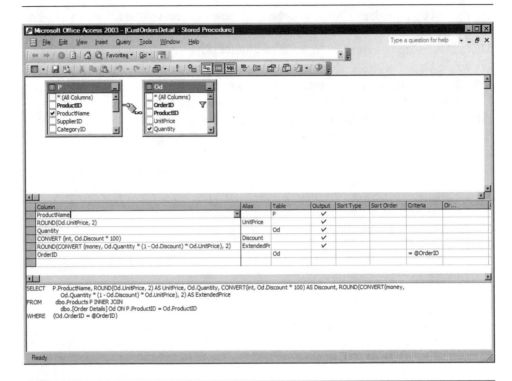

FIGURE 9-5   Stored Procedure Design view

environment automatically builds the SQL coding for the input parameters, and it isn't shown in the SQL pane. Here is the SQL code shown in the ADP SQL pane:

```
SELECT P.ProductName, ROUND(Od.UnitPrice, 2) AS UnitPrice,
    Od.Quantity, CONVERT(int, Od.Discount * 100) AS Discount,
    ROUND(CONVERT(money, Od.Quantity * (1 - Od.Discount) *
        Od.UnitPrice), 2) AS ExtendedPrice
FROM dbo.Products P INNER JOIN
    dbo.[Order Details] Od ON P.ProductID = Od.ProductID
WHERE (Od.OrderID = @OrderID)
```

Now let's look at the actual stored procedure code in the enterprise database:

```
CREATE PROCEDURE dbo.CustOrdersDetail
(
  @OrderID int,
```

```
    @Quantity smallint
)
AS
SELECT P.ProductName, ROUND(Od.UnitPrice, 2) AS UnitPrice,
   Od.Quantity, CONVERT(int, Od.Discount * 100) AS Discount,
   ROUND(CONVERT(money, Od.Quantity * (1 - Od.Discount) *
   Od.UnitPrice), 2) AS ExtendedPrice
FROM
   dbo.Products P INNER JOIN
   dbo.[Order Details] Od ON P.ProductID = Od.ProductID
WHERE
    Od.OrderID = @OrderID) AND (Od.Quantity = @Quantity)
GO
```

Note the initial Create Procedure syntax where the input parameter is defined. That is where the OrderID parameter is set as an integer value. Now let's make a slight change to the stored procedure in the ADP environment and set a second criteria parameter, and see what happens.

Add in "= @Quantity" to the criteria field for the Quantity column field (you're right—this makes no sense from the query standpoint, but it will illustrate the point). Then save the query. The new code is now saved on the server.

```
CREATE PROCEDURE dbo.CustOrdersDetail
(@OrderID int,
 @Quantity smallint)
AS SELECT P.ProductName, ROUND(Od.UnitPrice, 2) AS UnitPrice,
         Od.Quantity,
         CONVERT(int, Od.Discount * 100) AS Discount,
         ROUND(CONVERT(money, Od.Quantity * (1 -
              Od.Discount) * Od.UnitPrice), 2) AS ExtendedPrice
FROM dbo.Products P INNER JOIN
     dbo.[Order Details] Od ON P.ProductID = Od.ProductID
WHERE (Od.OrderID = @OrderID) AND (Od.Quantity = @Quantity)
GO
```

The ADP interface automatically added the @Quantity input parameter to the stored procedure. It also automatically sets the parameter type as smallint. If you look at the data type for the Quantity field in the Order Details table, it is in fact smallint.

While this automatic building of input parameters can make for quick and easy stored procedure coding, it can also limit the ability to create more complex stored procedures where input parameters that are used for other purposes are needed.

Exploring Tables and Queries

NOTE

Append queries can also be built, which are essentially stored procedures that insert data.

In the next chapter, we will explore building user functions on a sample database, which is very similar to building queries in the Design view.

ADP Database Utilities

The Database Utilities menu provides options that make managing the SQL Enterprise database from within the ADP easier. These tools can be useful for deploying the SQL database from one server to another.

On the Tools menu, when you select Database Utilities | Transfer Database, you can choose any SQL Server on your network, and supply login credentials and a database name. It then makes an exact copy of the SQL Server back-end database that you're using on the new server. This utility is ideal for moving an ADP back end from your development machine to a production server.

NOTE

If you want your ADP to point at the new database, you will need to change the ADP's connection string. This can be done by going to the File menu and selecting connection, and then updating the connection as appropriate to point to the new database.

The second option is pretty cool and can be useful even if you don't need to specifically work with an ADP. On the Tools menu, Database Utilities | Copy Database File gives you the option to make a SQL MDF file copy of a database. This option will make a copy of the physical file that holds the database on the server. That way, the database can be deployed to database servers and then attached within the target server.

NOTE

When this function is run, all current users are disconnected from the database.

In addition to these two options, you can also back up and restore a database, and an option is also provided for dropping a database.

Designing Relationships

We saw in the early chapters of the book that designing the relationships between the tables was critical for utilizing the querying capabilities of Access, and it is no different with ADPs.

When we build diagrams, we are actually creating SQL Server diagrams. The process is pretty much the same as it is for standard Access databases. Tables are added into the Design view and the links between the tables can then be drawn and set up as appropriate.

The Northwind database has no diagrams in it. Figure 9-6 shows a sample diagram based on the database structure.

The table relationships are all shown, and the diagram should look familiar. The diagram interface works a little differently than in a standard Access database, but not enough to cause any difficulties.

NOTE

If you right-click on any of the table relationships, the Table Properties dialog box pops up (we reviewed this earlier in the chapter). The constraints, relationships, and indexes/keys can all be managed from this view.

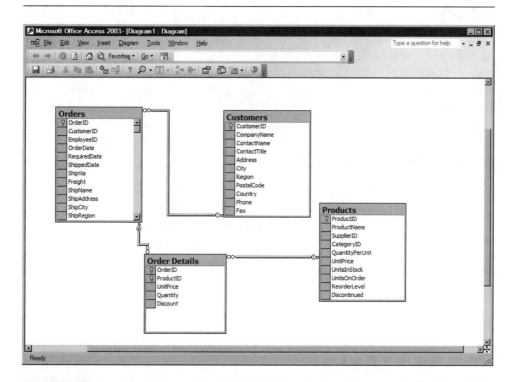

FIGURE 9-6   Sample database diagram

Designing Relationships

ADP Tips

One thing we cannot manage in ADPs is security for the SQL Server project. That will still need to be done through the traditional SQL Enterprise interface. It is important that the password used in the ODBC interface has the appropriate permissions to access the objects you want to work with in the ADP interface.

One of the more useful features of ADPs is the ability to link data from multiple sources. For example, you may have multiple enterprise SQL databases for which you want to be able to combine the data for reporting or updating. With ADPs, additional tables can be linked. Then, queries, forms, and reports can be built that utilize the multiple data servers. Figure 9-7 shows the concept.

Certainly Access isn't the only way to link tables in queries. It can also be done directly in SQL Server with Transact SQL (as is generated by Access), but Access provides a simple graphic environment for quickly building those queries.

Summary

Access Data Projects provide the best of both worlds—the graphical and wizard interfaces of Access with the full power of the SQL Server enterprise database engine. This combination can make for a powerful environment for building prototype applications that can be utilized for further development. It also provides an enhanced environment for designing databases and building supporting queries.

In the next chapter, we will build an enterprise database from scratch using the ADP interface. We will also explore building queries against the database using the Access tools but for the enterprise environment.

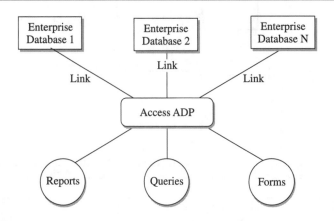

FIGURE 9-7   Linking databases in an ADP

Chapter 10

Building an Access Data Project

In the last chapter, we explored the basic concepts around Access Data Projects (ADP) and how they interface with SQL Server. We also explored the differences between traditional Access projects and ADPs.

In this chapter, we will build a sample ADP project from scratch. The table structure, queries, forms, and reports will all be created based on an initial database design.

Designing the Database

Our sample application will be focused on building administrative tools for managing an e-commerce store. These are the types of tools that would be used internally in an organization. We are going to build example administrative functions and reports that might be used by an IT shop to manage the database. The actual primary user interface might be built in ASP.NET or Visual Basic .NET and transact against the SQL Server, but in this example, we will see how ADPs can be a powerful tool for building and managing the enterprise database.

Business Requirements Overview

The e-commerce store is pretty straightforward. The primary product being sold is specialty pens, and the primary shoppers are consumers who do a lot of writing.

For the administrative tools, we want to be able to track and review individual orders. We also want to be able to update an order as required. From a reporting standpoint, we want to run reports on utilization of the store. We will also want to be able to export the order data to XML for processing in our internal fulfillment system.

Database Design

The database design is straightforward. The data starts with the product item data—this is the pen products that the shopper will buy. Next, the Basket table stores the core items that the shopper has selected.

The order and payment data is also stored for each order, and, finally, the shopper name and address data is stored as well. The following illustration shows the design of the database.

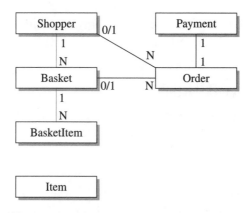

The database consists of six primary tables. The Shopper table holds the core shopper information. Shoppers will have multiple baskets. Each basket relates to one and only one shopper.

Each of the baskets will have a series of items in the basket. Note that a basket is only created when an item is selected by the shopper. So, there is always at least one item in each basket.

You will note that the Item table exists independently of any of the other tables. The reason the table is not linked is because as items are added into the shopping basket, a replica copy of the item data is stored in the BasketItem table. That way, if the item price or other facets change while the shopper is shopping or retrieves the basket at a later date, the original item they chose to purchase is still in their basket.

TIP

In a live system, we would want to implement business rules to ensure that if product data changes, then existing baskets that are invalid are updated. We would also want to ensure that baskets are cleared on a regular basis. Dead baskets can be archived for later analysis.

Some baskets will have an order. If there is an order, then there is only one related basket to the order. Likewise, each order relates to the shopper who placed the order. But, potentially there may not be orders for a shopper.

NOTE

Technically, we do not need the relationship between the Shopper table and the Order table. The orders for a shopper can be determined by looking for baskets with related orders. But, in this case, the small break in the normalization rules will allow for much easier analysis of shopper order history.

Designing the Database

That does it for the basic database design. Next, we will actually build the database tables via the ADP interface.

Setting Up the Database

Now we will go through the process of setting up the database. First, we will connect to the server and have the database created, and then the tables will be created using the table designer.

Connecting to the Server

Start up Microsoft Access. Select the New option on the File menu, and on the pop-up dialog box, select the Project Using New Data option. Save the file to an appropriate place. This will create a new Access Data Project and step through the process of creating the new database on the SQL Server.

The first dialog box in the setup process is the database connection setup. This is where we define the server and security access method for reaching the target SQL Server. Figure 10-1 shows the setup dialog box.

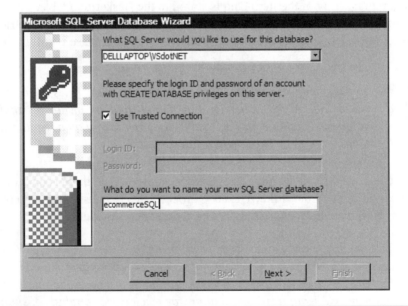

FIGURE 10-1   Setting the database connection

Enter the appropriate connection data for your SQL Server database, then click the Next button to go to the next screen. The next screen indicates that the wizard has enough information to create the database. When you click Finish, the wizard creates a new logical database on the SQL Server (this all happens behind the scenes). Now the database is ready for creating our database tables.

Building the Database

Our tables can be designed in the ADP interface. The table designer is available for defining the fields. Remember that the data types are based on the SQL Server engine and not the traditional Access data types.

To get started, click on Create Table in Design view to pull up the table Design view. Figure 10-2 shows the Design view for creating the table.

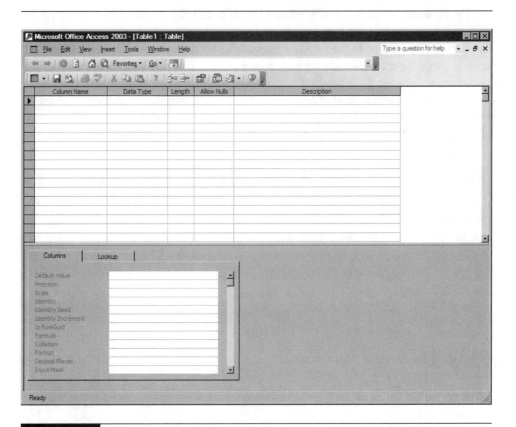

FIGURE 10-2 Table Design view

For each field, we are going to set up the field name, data type, length, and whether Nulls are allowed. In addition, we need to set any specific field-level settings such as Identity columns, etc.

Let's first create the Shopper table. This table will have all of the name and address fields for the shopper. Table 10-1 shows the fields for the Shopper table.

Each of the fields has its associated data type. Set each up in the database as appropriate, but note that the IDShopper field needs to be set up as an Identity field with the seed as 1. Also, set the IDShopper fields to be the primary key for the table. Save the table as Shopper. Figure 10-3 shows the final design of the table. For our design purposes, the fields can all allow Nulls except the IDShopper field.

Next, let's design the Basket table. The Basket table primary links the shopper, order, and basket items. We store some summary values for the basket items, including tax, shipping, and order total. Table 10-2 shows the fields and data types for the table.

The Basket table includes an identity column as its primary key. The DateCreated field defaults automatically to the value returned by the SQL GetDate() function—note that GetDate() is placed in the default value setting for the column. The three dollar amount fields are set to the data type of money to automatically handle the currency math properly. Figure 10-4 shows the design of the table.

Next, let's build the BasketItem table. In this case, we want to store all of the key item-related data, including name and price. We also need to store the quantity of the item ordered. Table 10-3 shows the field setup for the table.

Field	Data Type	Description
IDShopper	Int (Identity)	Unique ID (primary key) for the shopper – Identity generated
FirstName	VarChar(25)	First name of the shopper
LastName	VarChar(25)	Last name of the shopper
Phone	VarChar(15)	Phone number of the shopper
Street	VarChar(50)	Street address of the shopper
City	VarChar(50)	City of the shopper
State	VarChar(15)	State of the shopper
Zip	VarChar(15)	ZIP code of the shopper

TABLE 10-1   Shopper Table Fields

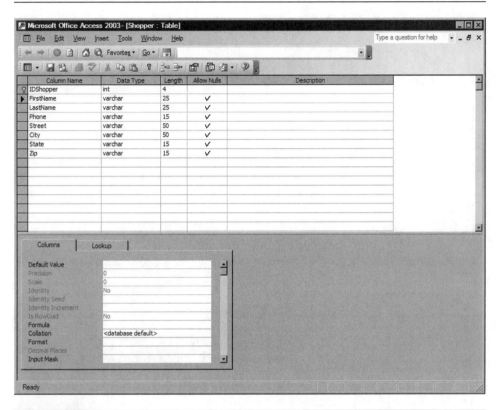

Column Name	Data Type	Length	Allow Nulls	Description
IDShopper	int	4		
FirstName	varchar	25	✓	
LastName	varchar	25	✓	
Phone	varchar	15	✓	
Street	varchar	50	✓	
City	varchar	50	✓	
State	varchar	15	✓	
Zip	varchar	15	✓	

FIGURE 10-3   Shopper table design

Field	Data Type	Description
IDBasket	Int (Identity)	Unique ID (primary key) for the basket – Identity generated
IDShopper	Int	Foreign key to the shopper table
DateCreated	DateTime	Date when the basket was created and defaulted to the GetDate() function, which returns current date and time
Subtotal	Money	Subtotal cost of the basket before shipping and tax
Total	Money	Total cost of the basket
Tax	Money	Tax cost of the basket
Shipping	Money	Shipping cost of the basket

TABLE 10-2   Basket Table Fields

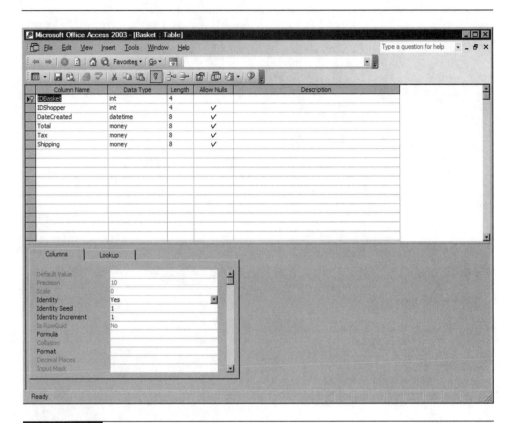

FIGURE 10-4 Basket table design

Field	Data Type	Description
IDBasketItem	Int (Identity)	Unique ID (primary key) for the basket item – Identity generated
IDBasket	Int	Foreign key relationship to the Basket table
Quantity	Int	The number of items added to the basket
Name	Varchar(100)	The name of the item at the time of purchase
Price	Money	The price of the product at the time of purchase
IDItem	Int	Original product ID

TABLE 10-3   BasketItem Table Fields

There aren't any surprises in this table. The ID of the added basket item is identity generated. The name and the price of the item at purchase time are stored in the basket. (See Figure 10-5.) The original ID of the added item is also stored.

The Item table is very similar. Table 10-4 shows the fields for the table. The name, description, and current price are all stored for the product.

For our example, we are using an Identity-generated key for the IDItem value. In many cases, this data might come from an external system that manages product inventory and creates SKUs for the items.

The Order table (see Table 10-5) defines the shopper data to be collected for orders. It includes the shipping contact information.

The Order table links everything up and indicates when the order is placed. Through the Order table we can get to the shopper, basket, and payment data. Note that we could store the payment data in the Order table, but by keeping it separate

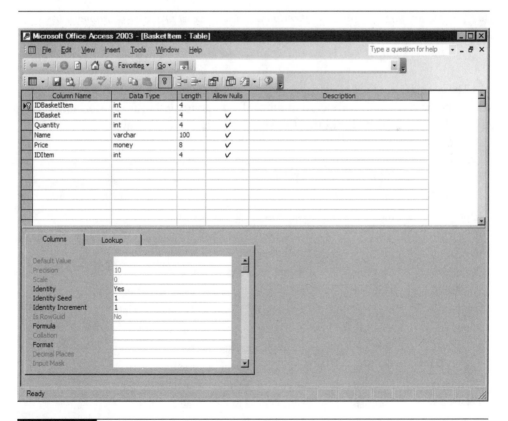

FIGURE 10-5   BasketItem Table

Field	Data Type	Description
IDItem	Int (Identity)	Unique ID (primary key) for the item – Identity generated
Name	Varchar(100)	The name of the item at the time of purchase
Description	Text	The description of the product
Price	Money	The price of the product

TABLE 10-4 Item Table Fields

we can ensure that the payment data can later be deleted with the shipping order data still intact. Figure 10-6 shows the design of the Order table.

Our last table is for payment data. The payment data stores the credit card information and billing data. Table 10-6 shows the fields for the table.

> **TIP** *Depending on your use of automatic credit card processing, some of this data may not be stored directly in the database. For example, the credit card number may never be stored, but passed to the credit card clearing house.*

The standard credit card data is collected, including the expiration date, card type, name on the card, and credit card number. Then the related billing information for the card is also collected. Figure 10-7 shows the design of the table.

Field	Data Type	Description
IDOrder	Int (Identity)	Unique ID (primary key) for the order – Identity generated
IDBasket	Int	Foreign key to the Basket table
IDShopper	Int	Foreign key to the Shopper table
IDPayment	Int	Foreign key to the Payment table
OrderDate	DateTime	Date the order has been placed
ShipFirstName	VarChar(50)	First name of the person the order is shipped to
ShipLastName	VarChar(50)	Last name of the person the order is shipped to
ShipStreet	VarChar(100)	Street address of the shipping address
ShipCity	VarChar(50)	City of the shipping address
ShipState	VarChar(15)	State of the shipping address
ShipZip	VarChar(15)	ZIP code of the shipping address
ShipPhone	VarChar(25)	Phone number of the shipping address

TABLE 10-5 Order Table Fields

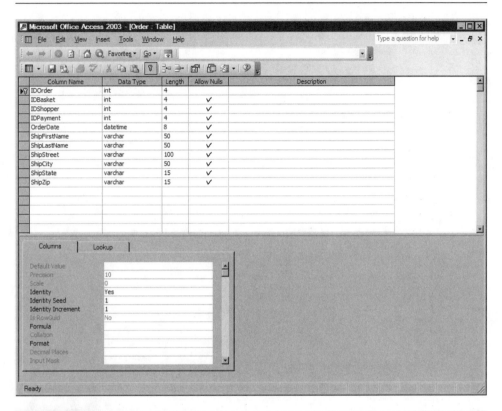

FIGURE 10-6   Order table design

Field	Data Type	Description
IDPayment	Int (Identity)	Unique ID (primary key) for the payment – Identity generated
OrderDate	DateTime	Date and time when the order was placed
CreditCardNumber	Varchar(50)	Credit card number data
CreditCardExpDate	DateTime	Expiration date of the credit card
CardType	Varchar(50)	Type of card
CardName	Varchar(100)	Name of the card owner
BillFirstName	VarChar(50)	First name of the person the order is billed to
BillLastName	VarChar(50)	Last name of the person the order is billed to

TABLE 10-6   Payment Table Fields

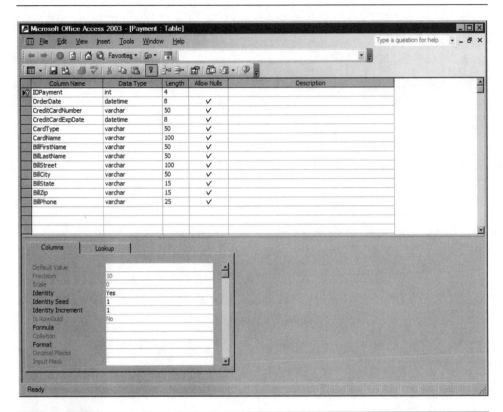

FIGURE 10-7 Payment table design

That completes the setup of the tables for the database. These tables have all been created on the SQL Server enterprise database and they are shown next in Enterprise Manager. Now, we can build the relationships between the tables.

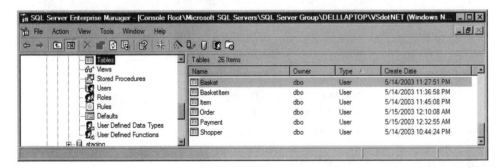

Building the Table Relationships

Now we will need to build the table relationships using the Database Diagrams feature of the ADP. This will create the diagram in the enterprise database as well.

To get started, select the Database Diagrams Objects, then click on the Create Database Diagram in Designer option. Add all of the tables to the diagram. Drag the foreign key values to the primary keys.

When the first relationship is set up, a dialog box is shown for defining the relationship. For these tables, we don't need to check existing data on creation, enforce replication, or cascade update of related fields. But, we can enforce cascading deletes. For example, when a basket is deleted, all of the related basket items can also be deleted. If we delete basket items, however, we do not want to delete related items. We do not want to delete shoppers if an order is deleted, and we might or might not want to delete baskets if an order is deleted—it depends on what scenarios we think we might want to enforce for cascading deletes. For each relationship defined, a constraint is set up in the enterprise database. Figure 10-8 shows an example of setting up the relationship.

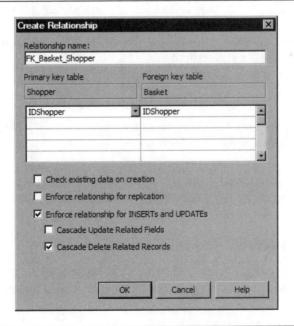

FIGURE 10-8   Setting up the shopper-to-basket relationship

Setting Up the Database

Once all of the relationships are set up, we can save the diagram (as ECommerce). When you choose to save, you will get a message asking if the tables can be saved. The reason this dialog box is displayed is to save the constraints for the tables.

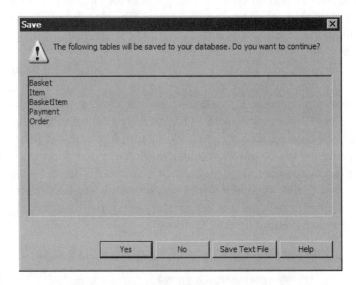

Cascade delete relationships are set up for all but the Shopper table–to–Order table relationship and the BasketItem table–to–Item table relationship. If a shopper is deleted, the corresponding baskets, basket items, and order and payment data are deleted.

NOTE *We might not want to delete order and payment data if a shopper is deleted. This might be needed for later analysis.*

With that last task, the database tables and relationships are set up. We can now begin using the rest of the ADP capabilities to work with the database.

Building Queries

Next, we are ready to begin building queries, stored procedures, and user functions for our database. We will explore using the designer to create each of the query types.

Query Creation

On the Queries Objects view, three options are listed for creating functions, views, and stored procedures in the Design view mode. In addition, if you click the New button, there are three options for creating the queries using the Create Text feature. These options allow us to bypass the traditional Design view and write the queries directly in a text format. Access will give us some templates for creating the various types of queries and functions.

One downside to using ADPs is that the wizards are gone. While the wizards aren't very useful when it comes to writing complex queries, they can be very handy for building lots of tedious select, update, and append (insert) queries. If you still want to use the wizards for query generation, consider creating a second Access database (not an ADP) and linking the SQL tables in the database and then use the wizards to create the queries. The queries can then be upsized to the database or the SQL copied directly to the ADP.

Creating SQL Views

We will first start with creating SQL views. These are our traditional select queries that were built in standard Access databases earlier in the chapter. We are going to create four sample views for this exercise. Table 10-7 lists the views and descriptions.

To get started, click the Create View in Designer option. What pops up is a familiar dialog box for adding tables into the query. As we reviewed in the last chapter, the Design view is different from the Design view in standard Access databases.

The first view will be a simple summary query that tells us how many baskets have been abandoned (e.g., did not turn into orders). This is an example of a useful report for administrative purposes to analyze the sales follow-through of the site.

In the blank Design view, add in the Basket and Shopper tables. From those tables, we want to display the IDBasket, DateCreated, Total, FirstName, LastName, and State fields. Add those fields into the design grid.

In order to get the baskets that are not orders, we need to get all of the baskets that are not associated with orders. The criteria for the IDBasket field needs to find

Query	Description
viewAbandonedBaskets	Lists all of the baskets that were not turned into orders
viewAllOrders	Lists all of the orders—will be used for reporting all orders
viewBasketItems	Lists all of the basket items—will be used for building an order data entry form
viewBaskets	Lists all of the baskets—will be used for building an order data entry form
viewOrders	List all of the orders—will be used for building an order data entry form

TABLE 10-7   View Queries

Building Queries

IDs not in the Orders table. This is done with a subselect query with the Not In check. The sub-select query is as follows:

```
NOT IN (SELECT IDBasket FROM [ORDER])
```

That goes into the criteria column for the IDBasket field. The final query that is generated is shown in the following listing:

```
SELECT dbo.Basket.IDBasket, dbo.Basket.DateCreated,
       dbo.Basket.Total, dbo.Shopper.FirstName,
       dbo.Shopper.LastName, dbo.Shopper.State
FROM dbo.Basket INNER JOIN
    dbo.Shopper ON dbo.Basket.IDShopper =
                   dbo.Shopper.IDShopper
WHERE  dbo.Basket.IDBasket NOT IN
       (SELECT IDBasket FROM ORDER]))
```

The Design view for the query is shown in Figure 10-9.

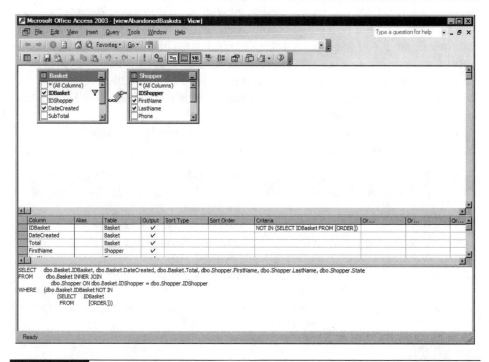

FIGURE 10-9   viewAbandonedBaskets Design view

In this view, we see the entire query setup, including the SQL code. Note the criteria field for the IDBasket field. When the query is run, the abandoned baskets are listed.

Our next query will join together all of the order data. This includes the Order, Payment, Basket, and BasketItem tables. Start a new view query in the Design view and add in each of the tables. From each of the tables, we want all of the non-key fields to be displayed. Select all of these fields and have them added to the design grid.

The result is a quickly built multi-join view. The SQL generated for the view is shown in the following listing:

```
SELECT  dbo.[Order].OrderDate, dbo.[Order].ShipFirstName,
        dbo.[Order].ShipLastName, dbo.[Order].ShipStreet,
        dbo.[Order].ShipCity, dbo.[Order].ShipState,
        dbo.[Order].ShipZip, dbo.[Order].ShipPhone,
        dbo.Payment.CreditCardNumber,
        dbo.Payment.CreditCardExpDate, dbo.Payment.CardType,
        dbo.Payment.CardName, dbo.Payment.BillFirstName,
        dbo.Payment.BillLastName, dbo.Payment.BillStreet,
        dbo.Payment.BillCity, dbo.Payment.BillState,
        dbo.Payment.BillZip, dbo.Payment.BillPhone,
        dbo.Basket.SubTotal, dbo.Basket.Total,
        dbo.Basket.Tax, dbo.Basket.Shipping,
        dbo.BasketItem.Quantity, dbo.BasketItem.Name,
        dbo.BasketItem.Price, dbo.BasketItem.IDItem
FROM    dbo.[Order] INNER JOIN
        dbo.Payment ON
        dbo.[Order].IDPayment = dbo.Payment.IDPayment
            INNER JOIN
        dbo.Basket ON
        dbo.[Order].IDBasket = dbo.Basket.IDBasket
            INNER JOIN
        dbo.BasketItem ON
        dbo.Basket.IDBasket = dbo.BasketItem.IDBasket
```

This is a great example of where the Access design tools make building queries much simpler and faster. Figure 10-10 shows the Design view for the query, including the SQL code.

The combined data in this query will be used to create an order report. Next, we will build three queries that pull the data from the Order, Basket, and BasketItem tables. These combined queries will be utilized to build an Access form for managing order data.

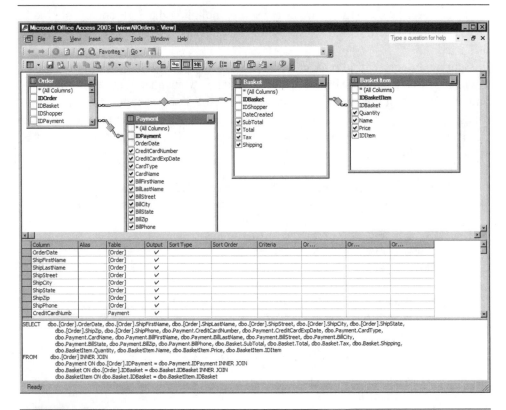

FIGURE 10-10 viewAllOrders Design view

Create a new View in the Design view. For the viewOrders view, we need the Order table added to the view. In this case, we are going to add all of the fields into the query. Here's the SQL generated by the Design view:

```
SELECT OrderDate, ShipFirstName, ShipLastName,
       ShipStreet, ShipCity, ShipState, ShipZip,
       ShipPhone, IDOrder, IDBasket, IDShopper,
       IDPayment
FROM dbo.[Order]
```

The Design view is straightforward as well. Figure 10-11 shows the setup.

Follow the same steps to create the viewBaskets and viewBasketItems views. This listing shows the SQL code generated for the viewBaskets view:

```
SELECT IDBasket, IDShopper, DateCreated, SubTotal,
       Total, Tax, Shipping
FROM  dbo.Basket
```

The following listing shows the SQL code generated for the viewBasketItems view:

```
SELECT IDItem, Price, Name, Quantity,
       IDBasket, IDBasketItem
FROM dbo.BasketItem
```

That completes the creation of the views we will be using to generate forms and reports against our enterprise database. As each view is built, it is created in the enterprise database. Figure 10-12 shows the view listing in the database.

That does it for creating the SQL views. Next, we will build a stored procedure for retrieving order data based on specific criteria.

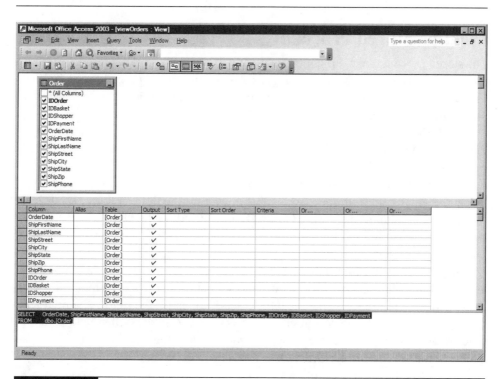

FIGURE 10-11   viewOrders query

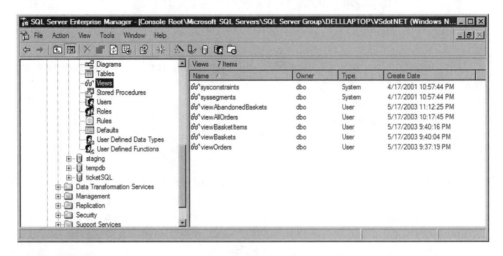

FIGURE 10-12   View listing in SQL Enterprise

Creating Stored Procedures

The stored procedure we are going to create will return the total order value and number of orders for a given date range. To create the stored procedure, select the Create Stored Procedure to start the Designer. There are two inputs into the stored procedure: the start date and the end date for the report.

In the Design view, add in the Order and Basket tables. We want to query for the orders and related baskets. We do not want to query for baskets that are abandoned (e.g., not related to an order).

The first column to be returned is the total value of the orders for the date range. Select the Total field from the Basket table, then alias the field as RangeTotal. In the Group By column (make sure Group By is selected on the Query menu) of the design grid, select Sum as the setting. This will sum up all of the basket totals for the items returned in the query.

Next, we want to sum up the number of records returned. The * should be set as the second column, which will be used to sum all of the rows returned (note it doesn't need to reference a specific table). Set the alias for the field as NumOrders. The last two entries in the design grid set the criteria. Add the Order Date field twice to the design grid. Set the Group By for both as Where.

Next, the criteria for the Order Date fields need to be set. For the first Order Date entry, set the criteria as follows:

```
>= @StartDate
```

This code checks for orders on or after the start date set by the call of the stored procedure. Set the second criteria as follows:

```
<= @EndDate
```

This code checks for orders that are on or before the date sent into the stored procedure. Note that for these two Order Date entries, the Output column is not checked since we do not want the Order Date to be returned.

Save the query as spOrderTotalsbyDateRange. Figure 10-13 shows the Design view for the query.

The SQL generated by the query in the Access Design view is shown in the following listing:

```
SELECT  SUM(dbo.Basket.Total) AS RangeTotal,
        COUNT(*) AS NumOrders
FROM    dbo.[Order] INNER JOIN
        dbo.Basket ON
            dbo.Basket.IDBasket = dbo.[Order].IDBasket
WHERE   (dbo.[Order].OrderDate >= @StartDate) AND
        (dbo.[Order].OrderDate <= @EndDate)
```

If you are familiar with building stored procedures, you know that this isn't all of the code for creating the stored procedure. The code that is actually saved in SQL Server is shown in the following listing:

```
CREATE PROCEDURE dbo.spOrderTotalsbyDateRange
(
    @StartDate Datetime,
    @EndDate DateTime
)
AS
SELECT  SUM(dbo.Basket.Total) AS RangeTotal,
        COUNT(*) AS NumOrders
FROM dbo.[Order] INNER JOIN dbo.Basket ON
    dbo.Basket.IDBasket = dbo.[Order].IDBasket
WHERE (dbo.[Order].OrderDate >= @StartDate) AND
      (dbo.[Order].OrderDate <= @EndDate)
GO
```

Building Queries

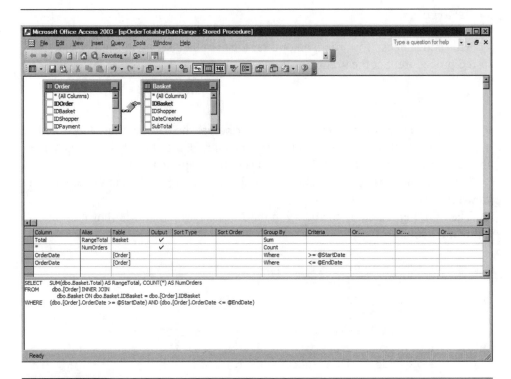

FIGURE 10-13   spOrderTotalsbyDateRange

Note the definition of the input parameters for the stored procedure. The ADP automatically built the structure and syntax of the stored procedure for you.

> TIP
>
> *As mentioned in the last chapter, this functionality of the ADP can be a good and bad thing. It is good from the standpoint of generating SQL code more quickly. It is bad from the standpoint of limited control over the stored procedure design. If you need more explicit control over the coding of the stored procedure, use the Create Text Stored Procedure option.*

Next, we will build some utility functions with the Access tools.

Creating and Working with Functions

Functions are very useful for encapsulating business logic within the SQL Server, and we can easily create user functions in our ADP project. In our example database, we are going to create four user functions as outlined in Table 10-8.

Function	Description
funcBasketShipping	Calculates the shipping total for a shopping basket. The amount is calculated as a percentage of the subtotal of the order.
funcBasketSubTotal	Calculates the subtotal of the basket based on the items and quantities in the basket.
funcBasketTax	Calculates the tax of the basket based on the subtotal of the order.
funcBasketTotal	Calculates the total price of the basket, including the subtotal, tax, and shipping.

TABLE 10-8 Functions

As you can see, each of these functions is focused on calculating components of the order cost. These functions could actually be utilized in the main e-commerce application. But, as we will see, they are relatively easy to build in the Access interface.

Let's first start working on the function that calculates the subtotal of the order. The function will take in the ID of the basket for the subtotal to be calculated. It will then multiply the price of each item in the basket times the quantity of the item purchased. That amount is summed up for each item.

For this function, let's use the text option for creating the function. Click the New button. The dialog box shown next pops up with the options for creating new stored procedures, views, and functions.

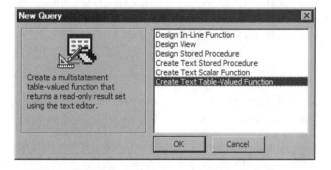

Select the Create Text Scalar Function option. Access then generates a text template for the function, which can then be modified. The following listing shows the template.

```
CREATE FUNCTION "Function1"
      (
      /*
      @parameter1 datatype = default value,
      @parameter2 datatype
      */
      )
RETURNS /* @table_variable TABLE (column1 datatype, column2 datatype) */
AS
      BEGIN
            /* INSERT INTO @table_variable
                     sql select statement   */
            /* alternative sql statement or statements */
      RETURN
      END
```

Now we can modify the template to create our subtotal function. The first step is to set the passed-in parameters of the function. In this case, it will be the ID of the basket we want to calculate the subtotal on. The parameter will be set as follows:

```
@IDBasket int
```

This indicates that the value passed in will be an integer data type. Next, we need to set the return data type after the RETURNS statement. In this case, we are returning a money data type for the subtotal.

Finally, we are ready to write the SQL logic for calculating the subtotal. Keep in mind that in the function, we need to return a specific value. The subtotal needs to be calculated and then stored in a variable that can be returned from the function. The following listing shows the SQL code:

```
Declare @SubTotal money

SELECT @SubTotal = Sum(Price * Quantity)
      FROM  dbo.BasketItem where IDBasket = @IDBasket
```

The first thing that happens is we declare a local variable @SubTotal as data type money. This is where the calculated subtotal is stored. Then, in the SQL query, the price of the item in the BasketItem table is multiplied times the quantity of items ordered. Those values are all summed up for the items in the specified basket. Note that the summed value is stored in the @SubTotal variable.

Now we can put the whole thing together to build our function. The following listing shows the complete function:

```
ALTER FUNCTION dbo.funcBasketSubTotal
     (
     @IDBasket int
     )
RETURNS Money
AS
     BEGIN
          Declare @SubTotal money

          SELECT     @SubTotal = Sum(Price * Quantity)
          FROM  dbo.BasketItem where IDBasket = @IDBasket
     RETURN @SubTotal

     END
```

Note at the end of the function, the RETURN statement has the @SubTotal variable being returned. Now save the function as funcBasketSubTotal, then double-click on the function to run it. When the function is run in the ADP, the dialog box shown next pops up asking for the input parameter (IDBasket) to be defined.

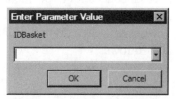

Enter in an appropriate IDBasket value. The subtotal is then calculated for that basket and returned in the standard Data Sheet view. Here's an example of a returned value.

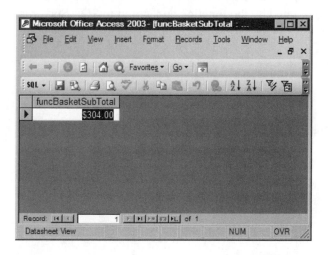

Let's next look at the calculation of the basket tax, but this time around let's use the Design view to create the function. Click the Create Function in Designer option. This will bring up the familiar Design view, which we utilized for creating views and stored procedures.

To calculate the tax, we need to know what state the order is being placed in. We only want tax for orders placed in Texas. To get the state value, we are going to need data from the Order table. We are also going to need to know the subtotal value for the basket. In order to get both of these sets of data, add the Order and Basket tables into the Design view.

The one output value is going to be the calculated Tax value. Set the first Column value in the Design view as follows:

```
dbo.Basket.SubTotal * .0675
```

Alias the column as Tax. This calculates the tax total as 6.75 percent of the subtotal. Next, we need to check to see if the order is being shipped to Texas. The ShipState value from the Order table needs be checked for a criterion of "TX".

Finally, all of this needs to be calculated for a specific basket. Just like calculating the basket subtotal, we need to pass in the ID of the basket we want to calculate tax on. For the last entry in the design grid, add in the IDBasket value from the Basket table. Set the criteria as follows:

```
= @IDBasket
```

Just as we saw with the stored procedures, the ADP will automatically build the input parameters for the function. Now the function has been set up using the Design view. Save the function as funcBasketTax. Figure 10-14 shows the Design view.

The SQL generated by the function and stored in SQL Server is shown in the following listing:

```
ALTER FUNCTION dbo.funcBasketTax
(
  @IDBasket int
)
RETURNS TABLE
AS
RETURN
(

SELECT dbo.Basket.SubTotal * .0675 AS Tax
```

```
FROM    dbo.Basket INNER JOIN dbo.[Order] ON
        dbo.Basket.IDBasket = dbo.[Order].IDBasket
WHERE   (dbo.[Order].ShipState = 'TX') AND
        (dbo.Basket.IDBasket = @IDBasket)
)
```

When you look at the syntax for this function versus the one for calculating the subtotal, you will note some subtle differences. The first difference is that the RETURNS statement shows that a table is returned—instead of specifically returning a single data type, in this case, the returned type is a table.

Secondly, the RETURNS statement actually returns the results of our select statement. The tax is not calculated and saved into a local variable, with that variable value being returned, as we saw in the last function.

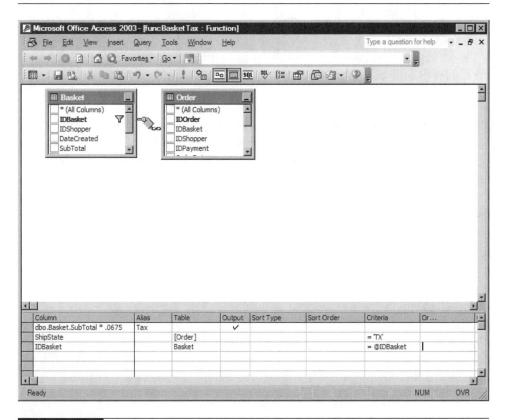

FIGURE 10-14   funcBasketTax in the Design view

The difference between the two is that the funcBasketSubtotal function is a scalar, because it returns only one value; thus, we invoke it differently. The funcBasketTax function returns a table that we can query against. We will see these differences in action a little later in this section.

The next function calculates the shipping for the order. This function is pretty straightforward and works like the tax function. The primary difference is that the state location is not checked. The shipping is simply calculated as a percentage of the subtotal value.

Create a new function with the Design view. In this case, we only need the Basket table to calculate the shipping. Add it into the Design view.

The first entry in the design grid is to calculate the shipping off of the subtotal. Set the column up as follows:

```
SubTotal * .02
```

Alias the column as Shipping. This will calculate the shipping fee as 2 percent of the order subtotal.

Next, set the next column as IDBasket from the Basket table. Set the Criteria parameter as follows:

```
= @IDBasket
```

That sets up an input parameter for sending in the ID of the basket to calculate the shipping. Save the function as funcBasketShipping. Figure 10-15 shows the setup of the function in the Design view.

The full SQL generated by the function and stored in SQL Server is shown in the following listing:

```
ALTER FUNCTION dbo.funcBasketShipping
(
    @IDBasket int
)
RETURNS TABLE
AS
RETURN
(
    SELECT SubTotal * .02 AS Shipping
    FROM dbo.Basket
    WHERE (IDBasket = @IDBasket)
)
```

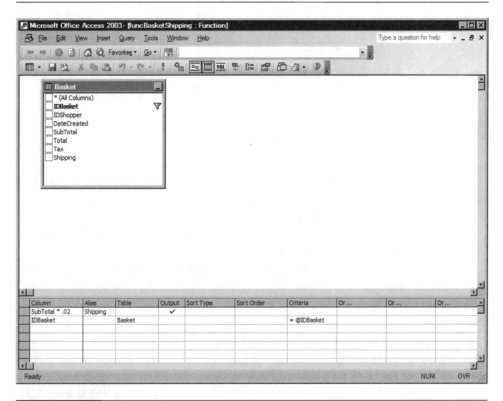

Building Queries

FIGURE 10-15   funcBasketShipping Design view

The SQL for the function is straightforward. Note that the return statement returns the value of the select query.

We will also build our last function as a scalar function. It will return the total cost of the basket. We will once again create this function using the Create Text Scalar Function option.

This function will add up the subtotal, tax, and shipping values to determine the total cost of the basket. The following listing shows the code for the function. Save the function as funcBasketTotal.

```
ALTER FUNCTION dbo.funcBasketTotal
    (
    @IDBasket int
    )
RETURNS Money
```

```
AS
      BEGIN
            Declare @Total money

            SELECT @Total = Subtotal + Tax + Shipping
            FROM   dbo.Basket where IDBasket = @idBasket

      RETURN @Total

      END
```

The parameter for the function is an integer data type that will be set to the ID of the basket. The function will return a value of data type money. A local variable is declared to store the calculated total.

The total is then calculated for the specified basket. The value in the @Total variable is then returned from the function.

That does it for our sample functions that handle the value calculations of the basket. So, how do we utilize these functions from within the Access environment? One example is to build a stored procedure that is called when we want to calculate all of the values of a particular basket.

To create this type of stored procedure in the ADP environment, we need to do it in the text mode versus the Design view because we are calling functions. Click the New button for the Query objects. Select the Create Text Stored Procedure option.

A text template for a stored procedure is created. The following listing shows the template:

```
CREATE PROCEDURE "StoredProcedure1"
/*
      (
            @parameter1 datatype = default value,
            @parameter2 datatype OUTPUT
      )
*/
AS
      /* SET NOCOUNT ON */
      RETURN
```

The template contains sections for setting the input parameters to the stored procedure and a section for the body of the stored procedure.

For our example, we need to calculate the different values step-by-step. First, the subtotal needs to be calculated and set for the basket. Then, the shipping and tax need to be calculated (based on the subtotal) and stored in the basket. Finally, the total of the basket can be calculated when all of the other values are set.

The following listing shows the completed stored procedure. Save the stored procedure as spCalculateBasketValues.

```
ALTER PROCEDURE spCalculateBasketValues
     (
          @IDBasket int
     )
AS

     Declare @Tax money
     Declare @Subtotal money
     Declare @Shipping money
     Declare @Total money

     select @Subtotal = dbo.funcBasketSubTotal(IDBasket)
      from Basket
      where IDBasket = @IDBasket

     update basket set subtotal = @subtotal
      where IDBasket = @IDBasket

     select @Tax=Tax from funcBasketTax(@IDBasket)

     update basket set tax = @tax
      where idbasket = @IDBasket

     select @Shipping=Tax from funcBasketTax(@IDBasket)

     update basket set shipping = @shipping
      where idbasket = @IDBasket

     select @Total = dbo.funcBasketTotal(IDBasket)
      from Basket
      where IDBasket = @IDBasket

     update basket set total = @total
      where idbasket = @IDBasket

RETURN
```

Building Queries

The first step is to set up the input parameter for the stored procedure. In this case, it is a data type of integer. The ID of the basket will be passed into the stored procedure, which in turn is passed to the functions.

In the body of the stored procedure, we first define local variables for each of the values we are going to calculate. The logic then follows step-by-step.

We first calculate the subtotal for the basket. Remember that the funcBasketsSubtotal function is scalar and returns a single value (versus a table). We can retrieve the value and set it to a local variable. The function is performed on the returned IDBasket value from the query, and the query retrieves the basket data for the basket specified in the input parameter, @IDBasket.

NOTE
We could pass the @IDBasket value into the function and get the same result since the value passed by the user and the value returned by the query are the same basket ID. But, in general, the values returned from the query should be used as input parameters for scalar functions.

Once the subtotal value is calculated and stored in the @Subtotal local variable, we can then update the specified basket's subtotal column.

TIP
The select and update statements are broken out in this example for clarity's sake. They could be combined into one update query.

After the subtotal is calculated, we are ready to calculate the tax and shipping. Remember that these two functions return tables for their results. We can actually query against the tables for the Tax and Shipping values.

For the queries, a from clause is set against the functions. The ID of the basket is passed into the functions to return the basket we are interested in. In this case, the functions only return one row and one column (a scalar). We are able to retrieve the shipping and tax values into the @Shipping and @Tax variables, respectively. Once the values have been retrieved, the values in the table can be updated.

Now that the other values have been updated in the tables, the final step is to calculate the basket total. As with the subtotal, the basket total is returned from a scalar function. The function is run on the returned basket ID from a query for the basket record. That value is then updated in the basket.

The result is a basket with completed values. Figure 10-16 shows a sample basket data set with all values calculated.

Note that two of the baskets do not have calculated values. That is because there are no associated order records with the baskets. Thus, no subtotal will be calculated and the other values will be returned as 0.

	IDBasket	IDShopper	DateCreated	SubTotal	Tax	Shipping	Total
▶	1	1	5/16/2003 4:20:50 AM	$304.00	$20.52	$20.52	$345.04
	2	2	5/16/2003 4:20:54 AM	$1,336.00	$90.18	$26.72	$1,452.90
	3	3	6/16/2003 4:20:55 AM	$696,996.00	$47,047.23	$13,939.92	$757,983.15
	4	4	8/16/2003 4:20:55 AM	$479.00	$32.33	$9.58	$520.91
	5	5	7/12/2003 4:20:56 AM	$1,008.00	$68.04	$20.16	$1,096.20
	6	1	7/2/2003 4:21:06 AM	$930,443.00	$62,804.90	$18,608.86	$1,011,856.76
	7	1	7/31/2003 4:21:10 AM	$439.00			
	8	1	9/23/2003 4:21:11 AM	$465,333.00	$31,409.98	$9,306.66	$506,049.64
	9	2	5/30/2003 4:21:12 AM	$132.00	$8.91	$2.64	$143.55
	10	3	6/6/2003 4:21:13 AM	$15.00	$1.01	$0.30	$16.31
	11	4	8/16/2003 4:21:13 AM	$1,916.00			
	12	5	9/22/2003 4:21:14 AM	$1,628,328.00	$109,912.14	$32,566.56	$1,770,806.70
*	(AutoNumber)		5/19/2003 11:40:23 AM				

FIGURE 10-16   Calculated basket values

That does it for our overview of views, stored procedures, and functions. The ADP project gives us full access to the SQL Server environment but also provides us with the design capabilities to make constructing queries easier. Next, we will build sample Access forms and reports based on these queries.

Building Forms

Now that we have our database and queries set up, we can use some of the form and reporting capabilities of Access. This is another area where utilizing Access in connection with SQL Server can be very helpful.

For our example, we are going to build a multitier order editing form. The form will allow for editing of the shipping, basket, and basket item data. In fact, this will be a form within a form within a form. The top-level form will have the core order data. The second-level form will have the basket data. The third-level form will have the basket item data for the basket.

The data feed for the forms will be the three view queries that we built for each of the sets of data—viewOrders, viewBaskets, and viewBasketItems. Note that we could use the Order, Basket, and BasketItem tables, but by using queries, we have the ability to abstract the data structure one level away from the user interface with the query. If, for example, we want to archive orders and their related data down the road, we can change the three queries to filter the archived records instead of changing the form logic.

To get started, we use the Form Wizard. This will allow us to set up the form data for the first-level orders. Select the Forms option on the Objects tab. Click the Create Form by Using Wizard option. The first dialog box for the wizard appears.

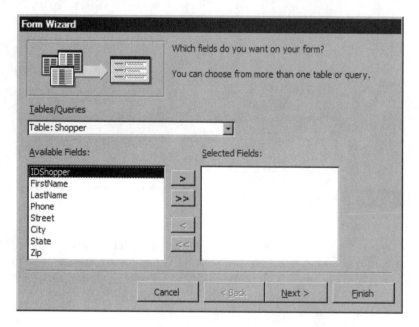

Select the viewOrders view from the Tables/Queries list. Select all of the fields except the primary key and foreign keys. Click the Next button to continue.

The next screen gives us options for selecting the style of layout for the form fields. In this case, the Columnar format will work fine even though we will have to do a little tweaking of the form layout when it is completed. Click the Next button to continue.

The next dialog box gives us options for the style of the form. Select whatever style suits your fancy and then click the Next button to continue. The last dialog box provides the option for naming the form—name the form Orders and click Finish.

The completed form provides the fields, laid out with label tags for each field. Each of the records in the form can be paged through with the standard Access record navigation buttons. Figure 10-17 shows the form with sample data.

That completes the first step for creating our order management form. The next step is to add in the basket detail to the form. This will actually be set up as a subform within the main Orders form.

To create the subform, open the Orders form in the Design view. Access will automatically create the subform for us by simply dragging the viewBaskets query onto the form. Go ahead and complete that step.

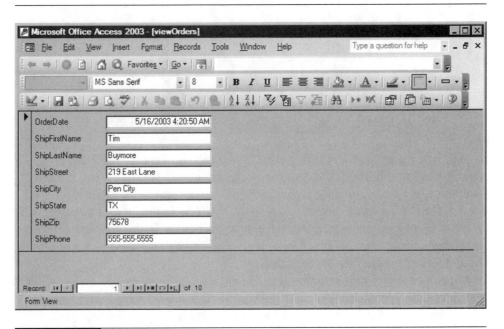

FIGURE 10-17   Orders form

When the viewBaskets query is dragged to the Orders form, a dialog box pops up asking us to define the links between main form and subform. In this case, the key link between the two sets of data is the IDBasket value. Select both fields for the main form and subform, as shown here:

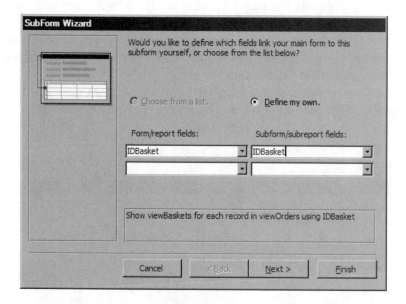

Note the message on the dialog box, "Show viewBaskets for each record in viewOrders using IDBasket." Thus, the link is defined. Click the Next button to continue. The dialog box asks for the name of the subform to be created. Save the form as Basket Subform. Figure 10-18 shows the form in the Design view.

Now when the form is run, the basket with each order is shown. Note that only one basket should exist per order since it is a one-to-one relationship. Figure 10-19 shows the active form with sample data.

As you page through the order data, the basket data changes along with it. We now have the Order and Basket data linked up and being displayed. The next step is to create the basket items subform to show the items for each basket.

Open up the Orders form in the Design view. Now drag the viewBasketItems query onto the Basket subform. Once again, the form design interface will ask us to link the two forms together. Select the IDBasket fields again for each of the

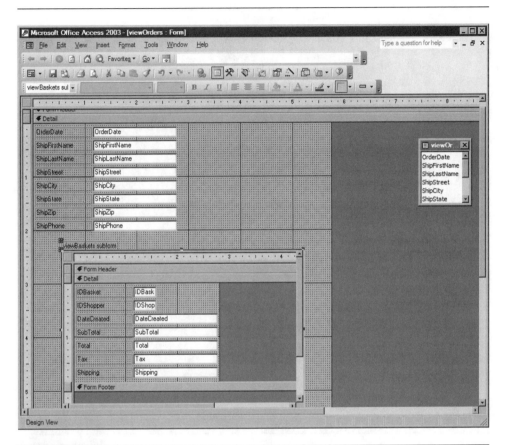

FIGURE 10-18   Orders form with Baskets subform in Design view

forms. That will create the link. Save the form as BasketItems Subform. Figure 10-20 shows the form in the Design view.

Now all of the data is set up and linked for display in the forms. Open the form in the View mode. This will bring up the order data, the associated basket, and the associated basket items.

To view the basket items for the basket, click the + sign next to the basket in the form. The basket item subform then expands to display the basket items for the basket. Figure 10-21 shows the form in the View mode.

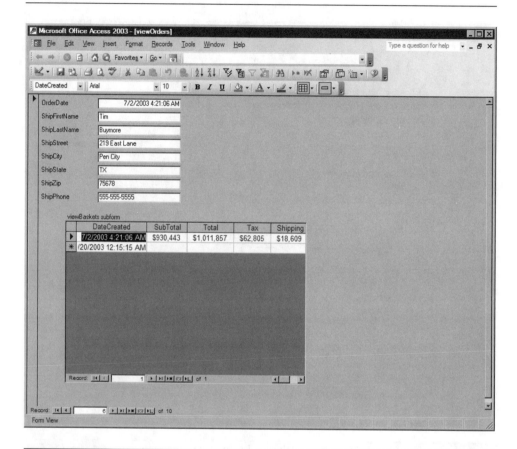

FIGURE 10-19   Orders form with Baskets subform

Now with the form, the orders can be paged through, updated as appropriate, etc. There are many additional features that could be added to harness the full power of Access. For example, if we need to change the items in the basket, we could build a pick list of existing items. We would also add in searching capabilities to find specific orders. In short, all of the client building tools that Access provides can be utilized against the SQL Server data and structure. Next, we will take a look at building reports against the enterprise data.

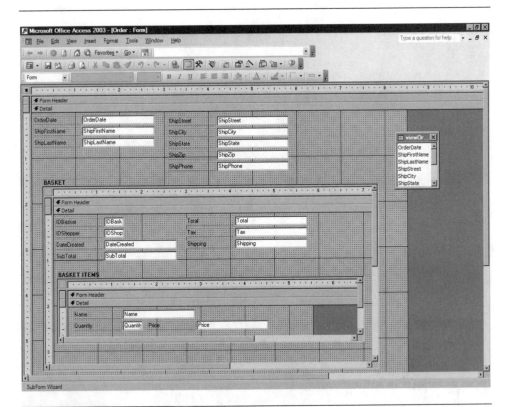

FIGURE 10-20 Order form with Basket and BasketItem subforms

Building Reports

Not only can we build forms against the enterprise data, we can also build reports. In many ways, the reporting capabilities of Access are some of the best features for utilizing against the enterprise data. All types of reports can be built.

For this example, we want to create a report that has all of the order details, including Order, Payment, Basket, and BasketItem. In fact, this turns out to be all of the data returned by our viewAllOrders view that we built earlier in the chapter.

To get started, click the Reports option on the Objects toolbar. As with reports, we have the option to use a wizard to create our report. Click the Create Report by Using Wizard option.

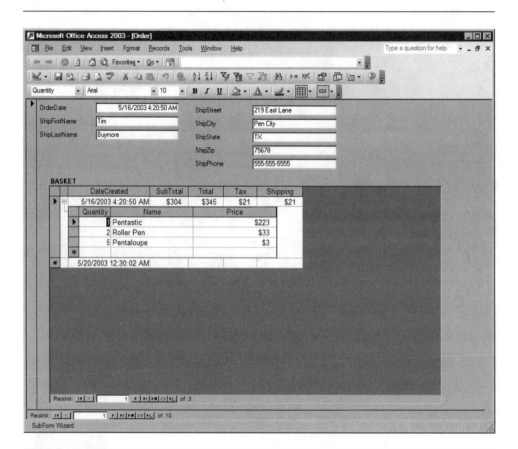

FIGURE 10-21   Order form in View mode

The first dialog box of the wizard asks for the tables/queries for building the report. Select the viewAllOrders view, as shown next. From that view, select all of the returned fields.

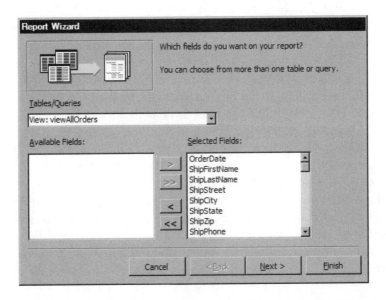

Click the Next button to continue. The next screen asks if we want grouping levels for the report. In this case, we want to group by date and then by the last name of the shipping data. Select both fields. Your form layout should look like this:

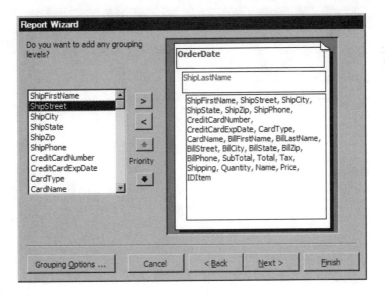

Click the Next button to continue. The dialog box gives us options for sorting the data. In this case, we are just interested in sorting by order date and last name. The groupings already take care of the sort.

Click the Next button to continue. The dialog box gives us options for how we want the report to be laid out. For our purposes, the stepped layout will work fine. As we will see, there is a little bit of work to do with the wizard output so that the report makes sense. Click the Next button to continue.

On the next screen, we have the option of picking the stylization of the form. Select whatever style suits your fancy. In the case of this example, the Corporate style was selected. Click the Next button to continue.

The final screen gives us the option to set the name of the report. We can also determine what happens when the wizard is finished. Save the report as viewAllOrders. Click the Finish button to complete the process.

The results of the wizard process can be seen in Figure 10-22. This doesn't look quite right. We see the order date grouping and then the last name grouping.

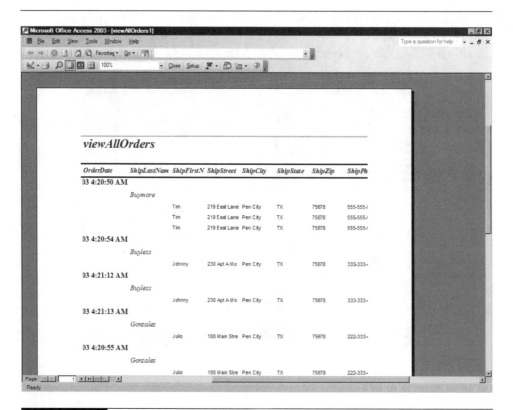

FIGURE 10-22   Wizard-generated report

But, the next list just shows the first name, street address, etc. If we page through the report, we will see that the data goes across many pages and there is a listing for each item in the basket. This isn't quite what we are looking for.

To fix this report up, go into the Design view for the report. What we see is that the Detail section of the report contains all of the fields for the order, payment, and basket. Thus, these data values are being repeatedly displayed with each basket item. What we need to do is move the fields we only want displayed once per order into the header section where the last name is being displayed. Figure 10-23 shows the current Design view.

Go ahead and rework the fields and lay them out as appropriate for the report. Figure 10-24 shows an example of how the report might be laid out. Note that the only fields in the Detail section are for the basket items.

Now the report can be viewed and the orders will be grouped by order date and last name, and the fields will be organized together properly. Figure 10-25 shows the report. Note the structure for the different orders.

With Access' fast and powerful reporting tools, creating administrative and analytical reports for maintaining a system is very useful and powerful. If you have

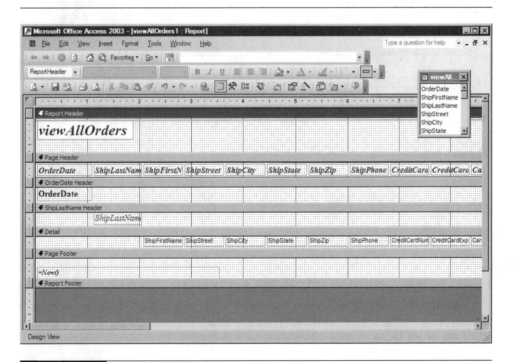

FIGURE 10-23   Wizard-generated report Design view

Building Reports

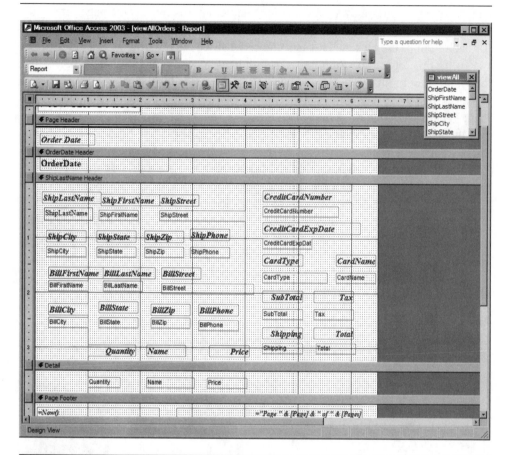

FIGURE 10-24   Reworked report in Design view

already built your database in SQL Server directly, consider setting up an ADP for the database just to utilize the extended reporting capabilities of Access.

Summary

Our Access Data Project example demonstrates how Access and SQL Server can work in harmony. The many benefits of Access can be leveraged against the SQL Server. Note that in this chapter we created a database from scratch. For existing SQL Server databases, ADPs can also be set up.

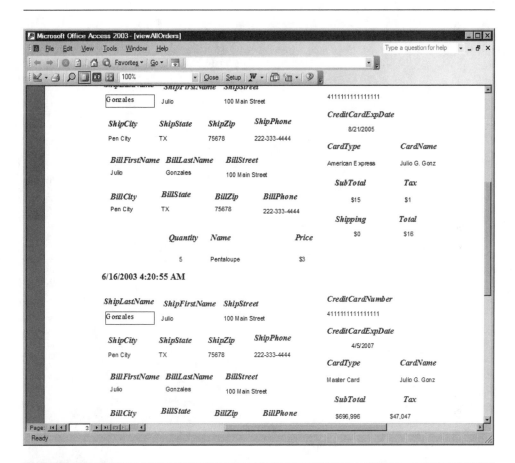

FIGURE 10-25   Reworked report

Keep in mind that ADPs can also be deployed to desktop users. If there are specific users who need extended data entry or reporting capabilities that go beyond the web browser, an ADP can be an excellent solution for the client interface to the database. Functionality is quick to build and easily deployed. In addition, ADPs are an excellent environment for quickly prototyping application functionality against SQL Server.

In the next chapter, we will explore issues surrounding database management for Access databases. The topics we will explore include replication, security, backups, and performance.

Chapter 11

Managing Access Databases

Access databases need to be properly managed even though they are not as sophisticated as enterprise-level databases. We have options for securing, replicating, backing up, and structuring the databases, and each must be considered in the context of the use of the database. In this chapter, we will explore the different database management techniques that can be utilized with Access.

Database Management Overview

When working with databases, it is important to implement the best practices for managing the database. Working with Access can be a little deceiving because it can be so simple to set up and deploy a database. One can get a false sense of safety because Access can be so simple to work with, but just consider what would happen if you linked up enterprise data in an Access Data Project (ADP) and didn't secure that Access interface…or, if you provided your Access database to users and they could access the underlying data structure, code, macros, etc. (Deploying copies of the data, backups, and other data management issues are also critical to consider.)

Fortunately, over the years Access has added features to the program that provide options for tackling each of these issues. While these features are not as robust or in-depth as those of SQL Server or other enterprise databases, if used properly they can meet the primary needs of the database manager.

Backup Strategies

Backing up databases is critical to preventing catastrophic data loss. With Access, the primary strategy is to back up the file to another location. With Office 2003, Microsoft added a new backup feature where the database can be backed up from the GUI interface. It effectively closes the database and then creates a file copy of the database:

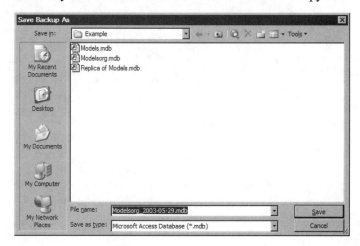

This is useful if you are in the middle of making major changes and want to save a copy before the changes are made. IT can be done in one step, without closing Access or going out to the file system.

From a production standpoint, it is important that Access databases are backed up frequently if they are not on some type of failover hard drive system (e.g., RAID). As with all backups, they should be taken offsite for safekeeping. Often, IT operations (especially in larger companies) will not focus on backing up Access data, but data is data, and data loss is painful no matter what!

Even with nightly or more frequent backups, there is still the chance that data will be lost between backups. To minimize data loss with Access, replication is required to capture all transactions to a second location (we will be discussing replication later in the chapter). In short, it is important to have a well-planned backup strategy and ensure that the potential for data loss is kept to acceptable levels and well understood.

Database Security

Another critical aspect of managing Access databases is security. There are several levels of security that can be implemented in Access. Each should be carefully reviewed to ensure that the proper level is implemented and supported.

Password and Encryption Security

The first level of security is a database-level password along with data encryption/ decryption. With the password security, the database cannot be opened without the password being entered. The password itself is stored in the database in an encrypted format.

To set the password, click the Tools menu and then the Security option. On the Security submenu, click the Set Database Password option. The dialog box shown next pops up to prompt for the password and verification entry of the password.

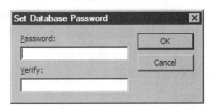

NOTE *If you do not have the database open for exclusive access, you will get a dialog box indicating it needs to be opened exclusively. Follow the instructions in the dialog box to open the database exclusively.*

Once the password is entered, subsequent attempts to open the database will require the password to be entered.

In addition to password protection, we can also encrypt the database. While the encryption is not key based, it does limit which non-Access utilities can easily read the contents of the MDB file. Combined with the password protection, these two techniques provide for a reasonably robust and simple security implementation. The problem is that they limit the granularity of the security to database objects and may limit what you can do with the database (such as replication). These techniques are especially useful for databases that are utilized by a limited number of people who need full access to the system.

One simple way to hide the structure of the database is to hide database objects. Right-click on any object and go to Properties. On the Properties dialog box, check the Hidden attribute.

These techniques provide some fairly simple and straightforward methods for securing Access data. These techniques can be useful when working with prototype databases, single-user systems, and other limited-use databases.

User-Level Security

The second major type of security is user-level security. This allows much more granularity of security levels by user. When the users start Microsoft Access, they enter their username and password. Users can be placed into defined groups, and security permissions can be defined at the group level.

NOTE   *We will first walk through the security options that Access provides. Once we are through the options, we will take a look at the Security Wizard, which assists with the automation to secure the database.*

Access uses the concepts of work groups to define and manage user-level security. A workgroup is a group of users in a multiuser environment that share data. If user-level security is defined, the members of a workgroup are recorded in user and group accounts that are stored in a Microsoft Access workgroup information file. Passwords are also stored in the workgroup information file. These security accounts can then be assigned permissions for databases and their tables, queries, forms, reports, and macros. The specific permissions for a database are stored in the database itself.

A default workgroup is created when Access is set up, and used as the default for all new databases. New workgroups can be set up using the Workgroup Administration tools.

User accounts are set up in the workgroup. It is important to ensure you have the proper workgroup selected when setting up user accounts. Before you create security accounts, you should choose a Microsoft Access workgroup information file where those accounts will be stored. It should be noted that it is good practice to create a new workgroup and not use the one installed by default. This helps to tighten up security.

NOTE   *You can use the same workgroup file for multiple databases.*

To demonstrate user-level security, let's first create a new workgroup file. Click the Tools menu, then the Security option. On the Security submenu, click the Workgroup Administrator option. A dialog box indicates that the current workgroup is the default one used at startup. We can either join that workgroup or we can create our own.

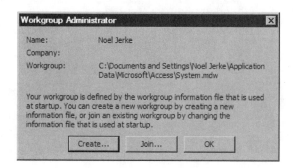

Click the Create option to create a new workgroup. The dialog box shown next asks us to define the workgroup. The name, organization, and workgroup ID need to be entered. The ID is how the workgroup will be identified.

Once the workgroup specifications are entered, Access queries where you want the workgroup file stored. Be sure to store it in a logical location where it can be properly backed up.

Once the workgroup is created, the details of the workgroup are recapped. Note that the dialog box indicates the importance of storing the data in a safe place.

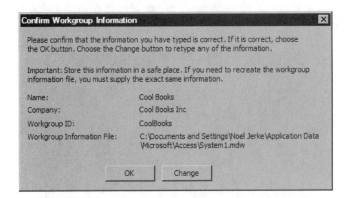

Now that the workgroups are set up, we can begin working on user-level security. As with security in Windows, we have groups that can be defined. Groups will have specific security access rights to objects in the database, and users can be a part of these groups. Managing security at the group level makes it easier to define general permission levels and move users in and out of the groups as needed.

To define users and groups, click the Tools menu and then click the Security option. On the Security submenu, click the User and Group Accounts option. There are three option tabs on the dialog box. The first is for managing users in the database, the second is for groups, and the third is for setting the admin logon password. The Users tab is shown here:

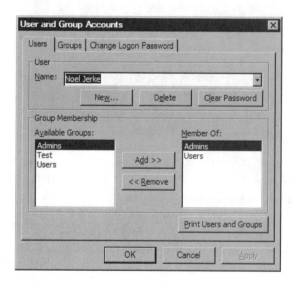

To create a new user, click the New button. Enter in the name and personal ID of the user. You will note in the drop-down box of users that there is only one user initially in the system, Admin. Once the new user is added, they can be added to additional groups.

Thus the new user, Noel Jerke, will have all of the permissions assigned to the Admins and Users groups. Now we can set up a new group. Click the Groups tab and then the New button. Enter in the name of the group and the ID for the group. Once the group is added, if you click back to the Users tab, you will see that the new group is available for assigning users.

TIP *Access has a useful feature that lets you print the security settings for a database.*

Database Security

Now that we have the users and groups set up, we can start working on permissions. Click the Tools menu and select the Security option. On the security submenu, select the User and Group Permissions option.

Permissions are set up by objects in the database (e.g., queries, tables, macros, etc.). Permissions are set on users and groups. Users in a group receive all of the permissions settings for the group.

In the Object Type drop-down box, you can select the type of object you want to set the security on. There are two basic types of security. The first is security for modifying the database structure for that object. For example, tables can be modified, read, and administered. This dialog box is for setting the object permissions.

The second set of permissions relates to the ability to change the data in the object. Options include reading, updating, inserting, and deleting data. Note that on forms, reports, and macros, there is an additional option to set Open/Run that defines if the user can utilize the object.

One of the objects that permissions can be set on is the entire database. In the Object Type drop-down box, select Database. The security options are shown here:

The Open Exclusive option indicates if the user can open the database exclusively and lock out other users. The Administer setting indicates that the user can manage administrative tasks such as security.

The second tab on the dialog box supports changing the owner of the different objects. This can be changed from the default administrator. Only the owner can save changes to the object and change the ownership of the object. This is very useful for large databases where there are multiple developers working on objects in the database. A good example of this is having a two-developer team where one developer is focused on the database tables and queries and the second developer creates forms and reports. By segmenting ownership, this helps to limit potential issues with developers overwriting each other's work.

Access also provides a wizard utility for setting up permissions in the database. The User-Level Security Wizard walks the user through a series of steps for defining permissions in the database. We will quickly walk through these steps.

The first screen handles the setting of the workgroup. If the default startup workgroup is used, then a new workgroup will have to be created. Figure 11-1 shows the first screen.

Database Security

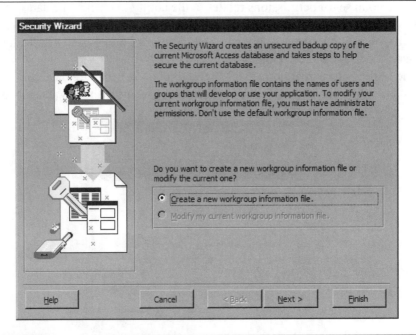

FIGURE 11-1   Setting up the workgroup

Click the Next button. You will notice that the workgroup ID (WID) is autogenerated to be a unique identifier. This value, along with the name, company, and location of the workgroup file, can all be modified. You also have options to determine if this workgroup should be the default or not.

The next screen allows you to select which objects you want to have secured. Select the appropriate set of objects that need to be secured. Some objects, such as forms or reports, may not need any specific security settings. Figure 11-2 shows the screen.

On the next screen, we have a series of groups that the wizard has defined for us. These are common groups that have very specific security level requirements. Select the groups that make sense for your application. Remember that you can always go and create your own groups after the fact, or modify the groups that the wizard is going to define. Select all of the groups and click the Next button to continue.

The next screen specifically asks what permissions the general users group should have. Note the big yellow warning on the screen that indicates that anyone with Access will be able to see what a user sees. This could potentially be a security issue and needs to be carefully considered. These permissions are set up

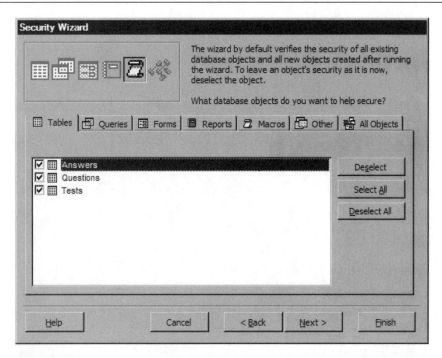

FIGURE 11-2   Security Wizard object selections

globally for the specific object. In other words, if you give Modify Design permissions to tables, the user will be able to modify the design of all tables. Figure 11-3 shows the dialog box.

The next screen handles adding users into the workgroup. Each user is given a name, password, and PID. The PID is automatically generated to be unique, but it can be changed as well. Once all of the users are added, the next screen provides the options for adding the users into their appropriate groups. You can either assign a user to specific groups or add users to a specific group.

When you finish assigning users to groups, the next screen indicates Access is ready to set up the new security model. It will create a backup of the database without the security settings and then create a version with all of the security settings. Note that in the process, we never actually defined security at the object level. This was essentially done by selecting the predefined groups that the wizard provided. You can, of course, still use the options outlined earlier to customize any of the security settings created by the wizard.

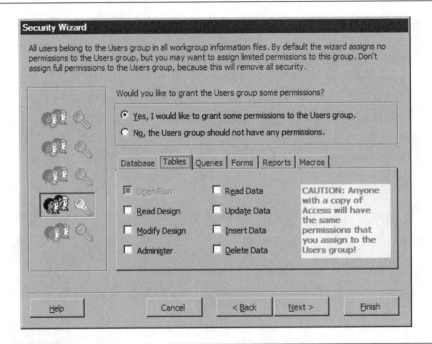

FIGURE 11-3   User account permissions setup

The wizard is very helpful in setting up the initial security structure for an Access database. In particular, if you can rely on the predefined groups the wizard provides, then setting up security can be fairly straightforward.

Splitting Databases

Access databases can be split into two databases. The first will have the tables and queries for the database. The second will have the macros, reports, forms, and VBA code in it. This provides a separation of the core data structure and the front end (interface and programmatic objects) of the database. This also allows front-end development to take place without also opening and exposing the table and query back-end objects.

To split the database, select the Tools menu and then the Database Utilities option. On the Database Utilities submenu, select Database Splitter. When you do so, a dialog box comes up indicating what will take place, along with the option to continue or cancel. Figure 11-4 shows the dialog box.

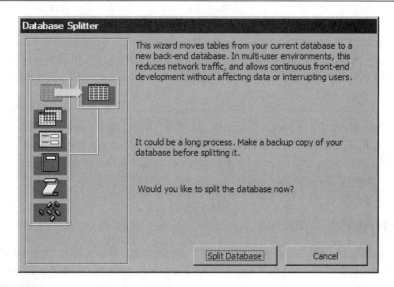

Database Security

FIGURE 11-4   Database Splitter dialog box

When you click on Split Database, a dialog box pops up that asks where the back-end database should be created. This is the database that will contain the tables and queries. Typically, this is going to be in a location other than where the front-end database is located. By having it in another location, you can enforce more security for the core data. Select an appropriate location and continue.

Now the database is split into two MDB files. The front-end database contains links to the back-end database for the tables and queries.

MDE and ADE Databases

One key consideration is how to secure Visual Basic for Applications (VBA) code. In general, you probably don't want this code readily available to end users if your database is going to be widely used. With Access, you can create MDE or ADE versions of the databases that do not contain source code. The MDE is for standard Access databases. The ADE is for Access Data projects.

When the MDE (or ADE) file is created, all of the module code is compiled and removed from the database. In addition, the destination database is compacted. The VBA code continues to run, but it cannot be viewed or edited. It also protects forms and reports without user-level security permissions being set up. Basically, the front-end components of the database cannot be imported, exported, modified, or viewed in design mode. It is important to note that tables, queries, and macros can still be imported or exported.

MDEs/ADEs provide an excellent method for distributing Access databases to end users. With a few additional permissions, tables and queries can be easily locked down. Or, these can be split out and centrally located and accessed by an MDE/ADE front end.

TIP   *Security is a hot issue at Microsoft. The Microsoft Developer Network (MSDN) provides extensive information on securing Access databases. Before any Access security plan is finalized, the latest information from Microsoft should be reviewed.*

Replication

Microsoft Access does provide replication capabilities. Many developers and DBAs are surprised to find out that Access supports replication, and it is fairly easy to implement.

Replication Overview

Replication can be very useful in certain situations where data needs to be frequently synchronized for backup purposes. It also makes it possible to share data in multiple locations and distributing updates. In some situations, replication can be detrimental to performance. If there are large sets of data and/or multiple replicas, keeping the data synchronized can significantly impact performance.

Access handles replication by creating replicas of the original (Design Master) database. These replicas are then synced with the original database. The replicas contain all of the tables, queries, forms, reports, macros, and modules of the design database. Only the Design Master can have changes made to the tables, queries, and other objects.

Before we dig into setting up replication, we need to understand replica visibility. The visibility of the replica determines what type of replicas you can create from it—whether it can act as the Design Master—in the replica set. It also determines how conflicts in synchronization are handled. Visibility also determines which replicas that replica can synchronize with. Note that you can't change a replica's visibility once you create the replica. Table 11-1 shows the three different visibility settings for a replica.

Visibility	Description
Global	Changes in the database are fully tracked. These changes can be exchanged with any other global replica in the set of replication databases. Global replicas can also exchange changes with local and anonymous replicas. Note that the Design Master is a global replica.
Local	A replica that exchanges data with its hub or a global replica, but not with other replicas in the replica set.
Anonymous	This replica is used when you don't need to track individual users. This is particularly useful for databases that are downloaded from the Internet.

TABLE 11-1   Replication Visibility

TIP   *The Access help provides additional information on anonymous replicas.*

When a database is set up for replication, changes are made to the database. The first change is that an s_GUID identifier is added for each record to uniquely identify the record. The s_Lineage is a binary field that contains information about the historical changes of each record. The final change is that an s_Generation field is added that stores information about groups of changes. In addition, for memo and OLE Object data types, a field is added called Gen_*Fieldname*.

As you can imagine, these changes are significant and are not easily undone. In addition, they add quite a bit of size to the database. Along with the fields, a series of system tables is also added.

The other key change is that autonumber fields are changed from incremental to random generation. If your tables rely on ordering by incremented autonumbers, this will be a significant issue.

Replication Demonstration

Let's set up a simple replication scenario. Create a new database or use one of the samples from earlier chapters. Click the Tools menu and select the Replication option. Select the Create Replica option on the submenu.

A dialog box will pop up that indicates the database needs to be closed. Click the Yes button to continue. Note that the dialog box indicates that the database will be converted into a Design Master. The dialog box shown next warns about the

Replication

changes that are required to create the Design Master. It also asks if you want a backup to be created. Click Yes to continue.

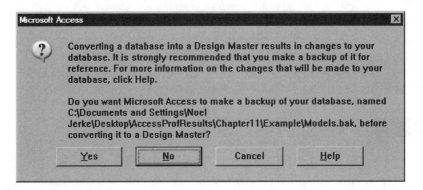

Next, Access queries for where you want the replica to be created and the type of replica. For our purposes, keep the global replica and select an appropriate location and continue. Now there are two MDB files, and the original is the Design Master. The second is the newly created replica.

Before we explore the changes made to the database, we want to show the system fields and tables to be able to view the changes. Click the Tools menu and select Options. Select the View tab of the dialog box. Check the System objects option. This will enable system objects to be viewed.

Figure 11-5 shows the Models database from earlier in the book converted into a Design Master replica.

Note the yellow double arrow icon tag on the tables of the database. Also note the number of system tables. The number of tables is about double that of a standard Access database. As mentioned earlier, these tables are added to support the replication.

Now select a table and go into the Design view. You will immediately see several changes. The first is that the autonumber field is now set to have a random generation. The new fields outlined earlier are also added into the table. Note that these fields will show up for every record in the table. Figure 11-6 shows the Models table in the Design view.

If you look at the table in the Design view, in the replica you will see the same structure. However, note that you can only see the Design view in read-only mode in the replica.

Now open up a table and change data in the table. Close the database and then open the replica. You will note that the changes do not show up in the replica. Changes have to be synchronized to show up.

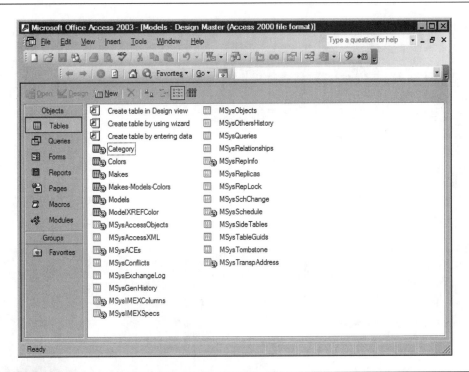

FIGURE 11-5 Models database Design Master

TIP *Changes can be programmatically synchronized between the replicas.*

Open up the Design Master or the replica and go to the Tools menu and select Replication. Click the Synchronize Now option to initialize the synchronization process.

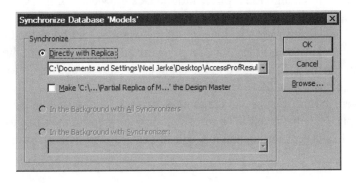

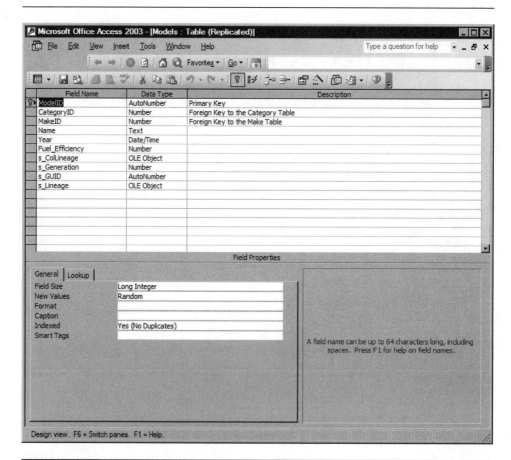

FIGURE 11-6   Models Table Design view

We are going to perform a direct synchronization, which is our only option. Note the option to change the replica into the Design Master. Click OK to continue with the synchronization.

Once the synchronization is done, all of the changes will be synced between the two databases. Because the data changes were only made in one of the databases, there are no conflicts. Even if we made changes in both databases, as long as it was to different records, there would be no conflicts.

If we were to make changes to the same record and field we would have a conflict from the replication that needs to be resolved. Make changes to the same record and field in both the Design Master and the replica. Then run the synchronization process.

For this example, the Category table data was updated in the Models database. The name of the category for the same record was updated in both the Design Master and replica. Then a synchronization was run. When the synchronization is complete, Access indicates that there is a conflict that needs to be resolved.

Upon completion of the synchronization, select the option to resolve the conflict (or select it from the Replication submenu). The Conflict Viewer is displayed in Figure 11-7.

The viewer shows several things to use to help resolve the conflict. First, the reason for the conflict is displayed. In this case, it is a conflict in updating the same records and fields. Access predetermines a winner and a loser based on Design Master versus the replica, time of the change, etc.

Note the name fields for the two records. This is where the change was made in both databases. We can now select which change we want to use as the final change. Or, we can postpone the resolution for a later date. Go ahead and select one of the data updates to be applied.

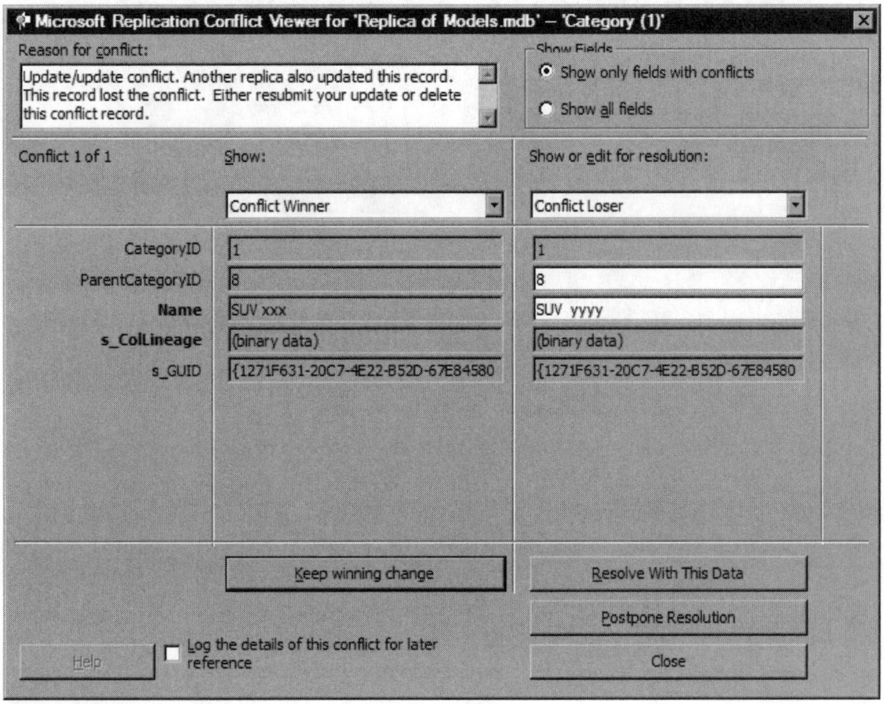

FIGURE 11-7   Conflict Viewer

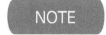
NOTE *The Microsoft Office 2003 Developer Kit comes with a Replication Manager tool as well as the Jet and Replication Objects (JRO). With these tools, additional capabilities are available for managing replication and synchronization.*

In addition to straight full database replications, we can also set up partial replication. This can be very helpful for segmenting via filters where data should be replicated. Access provides a Partial Replica Wizard that makes setting up partial replications easy.

Click the Tools menu and select Replication. On the replication submenu, select the Partial Replica Wizard option. The first screen of the wizard allows you to either set up a new partial replica or modify an existing replica. Select create and click the Next button to continue.

The next screen provides options for specifying where the replica will be stored and what type of replica will be created. There are also options for deciding if the replica will be read-only and preventing deletes of data.

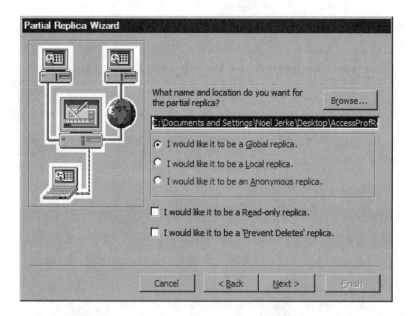

In this case, select a global replica and determine where the replica should be stored. Click the Next button to continue. The next dialog box provides options for filtering what data will go into the replica. This is where we can segment the data for the replica. An example of pulling all model data where the category is greater than 7 or less than 3 is shown here:

The next dialog box allows us to determine what related tables will be included in the partial replica. The records in these tables will be filtered to only pull records that are related to the returned records from the filter. You can choose which of these tables will be included.

Click Next to continue. The last dialog box indicates the replica will be created and generates a report of the tables and filters in the replica.

Now open up the partial replica. If you go to the Category table, you will find that only records with a category ID that meets the criteria show up. With this partial replication technique, we can segment data for management across multiple replicas and yet have the data still stored in a central repository.

Replication is a complicated topic that covers many different issues, techniques, and tools. We have touched on the key topics of replication, and there is much more to dig into that would cover several chapters. Microsoft's MSDN web site and the Office 2003 help system provide extended information on utilizing Access replica technology. In addition, the Replication Manager provides extended functionality that should be analyzed.

Summary

When Access is going to be deployed for enterprise use, it is important to consider backup, security, and replication as part of the database management strategy. Many developers believe that Access isn't robust enough to handle enterprise-level requirements in these areas. While Access would likely not be utilized to run a CRM or ERP system for a large company, it can be effectively used for very specific purposes, and it has the right tools for ensuring that data availability and security can be managed properly.

Chapter 12

Visual Basic for Applications

In a couple of the earlier chapters we utilized a little Visual Basic for Applications (VBA) in our examples. In this chapter, we are going to explore some of the basics of programming within the Access environment.

Overview

Visual Basic for Applications is a lightweight version of the full-fledged Visual Basic programming language. It is specifically built into applications such as Access, Excel, Visio, etc., and within Access it allows us to build complex applications based in the Access interface.

> NOTE
>
> *Visual Basic is a stand-alone tool for creating separate software components, such as executable programs. VBA offers the same powerful tools as Visual Basic in the context of an existing application, and is the best option for customizing software that already meets most of your needs. VBScript is a lightweight version of the Visual Basic language, and is designed specifically for use on web pages. VBA is the premier technology designed specifically for application automation.*

When you utilize VBA, it provides a complete integrated development environment (IDE) that features the same elements familiar to developers using Microsoft Visual Basic, including a Project window, a Properties window, and debugging tools. VBA also includes support for Microsoft Forms (for creating custom dialog boxes) and ActiveX Controls.

With VBA, your Access applications can be tailored to fit specific business needs. When you utilize VBA within Access, you are able to take advantage of all of the Access features such as the database engine (tables and queries), forms, reports, etc., which can reduce the amount of required custom programming to build the application.

Object Model

Microsoft Access is built upon a series of objects. Many of the primary objects are familiar, such as tables, queries, forms, data access pages and reports. When you work with VBA programming, you are manipulating these objects in the Access environment.

Access has two major object hierarchies, the Access application itself and the ActiveX Data Objects (ADO). The application layer consists of all the menu bars, toolbars, windows, etc., for creating and working with the database. ADO is utilized for interfacing with the data itself.

The object model is fairly detailed and complex. We will utilize a few of the objects in our examples in this chapter. Once you get the hang of using VBA in the Access environment, a good object model reference will be useful for accomplishing your programming tasks.

TIP   *For more on the Access object model, see* Microsoft® Office Access 2003: The Complete Reference *(McGraw-Hill/Osborne, 2003).*

Hello World—Access Style

To get familiar with the VBA development environment, we will build a very simple Hello World application. Create a new Access database and save it as Hello.mdb.

NOTE   *For this chapter, we are assuming you have a fundamental understanding of programming concepts and some experience with the Visual Basic language.*

Once the database is open, click on the Modules option in the Objects window. This will take you to the list of VBA modules created in the database (of course, right now we don't' have any).

Click on the New button to create a new module. When you do that, the IDE for VBA opens up separately from Access. The IDE, shown in Figure 12-1, is specifically designed for writing VBA code.

The IDE has three primary windows. The first is the Project window. This is where modules and other code created in the database are listed. Note the ACWZMain project listed. This is the code for all of the wizards in Access. Our Hello database has its code and modules listed, which for the moment is for our new module (module1).

The Properties window will list our properties for the various objects we will be utilizing, including our modules. The final window is for the VBA code, which is where code for the application will be written.

We are going to start out our coding by building a simple public function in our module. This function will pop up a dialog box that says "Hello World!". Before we get started, save the module as HelloMod.

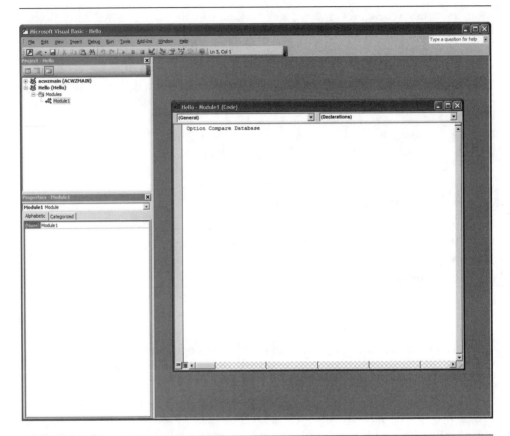

FIGURE 12-1   Access VBA IDE

Now, enter the following code in the module:

```
Public Function HW()

   MsgBox "Hello World!"

End Function
```

Your IDE should now look like Figure 12-2.

This code creates a public function called HW. The public part means we will be able to call it outside of our HelloMod module. Within the function, we are calling the MsgBox function, which will pop up a message box that says "Hello World!". Be sure to save the module.

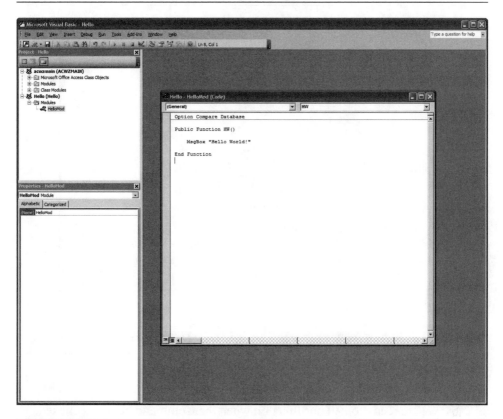

FIGURE 12-2   HelloMod module with code

To test the function, click the cursor anywhere inside the function. Then, click on the Run Sub/UserForm button on the toolbar. When the button is clicked, the subroutine is run and the message box pops up. Figure 12-3 shows the message box. Note that the Access interface comes into focus to show it.

Now let's show how we would use this function from within the Access environment. Specifically, we will call our function from a button on a form.

Click on the Forms option on the Objects listing. Click on the New button to create a new form in the Design view. Save it as HelloForm. From the toolbox, select the Command button and then draw a new button on the form. When you do that, a Command Button Wizard will pop up. Click on cancel.

Change the text on the Command button to be "Say Hello!". Right-click on the button, and on the pop-up menu select Properties. On the All tab of the Properties window, change the name to cmdHello.

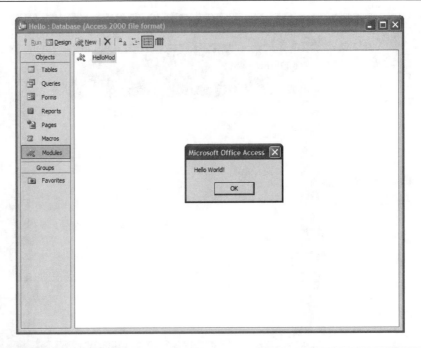

FIGURE 12-3 Hello World! in action

Now we are ready to call our function when the Command button is clicked. On the Properties window, select the Event tab. This lists a set of events for the command button object so that we can programmatically control what happens when the event fires. In this example, we want to call our function when the button is clicked. Place the mouse cursor in the On Click event text box. Then click the "..." button. A dialog box pops up asking which builder you want to use to define the click event action. In this case, select the Code Builder.

We are brought back to the VBA IDE. A new code window is opened up for the form. The name of the code object is called Form_HelloForm, and a private subroutine, cmdHello_Click, is created for the click event. In this subroutine, we can call our function. The subroutine should look like the following listing:

```
Private Sub cmdHello_Click()

    HW

End Sub
```

The code is simple with the call to our HW function. Now save the changes and close out of the VBA IDE. Close the Properties window for the Command button. Now we are ready to see our form in action. Change to the Form view. Figure 12-4 shows the form.

Now click on the button to see the Hello World! message. That does it for our simple example. It shows the basics of building VBA code within Access.

Building a Customer Query

In our next example, we will get a little more sophisticated in our use of VBA. We are going to build a scenario where a custom query and Excel report will be created based on user selections.

Building the Sample Data

To get started, we will need a sample database to show off our techniques. In this case, we are going to build a database of prospects, mail campaigns, and mailings. The idea is to be able to build a mail campaign to a targeted list of prospects.

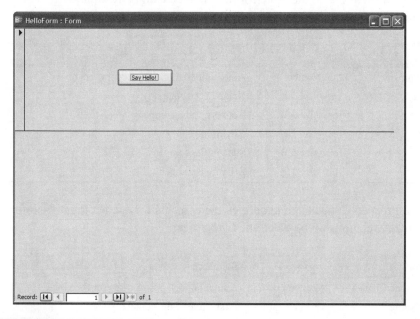

FIGURE 12-4   HelloForm

We will have four tables in our sample database, as outlined here:

Table	Description
Campaigns	Defines the mail campaigns including subject, body, and signature
Mailings	Lists all of the mailings that each prospect has received
ProspectCompany	List of companies for our prospects
ProspectContacts	List of individual prospects

Create a new database and save it as mailingdb.mdb. We will first create the Campaigns table. Add the following fields to the table:

Field	Type	Description
IDCampaigns	AutoNumber	Autonumbered primary key for the table
Subject	Text (size 50)	The subject of the campaign
BodyText	Memo	The text of the body of the campaign
Signature	Memo	The signature text of the campaign

Next, we will create the table for the ProspectCompany table with the following fields:

Field	Type	Description
IDCompany	AutoNumber	Autonumbered primary key for the table
Name	Text (size 50)	Name of the company
Address	Text (size 50)	Address of the company
City	Text (size 50)	City of the company
State	Text (size 50)	State of the company
Zip	Text (size 15)	ZIP of the company

The ProspectContacts table defines the contacts for each company. Note the foreign key relationship between the two tables.

Field	Type	Description
IDProspectContact	AutoNumber	Autonumbered primary key for the table
FirstName	Text (size 50)	First name of the contact
LastName	Text (size 50)	Last name of the contact
Phone	Text (size 20)	Phone number of the contact

Field	Type	Description
Email	Text (size 50)	Email address of the contact
IDCompany	Number	Foreign key for the ProspectCompany table

The final table is utilized for the historical tracking of the mailings each contact has received. The Mailings table fields are shown here:

Field	Type	Description
IDMailHistory	AutoNumber	Autonumbered primary key for the table
IDProspectContact	Text (size 50)	Foreign key that relates the contact to the mailing
MailDate	Text (size 50)	Date the mailing was created
IDCampaigns	Text (size 20)	Foreign key that relates the campaign to the mailing

NOTE *You will want to populate the database with sample data.*

That does it for our table structures. Now we will need to create one query. This query will be utilized to return a distinct list of states from the ProspectCompany table—the idea being we will want to send campaigns by state.

Click on the Queries option on the Objects listing. Create the new query in the Design view. Add in the ProspectCompany table to the query. Add the State field to the grid and set the Sort to be Ascending. Now we have to adjust the SQL to only return distinct states. That way, if there is more than one company in a state, the state will only show up once in the list. The following listing shows the code for the SQL:

```
SELECT DISTINCT ProspectCompany.State
FROM ProspectCompany
ORDER BY ProspectCompany.State;
```

Note the addition of the DISTINCT clause in the SQL code. This ensures that only distinct states are listed. Now save the query as DistinctStates. When you run it, the states from the table are listed. That does it for setting up the database.

Building the User Form

Next, we will build a form that will do a number of things for us. In the form, the user will define the details of a mailing campaign they would like to create. The user will select the campaign and the target state. Then, through VBA code, a number of steps will be taken to get the data, update the Mailing table, and create an Excel spreadsheet for the mailing.

To get started, click on the Forms option on the Objects listing. Create a new Form in the Design view, and save the form as CampaignBuilder.

We are going to add four controls to our blank form. The first two are combo boxes. For the first combo, when the dialog box comes up to help you set up the combo box, click Cancel. We will be customizing it ourselves. Follow these steps to set up the combo box:

1. Set the label text to be "Campaigns:".

2. Right-click on the combo box and select the Properties option.

3. Select the All tab.

4. Set the name of the combo box to be cboCampaigns.

5. Set the Row Source Type to be Table/Query.

6. Set the Row Source to the following query:

```
SELECT Campaigns.IDCampaigns, Campaigns.Subject
FROM Campaigns ORDER BY [Subject];
```

7. Set the Bound Column to a value of 1.

These steps basically set up the combo box to pull the list of campaign ID values and campaign subjects. The bound column defines the value of the control for the selected item—in this case, the ID of the campaign. For the second combo box, follow these steps to set it up:

1. Set the label text to be "State:".

2. Right-click on the combo box and select the Properties option.

3. Select the All tab.

4. Set the name of the combo box to be cboStates.

5. Set the Row Source Type to be Table/Query.

6. Set the Row Source to the DistinctStates query.

7. Set the Bound Column to a value of 1.

Like the first combo box, we are setting up the data source and the value of the control. In this case, we are using the DistinctStates query and setting the control value to the ProspectCompany state field.

Next we need to add a text box to our form. This text box will be utilized to enter the name of the query that will be saved for the campaign. For each campaign that is created, a query that retrieves the mail list will be created in the database. That way, the original data can be retrieved if needed. Add the text box to the form and follow these steps for setting it up:

1. Set the label text to be "Query Name:".

2. Right-click on the text box and select the Properties option.

3. Select the All tab.

4. Set the name of the text box to be txtQueryName.

Our final control on the form will be Command button. When clicked, it will initiate the creation of the campaign. Draw the control on the form. When the wizard starts up to set up the control, click Cancel. Follows these steps to set up the Command button:

1. Set the text of the control to be "Build Mailing".

2. Right-click on the text box and select the Properties option.

3. Select the All tab.

4. Set the name of the Command button to be cmdBuildQuery.

That does it for setting up the form. Your final form layout should look something like Figure 12-5.

Now switch to the Form view to utilize the form. The combo boxes should be populated with appropriate data. At this stage when you click on the button, nothing will happen. Figure 12-6 shows the form in the Form view.

That does it for setting up the form. Now we are ready to dig into the VBA coding.

Building the VBA Code

The action for our mail campaign logic will happen behind the click event of the Command Button. All of our logic will be placed in that event.

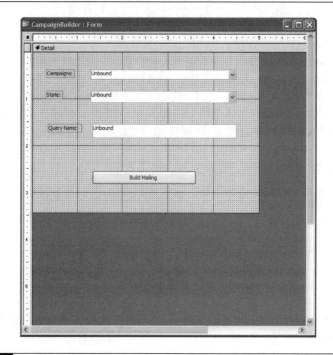

FIGURE 12-5 Form layout

Before we dig into the code, let's outline the basic requirements for the VBA code. The following listing outlines each requirement:

1. Pull the data from the form and ensure appropriate values have been selected and entered.

2. If values were not selected/entered, notify the user and quit processing.

3. Check to ensure that the query name entered by the user has not already been used.

4. If the query name has been used, notify the user.

5. Update the Mailings table to show that a mailing has been done to the selected prospects.

6. Create a query to retrieve the mailing data.

7. Export the query data to an Excel spreadsheet.

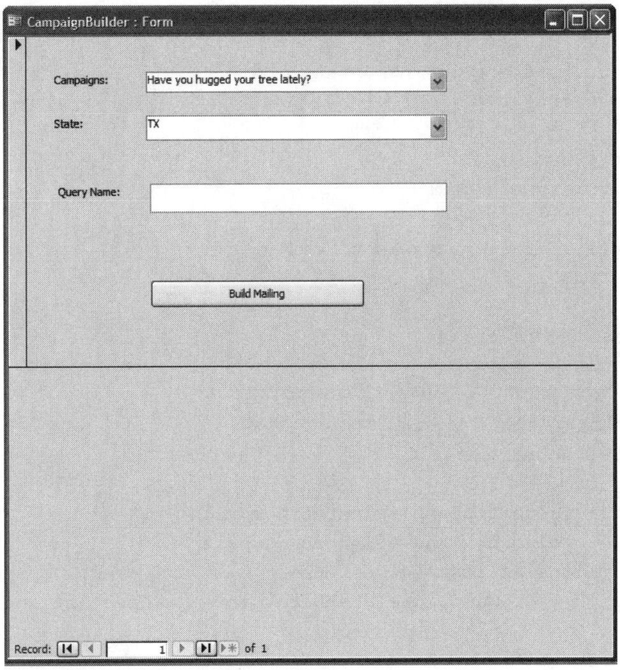

FIGURE 12-6   Form view

To get started, we need to create the VBA code structure for the Command button click event, just like we did in the Hello World! example. Right-click on the Command button and select the Properties option. On the Properties dialog box, select the Event tab. Then select the On Click event. Click on the "…" button that appears for the event. In the dialog box that pops up, select the Code Builder option. When you do this, the VBA IDE is opened up and the click event subroutine is created.

Add the following code in Listing 14-1 to the click event:

Listing 14-1.

```
Private Sub cmdBuildQuery_Click()

'  Dimension our variables
Dim queryName As String
Dim queryState As String
```

```
Dim queryCampaign As String
Dim Result

'  Set the focus to the query name text box
txtQueryName.SetFocus

'  Get the query name
queryName = txtQueryName.Text

'  Set the focus to the states combo box
cboStates.SetFocus

'  Get the name of the state
queryState = cboStates.Text

'  Set the focus to the campaigns combo box
cboCampaigns.SetFocus

'  Get the index value for the selected campaign
'  Get the index value for the selected campaign
If Trim(cboCampaigns.SelText) <> "" Then
    queryCampaign = cboCampaigns.ItemData(cboCampaigns.ListIndex)
Else
    queryCampaign = ""
End If

'  Check to ensure values were entered for all three data entry fields
If Len(Trim(queryName)) = 0 Or _
   Len(Trim(queryState)) = 0 Or _
   Len(Trim(queryCampaign)) = 0 Then

    '  Indicate a field wasn't filled out
    MsgBox "You did not make all of the appropriate selections"

Else

    '  Loop through the current list of queries
    For N = 0 To CurrentDb.QueryDefs.Count - 1

        '  Check for a similar query name
        If LCase(Trim(CurrentDb.QueryDefs(N).Name)) = _
           LCase(Trim(queryName)) Then

            '  Indicate a match was found
            Flag = 1
```

```
            '   Exit the loop
            Exit For

    End If

Next N

'   If there was not a match
If Flag <> 1 Then

    '   Insert mailing list data
    CurrentProject.Connection.Execute "INSERT INTO mailings " & _
        "(idProspectContact, MailDate, idCampaigns) " & _
        "SELECT ProspectContacts.idProspectContact, " & _
        "Date() AS MailDate, " & queryCampaign & _
        " AS idCampaign FROM ProspectCompany " & _
        "INNER JOIN ProspectContacts ON " & _
        "ProspectCompany.IDCompany = ProspectContacts.IDCompany " & _
        "WHERE (((ProspectCompany.State)=""" & queryState & """))"

    '   Build query to retrieve the campaign data
    Result = Application.CurrentDb.CreateQueryDef(queryName, _
            "SELECT ProspectContacts.FirstName, " & _
            "ProspectContacts.LastName, " & _
            "ProspectCompany.Address, ProspectCompany.City, " & _
            "ProspectCompany.State, ProspectCompany.Zip, " & _
            "Campaigns.Subject, Campaigns.BodyText, " & _
            "Campaigns.Signature FROM Campaigns INNER JOIN " & _
            "((ProspectCompany INNER JOIN ProspectContacts ON " & _
            "ProspectCompany.IDCompany = " & _
            "ProspectContacts.IDCompany) " & _
            "INNER JOIN mailings ON " & _
            "ProspectContacts.idProspectContact = " & _
            "mailings.idProspectContact) ON " & _
            "Campaigns.IDCampaigns =" & _
            "mailings.IDCampaigns WHERE " & _
            "(((Campaigns.IDCampaigns)=" & _
            queryCampaign & ") AND " & _
            "((mailings.MailDate)=Date()) AND " & _
            "((ProspectCompany.State)=""" & _
            queryState & """))")

    '   Indicate the query was created
    MsgBox "Your Query was Successfully Created!"

    '   Export the campaign data to Excel
```

```
        DoCmd.OutputTo acOutputQuery, queryName, _
                    acFormatXLS, queryName & ".xls", True

    Else

        '  Indicate that a query already exists
        MsgBox "A query with that name already exists!"

    End If

End If

End Sub
```

In the first part of our subroutine, we dimension the variables we will be using. While it isn't strictly required that we dimension them, it is always a good idea.

> **NOTE** *You can use the Option Explicit keywords at the top of the form code, which requires that all variables be dimensioned.*

Next in the code, we have to retrieve the data selected and entered by the user. In order to retrieve the values of the controls, we have to set the focus to each and then get the data.

First, the query name text box is retrieved and stored in a variable. We just reference the Text property to get the user-entered value. Next, we set the focus to the cboState control. In this case with the state control, we can just get the text value of the current item since we are not explicitly retrieving a primary key value.

> **NOTE** *We are assuming that all states will be entered by their abbreviation (e.g., TX). We will be actually querying on the name of the state versus an autonumber-generated primary key value for the state. In reality, we might want to have a lookup table of states with a unique ID for each state.*

Finally, the focus is set for the cboCampaigns control. First, we check to ensure something is selected. If we don't, we will get an error trying to retrieve the campaign ID.

To retrieve the IDCampaigns field value for a selected campaign, the ItemData property is utilized. We have to index into the ItemData collection to retrieve the ID value of the currently selected campaign. To do this, the ListIndex property is used to get the index value of the selected item in the list.

Once we have the available values, we do a quick check to ensure all of them are set. If they are not, we inform the user and then end the process.

Our next check ensures that a query with that name doesn't already exist. To do this, we are going to reference the CurrentDB object. The QueryDefs object collection is part of the CurrentDB object hierarchy. We can iterate through the collection and get the name of each existing query and check it against the user-entered query name. If we find a match, we set a flag and then exit the For loop.

Next, we check the flag and if it is not set, we are ready to create the query and follow the rest of our tasks.

The first thing we do is insert the mailing data into the Mailings table as a record of the campaign being sent to those prospects. We utilize an Insert Into SQL statement, which inserts the data from a Select statement.

The Select statement retrieves the ID of the prospect contact, the mail date, and the ID of the campaign. The mail date uses the Date() function to get the current system date. The ID of the campaign comes from the user-selected campaign.

We have to join together the ProspectContacts and ProspectCompany tables so that we can only retrieve prospect contacts whose companies are in the user-selected state.

To execute the query, we use the database connection for the current project. The connection object has an Execute method that will run any action queries (e.g., updates, deletes, and inserts). Once the query is run, the new records are inserted into the Mailings table.

NOTE
The CurrentProject object allows us to reference any of the objects in our Access project (ADP or MDB). It contains the AllForms, AllReports, AllMacros, AllModules, and AllDataAccessPages collections.

Next we are ready to create the campaign query. This will return the name of the prospect contact, the address data for the contact, and the campaign details. The idea is that this data will generate a mail list set of data that can be used to send the campaign out the door.

To create the query, the CreateQueryDef method will be utilized. The method is part of the CurrentDB object hierarchy, which is a subhierarchy of the Application object. We reference through the "." method, as in:

Application.CurrentDB.CreateQueryDef.

The Application object allows us to reference anything in our Access application. This can include menus, tables, queries, etc. The CurrentDB allows us to reference the currently open database.

Building a Customer Query

The CreateQueryDef method takes two parameters. The first is the name of the query to be created. The second is the SQL syntax of the query. That long set of SQL syntax in the code builds the select query that joins together Campaigns, ProspectCompany, ProspectContacts, and Mailings data to build the campaign mail data.

> **TIP** *When building complex queries like this on the fly in VBA code, use either the message box (msgbox) or show the query in a text box to easily debug the query syntax being built. If you don't create a valid query, an error will be generated.*

> **TIP** *For both the Insert Into and Select queries, the query wizards of Access can be used to generate the SQL template. Then the SQL code is pasted into the VBA IDE, and the VBA code to construct the query is built.*

Next, we tell the user that the query was created successfully. The MsgBox() function is used, as we saw in our earlier example.

Finally, in our code, we are going to export the query data into an Excel spreadsheet. To do this, the powerful DoCmd object is utilized. It allows us to perform a basic Access action. Actions allows us to do things like close windows, open forms, and, in this case, export data.

To export the data, we will use the OutPutTo action of Access. With this method, we can export data into a number of formats. The action takes seven parameters:

Parameter	Description
Object Type	The type of object containing the data to output. These can include tables, queries, forms, reports, etc. A series of constants is available for each type.
Object Name	The name of the object to be output.
Output Format	A series of constants that represent the format of the output.
Output File	The name of the file, including the path as to where the file should be created.
Auto Start	Set this to true if you want the target application to be started automatically to show the file (e.g., show the exported file in Excel).
Template File	Indicates the template file to be used for exporting to HTML, HTX, or ASP pages.
Encoding	Sets the encoding format.

In our example, we are going to export the data to excel from our newly created query. We indicate the output object type is a query by using the acOutputQuery constant. Next, we specify the query name entered by the user.

The format of the output will be for Excel, so the acFormatXLS constant is used. Next, we indicate that the name of the file should be the same as the query, including a ".XLS" extension. Finally, we indicate we want Excel to start up automatically and show the file.

That does it for our VBA code. Now we are ready to see it all run.

Utilizing the Application

Finally, we are ready to see our VBA application in action. We will build a couple of campaigns and see the power of VBA in action.

Switch to the Form view for our form. Select an appropriate campaign and state. Then enter a query name (be sure it is unique). Figure 12-7 shows a completed form.

Once the data is selected, we are ready to click our Command button and fire off the VBA code for the click event. As long as everything was filled in correctly

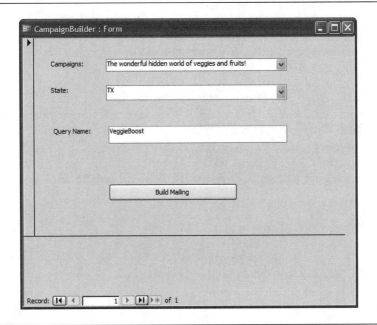

FIGURE 12-7   Campaign data selection

and the query name was unique, you should get a message box indicating the query was created. Click OK on the message box to continue.

Next, the Excel spreadsheet should open up with the exported data. A column for each field returned in the query is created. Figure 12-8 shows a sample exported spreadsheet.

> **NOTE** *If you do not specify a path for the spreadsheet to be saved, it will automatically be saved in the My Documents folder.*

Now go back to the Access database and go to the query objects listing. You will see that a query was created with the query name that you entered. Open up the query in the Design view.

You will note that the structure of the table includes all of the tables. The state will have a criteria set to the state you selected in the form, and the campaign ID is set to the campaign selected in the form. Figure 12-9 shows a sample Design view of the query.

The SQL for the query is shown in the following listing:

```
SELECT ProspectContacts.FirstName,
       ProspectContacts.LastName,
       ProspectCompany.Address, ProspectCompany.City,
       ProspectCompany.State, ProspectCompany.Zip,
       Campaigns.Subject, Campaigns.BodyText,
       Campaigns.Signature
FROM Campaigns INNER JOIN
     ((ProspectCompany INNER JOIN ProspectContacts ON
      ProspectCompany.IDCompany = ProspectContacts.IDCompany)
      INNER JOIN mailings ON
       ProspectContacts.idProspectContact =
       mailings.idProspectContact) ON
       Campaigns.IDCampaigns = mailings.IDCampaigns
WHERE (
        (
        (ProspectCompany.State)="TX") AND
        (
            (Campaigns.IDCampaigns)=4) AND
            ((mailings.MailDate)=Date())
        )
     );
```

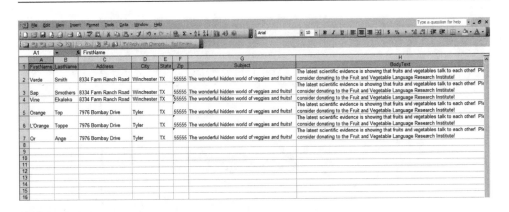

FIGURE 12-8 Sample exported spreadsheet

All of this was done with a fairly straightforward set of VBA code. Now let's try and break our form. Go back to the form and try and run it again with the same query name. You will get a message indicating a query with that name exists. Figure 12-10 shows the message.

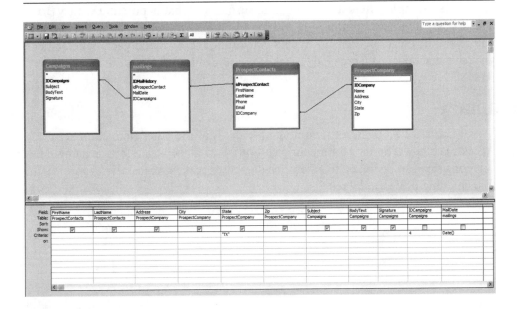

FIGURE 12-9 Sample query

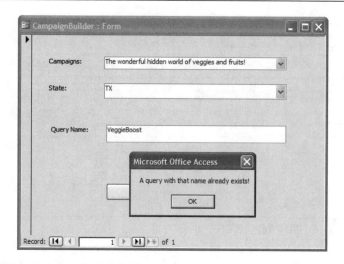

FIGURE 12-10 Duplicate query error message

Likewise, try not selecting a campaign name or state or not entering in a query name at all. You will get a message indicating the form is not completely filled out.

In this example, we just scratched the surface of what is possible with VBA and Access. If you are comfortable with programming in Visual Basic, the key to unlocking the power of VBA in Access is learning the Access object model. Once you have that down, you are ready to take your utilization of Access to the next level.

Summary

Visual Basic for Applications, combined with all of the other rich features of Access, is a powerful tool for meeting enterprise data needs. Building custom data solutions that can be linked to enterprise databases makes Access even more useful for achieving professional results.

Appendix A

Access 2003 XML Objects

This appendix outlines the XML methods supported in Access 2003. These methods provide the ability to import, export, and transform XML data using Visual Basic for Applications (VBA) code.

ExportXML Method

This method provides support for exporting data into an XML format. The data itself can be exported into an XML format. The schema definition is also exported. In addition, presentation data can also be exported.

Parameters

Table A-1 defines the parameters in order for the ExportXML method.

OtherFlags Parameter Options

Table A-2 outlines the option settings for the OtherFlags parameter.

Note that the OtherFlags are summed to determine the value of the Values parameter. For example, if you want to embed the schema and not export the primary keys and indexes, then the OtherFlags parameter would have a value of 3 (2+1).

AdditionalData Object

The AdditionalData object allows for related data to the main export object to also be exported. Table A-3 shows the methods of the object.

Table A-4 shows the properties for the AdditionalData object.

TransformXML Method

TransformXML loads the data from the data source into a DOMDocument (top level of the XML source) and then applies the specified transformation to the data. Once the data is transformed, it is stored in the specified source.

Parameters

Table A-5 defines the parameters in order for the TranformXML method.

Parameter	Type	Optional	Description
ObjectType	AcExportXMLObjectType	No	The type of object to be exported (e.g., table = acExportTable).
DataSource	String	No	The name of the object to be exported.
DataTarget	String	Yes	The filename, including the path for where the data should be exported.
SchemaTarget	String	Yes	The filename, including the path for where the XML schema should be exported.
PresentationTarget	String	Yes	The filename, including the path for where the presentation data should be exported.
ImageTarget	String	Yes	The path where images should be exported.
Encoding	AcExportXMLEncoding	Yes	The type of text encoding to be used for the exported data. The default is UTF8.
OtherFlags	Long	Yes	Sum of the values specifying the other flags (see below).
UserFilter	Boolean	Yes	Specifies if the filter of the object to be exported should be utilized to determine what data should be exported.
UseSort	Boolean	Yes	Specifies if the sort property of the object should be used to determine the sort order of the exported data.
AdditionalData	AdditionalData	Yes	Determines what other related data should be exported. See below for more information on AdditionalData.

TABLE A-1   Export XML Parameter Definitions

Flag	Value	Description
acEmbedSchema	1	The type of object to be exported (e.g., table, query, report).
acExcludePrimaryKeyandIndexes	2	Primary key fields and indices aren't exported.
acRunFromServer	4	Creates an ASP wrapper instead of an HTML wrapper.
acLiveReportSource	8	Connection information for a report containing live data.
acPersistReportML	16	Export the Report ML.

TABLE A-2   OtherFlags Parameter

TransformXML Method

Method	Parameters	Description
Add	Name as String	Creates a new AdditionalData object for the specified object (e.g., table).
Item	Index as Integer	Returns the AdditionalData object corresponding to the index referenced.

TABLE A-3   Additional Data Methods

Property	Description
Count	The number of AdditionalData objects added.
Name	The name of the AdditionalData object.

TABLE A-4   Additional Data Methods

Parameter	Type	Optional	Description
DataSource	String	No	The name and past of the XML file to import. This can be a URL or a file path.
TransformSource	String	No	The XSL file to apply to the DataSource.
OutputTarget	String	Yes	The filename and path for the results after applying the transform. Note that the source can be overwritten.
WellFormedXMLOutput	Boolean	Yes	If True, the TransformNodetoObject method of the DOM is used. This requires that the output be well-formed XML. If False, the TransformNode method of the DOM is used.
ScriptOption	AcTransformXMLScriptOptions	Yes	If set to ACPromptObject, the user will be prompted before creating any objects in the script. For the acEnableObjects, any script will run. If set to acDisableObjects, the transform fails if an object is to be created. Default is acPromptObjects.

TABLE A-5   Transform XML Parameter Definitions

Parameter	Type	Description
DataSource	String	The name with the path information of the XML data to import.
ImportOptions	String	Indicates options for the import (see below).

TABLE A-6   ImportXML Parameters

ImportXML Method

The import XML method imports data and/or presentation data into Access objects. If the objects already exist, they will be overwritten.

Parameters

Table A-6 defines the parameters in order for the ImportXML method.

Import Options

Table A-7 defines the ImportOptions parameter for ImportXML.

Note that the parameters can be combined. For example, if you want to import structure and data as well as append the data, the parameter value would be 3 (2+1).

Flag	Value	Description
acStructureOnly	0	Import the schema only.
acStructureAndData	1	Import schema and data.
acAppendData	2	Append the data to the existing table.

TABLE A-7   OtherFlags Parameter

Appendix B

PivotTable and PivotChart Basics

The Office PivotTable and PivotChart components were integrated into Access 2003 to provide additional views for data. These components are a set of ActiveX controls integrated right into the application.

In this appendix, we are going to explore the basic setup and utilization of PivotTables and PivotCharts within Access, and we will be exploring these capabilities in various sections of this book.

Setting Up the Sample Data

We will build a sample database that will demonstrate the capabilities of PivotTables and PivotCharts. Our data will be modeled off of simple order data, contained in two tables, Orders and Customers. The Orders table is defined as follows:

Field	Type	Description
OrderID	AutoNumber	The primary key and order identifier
OrderAmount	Currency	The dollar amount of the order
OrderDate	Date/Time	The date the order was placed
CustomerID	Number	The ID of the customer who placed the order (foreign key to the Customers table)

The simple order data includes the amount of the order, the date the order was placed, and the ID of the customer who placed the order. Note that we are not going to build any tables to track product items, etc. The Customers table is defined as follows:

Field	Type	Description
CustomerID	AutoNumber	The primary key and customer identifier
CustomerName	Text	The name of the customer
PremierCustomer	Yes/No	Flag indicating if the customer has premier status or not

The Customers table includes the identifier and the name. In addition, we have a flag which segments customers into premier and nonpremier status. We will use this flag to demonstrate some of the filtering techniques of the PivotTable and PivotChart.

Once the tables are set up, we will need to have sample data entered into each table to build our PivotTable properly. The following table has a sample set of data for the Customers table.

CustomerID	CustomerName	PremierCustomer
1	Ralph's Linguistic Lab	Yes
2	Martinez Scientific Inc.	Yes
3	Kwami Flight Operators	No
4	Consuelo's Eatery	No

The following table has the sample order data. Note the order dates are for a specific period of months with varying orders per month.

OrderID	OrderAmount	OrderDate	CustomerID
1	$500.00	1/1/2003	1
2	$2,500.00	1/2/2003	1
3	$234.58	1/3/2003	2
4	$2,900.00	2/3/2003	2
5	$2,541.25	2/5/2003	3
6	$600.00	2/10/2003	3
7	$350.00	3/12/2003	4
8	$221.00	3/18/2003	4
9	$698.00	3/20/2003	1
10	$456.00	3/25/2003	2
11	$235.00	3/30/2003	3
12	$21.00	3/30/2003	4
13	$7,500.25	4/8/2003	4
14	$689.21	4/9/2003	3
15	$587.00	4/11/2003	2
16	$6,325.00	4/15/2003	1
17	$425.00	4/18/2003	1
18	$985.00	4/24/2003	2
19	$6,587.25	5/30/2003	3
20	$536.00	6/1/2003	4
21	$125.58	6/8/2003	4
22	$35.25	7/2/2003	4
23	$98.52	7/14/2003	4
24	$214.58	7/21/2003	4
25	$77.56	7/24/2003	2
26	$65.89	7/25/2003	2
27	$899.65	8/2/2003	2

OrderID	OrderAmount	OrderDate	CustomerID
28	$235.25	8/4/2003	1
29	$453.25	9/6/2003	1
30	$658.66	9/19/2003	3
31	$785.21	10/1/2003	3
32	$9,875.25	10/26/2003	3

Finally, we will need a query that combines the two sets of data together, which will be used for our examples. Click to the Queries objects view. Click the Create Query in Design View option. Add both of the tables to the query.

Select the * option on each table to add all of the fields to the query results. Save the query as CustomerOrders-PivotChart. This query will be used to build the sample PivotChart. Your final results should look like Figure B-1.

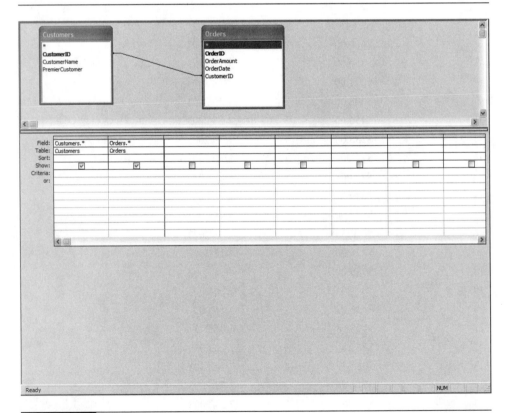

FIGURE B-1   CustomerOrders-PivotChart query

Now make a copy of the query and name it as CustomerOrders-PivotTable. We will use this query to build the sample PivotTable.

PivotTable Basics

A PivotTable is a way of viewing table data that is useful for analysis. It not only allows you to organize data into logical groups, it also provides for powerful summary reporting of data. In some ways it is similar to crosstab queries in Access, but it provides much more flexibility.

> NOTE *PivotTables and PivotCharts are especially useful when utilized in Access Data Projects (ADPs). Since Microsoft SQL Server does not natively support PivotTable and PivotChart capabilities, Access can be utilized for that type of analysis.*

Another powerful feature of PivotTables is the ability to drill into the high-level summary of data. If there is a specific set of summary data that looks intriguing, you can drill into it and view the underlying data.

> NOTE *Data viewed in a PivotTable cannot be updated; it is read-only.*

Open up the CustomerOrders-PivotChart query. To switch to the PivotView, click the View icon on the toolbar and select PivotTable View. Figure B-2 shows the blank PivotTable screen.

The PivotTable screen has four "drop" areas, which are listed and defined in the following table. In these areas we can drop fields or calculations on fields (e.g., sum, count, average, etc.).

Area	Description
Filter fields	Fields from the data can be added to this area. Then criteria can be selected to determine what detail and summary data is displayed.
Column fields	The column fields show what detail data and summary data is displayed for each row. You need to be careful and ensure that this data is fairly unique and has a reasonably limited number of values. For example, showing the number of quarters or months in a year would be reasonable to display, whereas showing each day of year is probably too many fields to easily view.
Row fields	The row fields define how the data is grouped horizontally. The number of rows isn't as big an issue as with columns. The rows are like viewing data in the datasheet view of a table.

Area	Description
Totals and/or Detail fields	This is where the main data will be displayed, for example, the order data for a customer. Both the individual data values or totals and calculations of data can be displayed.

Utilizing our sample data, we are going to build a PivotTable that shows the number of sales by quarter for each customer and summarize the total sales by customer for the year. In addition, we will set up the PivotTable to be able to filter between premier and nonpremier customers.

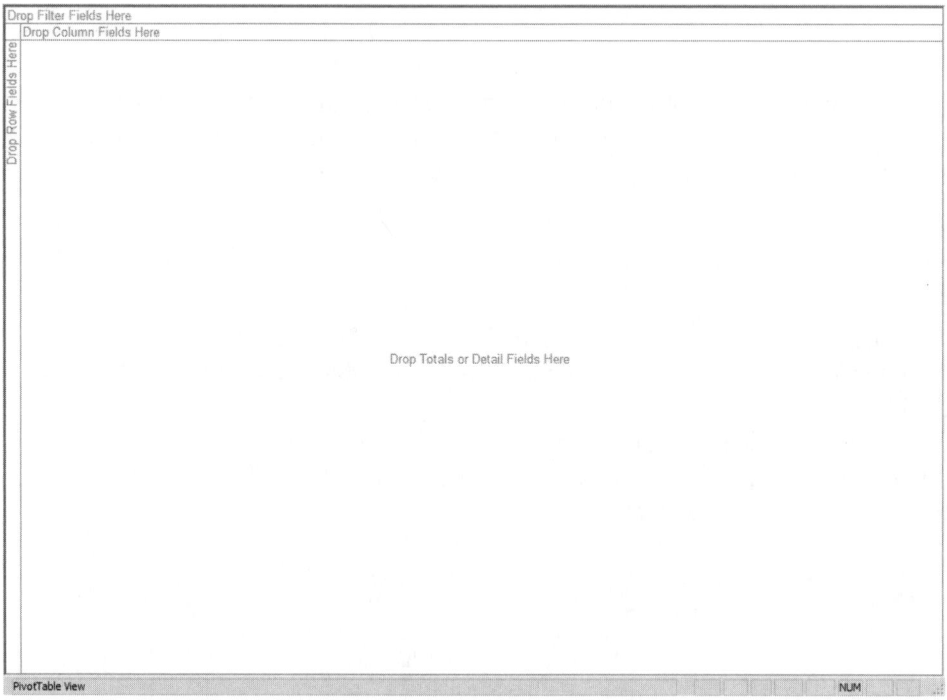

FIGURE B-2   Blank PivotTable screen

The field list window lists all fields available in the table or query. From this window we will drag the desired fields to the PivotTable screen. The PivotTable Field list is shown here:

Note on the field list two fields that were not included in our original tables and returned from the query. The OrderDate By Week and OrderDate By Month fields are automatically created for the OrderDate field. This allows us to easily group data by these two methods. If you expand the list of fields, under each you will see options to view by quarter, month, week, day, hours, minutes, and seconds.

Drag the Quarters subfield from the OrderDate By Month field onto the Column Fields section of the PivotTable screen. Note that each quarter can be expanded to show the months of the quarter. The months can then be expanded to show the days the orders were placed. This is a great example of the drill-down capabilities of PivotTables. Figure B-3 shows the PivotTable screen with the quarter detail displayed.

Now we are ready to add in the rows that will show the customers' names. Drag the CustomerName field to the Row Fields section of the PivotTable screen. The grid is now set up to show customer orders by month. Figure B-4 shows the updated PivotTable.

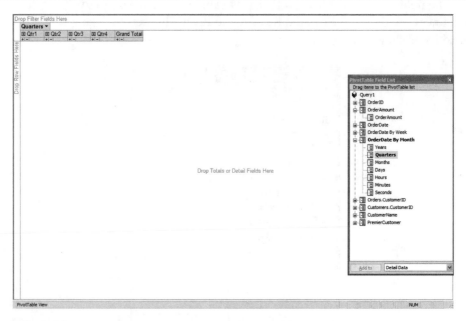

FIGURE B-3   PivotTable with OrderDate columns

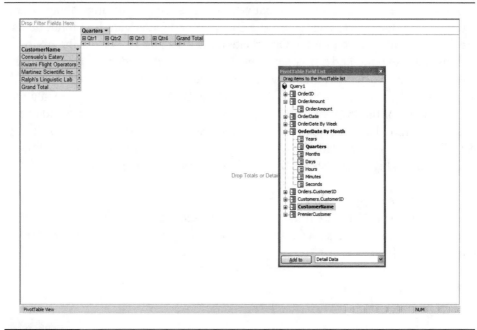

FIGURE B-4   PivotTable with CustomerName rows

Next, we can add in the order data detail. Drag the OrderAmount field to the Totals/Detail area of the PivotTable screen. The detail of each order by month is then displayed on the screen shown in Figure B-5. Note that the orders for each quarter are listed.

Next, we are ready to calculate the totals for the year. With the OrderAmount data selected (click it in the screen), click the PivotTable menu. Then select the AutoCalc option and click Sum. Doing so will automatically add a new field, Sum of OrderAmount, to the PivotTable, which will be added under a list of Totals fields in the field list. Figure B-6 shows the updated field list and PivotTable screen. Note that the Sum of OrderAmount was automatically added to the Totals/Detail area of the screen.

We still show the detail of each order by quarter being listed. If we had hundreds or thousands of orders this would be very detailed and difficult to view. But, we can hide these details and roll up the data by quarter and by customer. Start by right-clicking on the PivotTable screen and then select the Hide Details option. Now the order data for each quarter has been summed up. In fact, the column header for each quarter has been changed to "Sum of OrderAmount". Figure B-7 shows the hidden details.

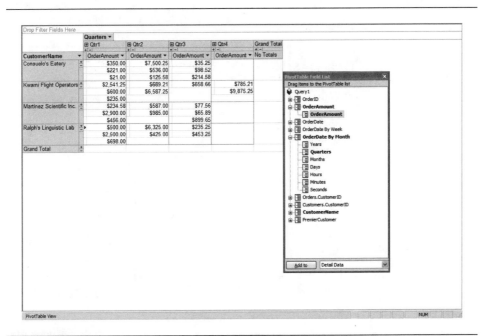

| FIGURE B-5 | PivotTable with customer orders |

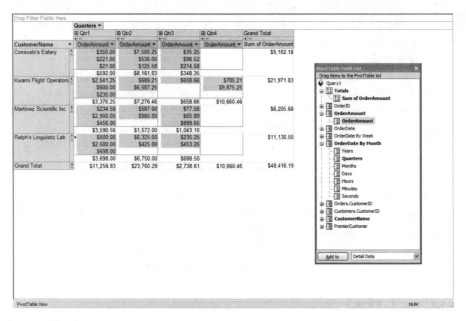

FIGURE B-6   PivotTable with OrderAmount Sum

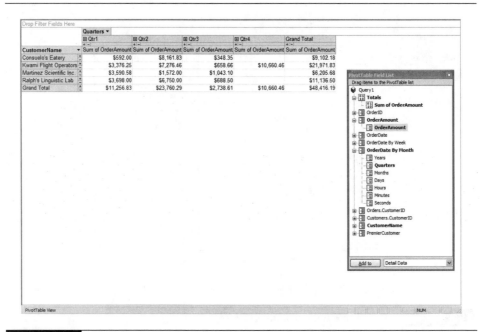

FIGURE B-7   PivotTable with hidden detail

Now we have a nice, neat view of customer orders by quarter with a total for the year. If you look at the column and row headers, you will see plus (+) and minus (-) signs above all of the headers. We still have the flexibility drill-down into the details of any of the sums. For example, if we click the plus sign for Ralph's Linguistic Lab, we can see that customer's specific orders for each quarter. And, the totals for each quarter are still calculated. Figure B-8 shows the detailed data.

The last option we have is to set filter fields for the PivotTable. Remember our premier customer flag? We can utilize that to show premier and nonpremier customers in the data. From the field list, select the PremierCustomer field and drag it to the Filter Fields section of the screen. Figure B-9 shows the updated screen.

If you select the down arrow next to PremierCustomer, you will see options to set the filter. Set the filter so that only Yes is selected and then click OK. By doing so, all nonpremier customers are removed from the PivotTable screen. Figure B-10 shows the updated screen.

We do, however, have many other options to filter the data. There are filter options for the CustomerName field and Quarters field. We can even filter down to look at a specific month for a specific customer if we like.

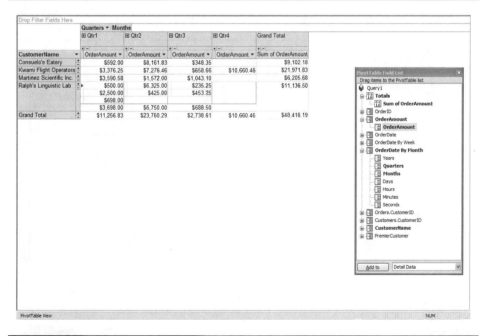

FIGURE B-8   Detailed customer order data

PivotTable Basics

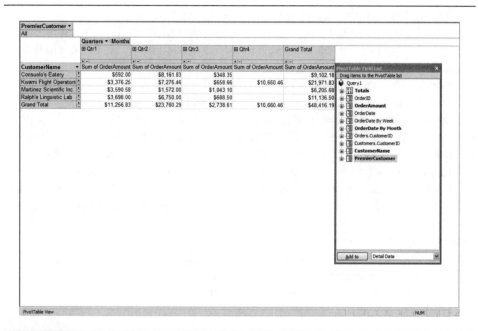

PivotTable with Filter Fields

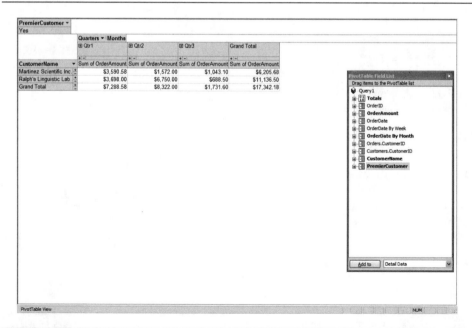

FIGURE B-10 PivotTable with Premier Customers

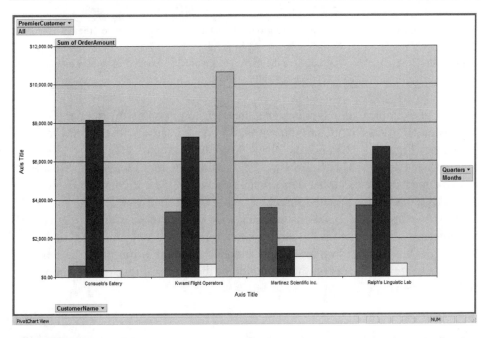

FIGURE B-11   PivotChart view of our PivotTable

Finally, now that we have the PivotTable built, we can switch to the PivotChart view to see a PivotChart version of the table. First, be sure to have all customers shown in the PivotTable. From the View toolbar option, select the PivotChart View. Our data is graphed by quarter, customer, and the sum of the order amount. Figure B-11 shows the PivotChart.

That does it for the basics of building PivotTables. Next we will look at building the same version of the PivotChart from scratch.

PivotChart Basics

We'll follow a similar process and build a PivotChart from our query data. There are four drop areas for setting up the PivotChart. The following table outlines each.

Area	Description
Filter fields	Fields from the data can be added to this area. Then criteria can be selected to determine what detail and summary data is displayed.
Drop Series fields	Utilized to create a data series based on one or more fields. A series is a group of related data points that are charted on the vertical (y) axis. These fields should be non-unique and small in number.

Area	Description
Category fields	A category is a group of related data that is plotted on the horizontal (x) axis.
Data fields	This is where the data to be graphed is dropped. Any data dragged into this area is by default totaled.

For our example, we will once again show customer orders by quarter. Open the CustomerOrders-PivotChart query that we created earlier. Set the view to PivotChart. Figure B-12 shows the blank PivotChart screen.

First, let's drag the CustomerName field to the Category Fields drop area. After you've done this, the customer name data is shown on the horizontal (x) axis. Figure B-13 shows the updated screen.

Next, we are ready to set up the categories of data to be graphed for each customer. In this case we will want to show quarterly order amount totals. Select the Quarters field under OrderDate By Month and drag it to the Series Fields drop area, which is on the right side of the screen. Figure B-14 shows the updated screen.

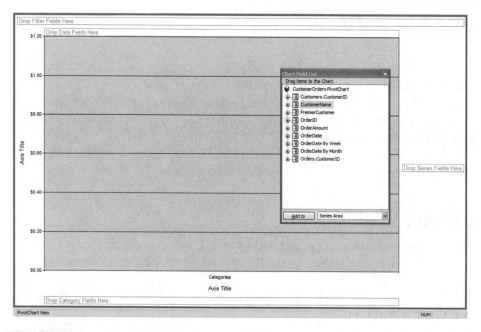

FIGURE B-12   Blank PivotChart screen

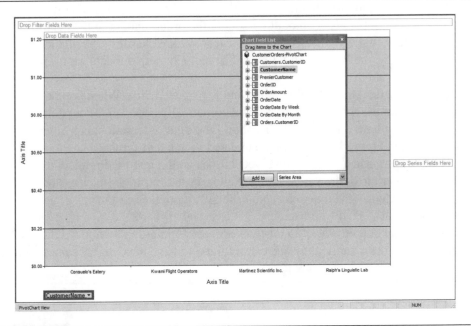

FIGURE B-13   PivotChart with the CustomerName field

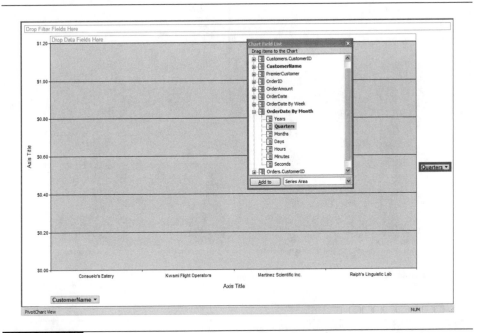

FIGURE B-14   PivotChart with Quarters OrderDate categories

Now we are ready to add the data for the PivotChart. In the PivotTable we had to create a sum of the order amount by adding the order amount to the detail area and then selecting the sum calculation. Because we are charting data and need sums for display, the PivotChart will automatically sum up the data we drop into the Data Fields area.

Drag the OrderAmount field to the Data Fields drop area. When you do that, note that a Sum of OrderAmount field is automatically added to the field list under Totals. We now have a PivotChart that shows the total order amounts by quarter for each customer. Figure B-15 shows the updated PivotChart screen.

Next, we can add a filter to the PivotChart as well. Drag the PremierCustomer field to the Filter Fields drop area. This will allow us to determine which customers are shown on the chart. This time select No to show nonpremier customers. Figure B-16 shows the updated PivotChart screen.

Now set the chart to show all customers again. You probably noticed the Axis Title labels on the x and y axes. We can set these to have meaningful names. Select

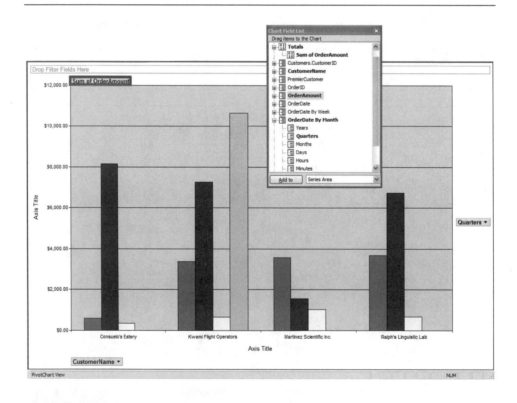

FIGURE B-15   PivotChart with order amount data

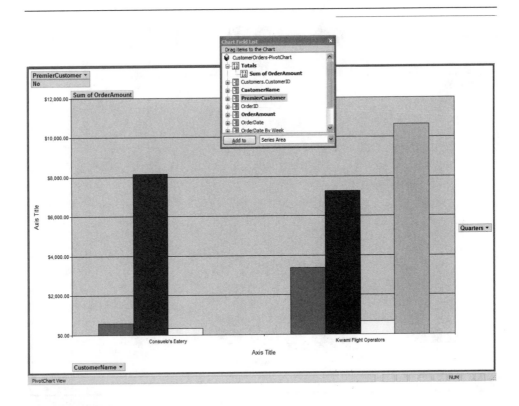

FIGURE B-16   PivotChart with nonpremier customers

the x axis label and then right-click it. Select the Properties option on the pop-up menu. In the dialog box, select the Format tab. Change the caption to **Customers Orders by Quarter**. Change the other axis label to **Total Order Amount**. Figure B-17 shows the updated PivotChart screen.

We can also change the type of chart that we are viewing. For example, we can choose a nice, three dimensional view of the data that will make it easy to compare customer trends.

Right-click anywhere on the PivotChart screen and select Chart Type on the pop-up menu. From the list of chart groups, select Column. From the list of charts for line, select the 3D Line style. As soon as you click the 3D Line style, the chart automatically changes to the new format.

Select the Data Details tab on the Properties window. Click the Series Orientation icon to flip the orientation and move the quarters to the bottom left and the customers

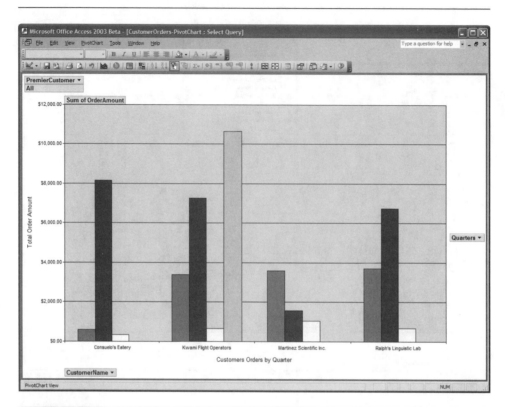

FIGURE B-17   PivotChart with updates axis labels

to the bottom right. Also click the 3D View tab and play with the view until you have it the way you want it. Figure B-18 shows the updated chart.

From this view it is a bit easier to see that Consuelo's Eatery, Kwami Flight Operations, and Ralph's Linguistic Lab all had high order volume during the second quarter. But, it looks like the third quarter was pretty dead for all of the customers. And, in the fourth quarter, only Kwami Flight Operations was placing any orders and they spiked way up.

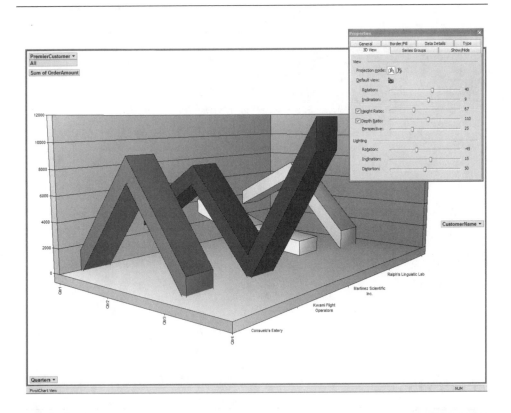

FIGURE B-18   3D Line chart

Finally, from this high-level chart view, we can always switch back to the PivotTable view to drill down into the details of the data. From the View icon on the toolbar, select PivotTable. Figure B-19 shows the PivotTable screen, which should look very familiar. It is basically the same pivot table that we created in the last section. We can easily switch between the two views to look at a high-level graphical representation or drill into the relational details of the data.

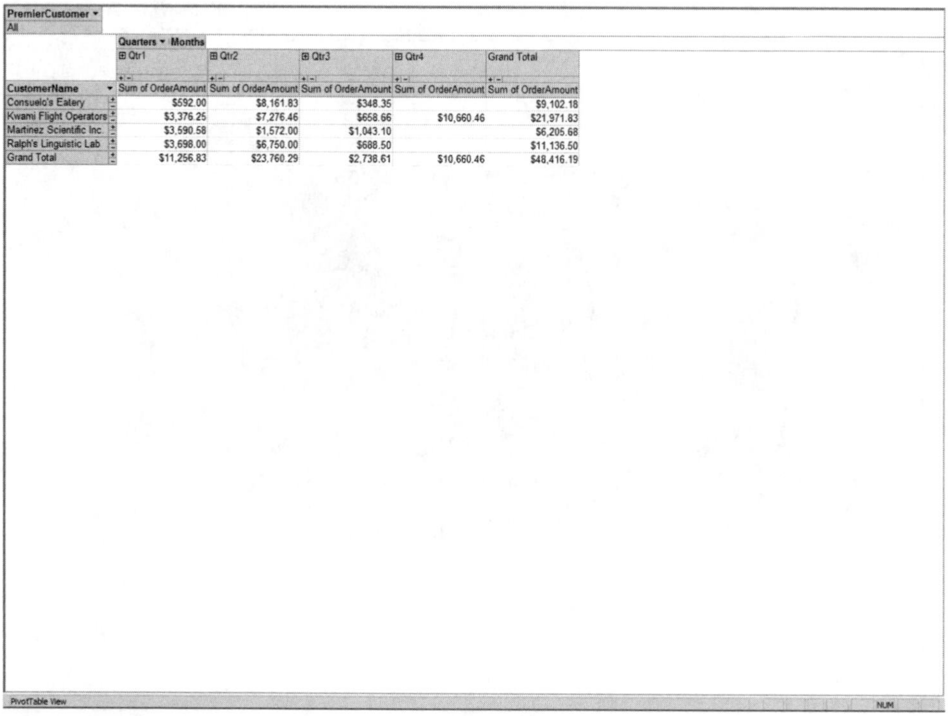

| PremierCustomer ▼ | | | | | |
| All | | | | | |

Quarters ▼ Months					
	⊞ Qtr1	⊞ Qtr2	⊞ Qtr3	⊞ Qtr4	Grand Total
	+│−	+│−	+│−	+│−	+│−
CustomerName ▼	Sum of OrderAmount	Sum of OrderAmount	Sum of OrderAmount	Sum of OrderAmount	Sum of OrderAmount
Consuelo's Eatery	$592.00	$8,161.83	$348.35		$9,102.18
Kwami Flight Operators	$3,376.25	$7,276.46	$658.66	$10,660.46	$21,971.83
Martinez Scientific Inc.	$3,590.58	$1,572.00	$1,043.10		$6,205.68
Ralph's Linguistic Lab	$3,698.00	$6,750.00	$688.50		$11,136.50
Grand Total	$11,256.83	$23,760.29	$2,738.61	$10,660.46	$48,416.19

PivotTable View   NUM

FIGURE B-19   PivotTable view

PivotTable and PivotChart Summary

These two tools provide powerful views of data within the Access environment. PivotTables and PivotCharts can also be used against table data and data displayed in forms. An example of how PivotTables will be utilized in this book is to analyze and verify imported data. With the PivotTable view, we can view data relationships and drill down into the data details.

> **NOTE** *PivotTables and PivotCharts can be used in the other office applications for working with data. In particular in Microsoft Excel, worksheet data can be viewed in PivotTables and PivotCharts.*

Appendix C

Data Access Pages

Data Access Pages enable you to create data-bound HTML pages from within the Access user interface. These pages can be viewed in Microsoft Internet Explorer 5 or later and can contain static or live data that is distributed by email.

Typically, Data Access Pages are intended for internal use on an intranet. They can be used on a public Internet site but should be done so with caution to ensure proper security precautions. In addition, Data Access Pages can be used within the Access environment.

Choosing Data Access Pages over Forms and Reports

Access provides three primary methods for delivering data to end users—forms, reports, and Data Access Pages. Forms are utilized for delivering data in a standard Windows form interface, and depending on the form, data can also be updated. Reports are primarily created for printing data on paper. Data Access Pages can be used for all three and the delivery interface is through the web browser.

One of the best benefits of Data Access Pages is the ability to distribute live data via email. In addition, as with reports, you can send static data (snapshots) as well. This allows for data to be easily distributed and updated through a common medium, email.

Utilizing Data Access Pages

Data Access Pages are created and designed with the Page tools in Microsoft Access. A page is actually stored as a separate file outside of Access. Access keeps a list of shortcuts in the database window.

Data Access Page design is similar to that of forms and reports. A list of available fields is provided, a toolbox for creating elements, the Sorting and Grouping dialog box, and so on. The three primary approaches to designing pages are outlined here:

Type	Description
Interactive Reporting	This type of reporting provides drill-downs and passages through the data to view different details. For example, we might have top level e-commerce order data that shows sales for the year. We can then drill down into sales by month. We then might jump to sales by customer. This type of data is typically not edited and is read-only.
Data Analysis	This type of report is similar to interactive reporting but it expands the ability to work with the data. You might change values to build what-if scenarios. You might also incorporate advanced queries and views to look at the data differently and analyze it.

Type	Description
Data Entry	This type of page is essentially used for managing data. Records can be reviewed and updated, or, new data can be inserted.

One way to think about data entry pages is that they combine the capabilities of reports and forms, all in a browser interface.

Data Access Pages are accessed just like any other web page in Internet Explorer. When users view a page, they are grabbing a copy from the server and looking at it in their browser. Only data (if supported on the page) can be updated. The page itself can be modified, and no settings on the page (such as sort settings) will be saved in the database.

TIP   *Users need to have at least Internet Explorer 5 or above and a license for Office.*

Data Access Pages can also be viewed within Microsoft Access. When the page is opened, you can switch between design and view modes. This allows you to work with the page easily without having to open the page directly in Internet Explorer.

Building a Data Access Page

We will first build a simple Data Access Page to show how the process works. We will use the wizard, which, like queries, is useful for building simple solutions. We will also explore how PivotCharts and PivotTables can be created in the Data Access Page and displayed as well.

For our demonstration, we will use the e-commerce database set up in Appendix B. Review the section of that appendix, which describes the structure and details of the data. Once the database is set up, click the Pages objects option on the Database window.

Next, click the Create Data Access Page By Using Wizard to create our first Data Access Page. The first dialog (Figure C-1) shows the initial screen. As with the other wizards in Access, the first step is to select our data source.

In the dialog, select the Customers table then click the double arrow to select all of the fields. Now select the Orders table and click the double arrow to select all of its fields. Click the Next button to move to the next screen.

In the next dialog, we have the option of determining if we would like our data grouped in any way. In this case, let's select the CustomerName field to group the display of the data. This will allow us to see customer orders by customer. Figure C-2 shows the screen with the CustomerName field selected.

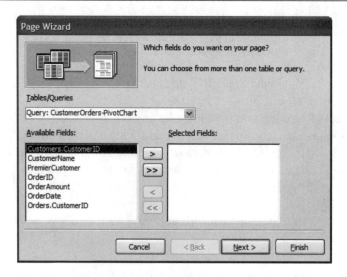

Page Wizard—Data source selection

Click the Next button to continue. The next screen gives us options for sorting the data. In this case, let's sort by OrderAmount, which will sort the orders for each customer by amount. Figure C-3 shows the dialog.

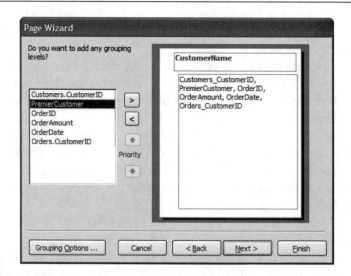

Page Wizard—CustomerName grouping

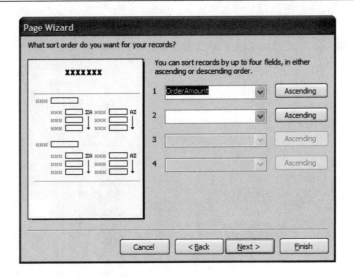

Building a Data Access Page

FIGURE C-3 Page Wizard—Sort options

On the final screen, save the page as Customers and then click Finish. The Design view of the page comes up. The Design environment for the page is straightforward. A toolbox is provided for dragging the standard HTML elements to the page, which includes radio buttons, check boxes, and so on.

We can also drag objects such as PivotTables and PivotCharts. A field list of the data we can pull from in the Access database is also shown on the right. Figure C-4 shows the design created by the Wizard.

Now click the View button on the toolbar and change the view to Page view. When the page comes up, a plus sign appears next to the customer name. Click the plus sign to expand the view. Within that view the order detail for the customer comes up. Navigation is provided for browsing through both the order and customer data. Figure C-5 shows the page.

The navigation toolbar also provides options for sorting, help, and so on. Now save the page. When you do so, Access is going to ask where you want the page saved. Although it will default to the location of the Access database file, you can choose to locate it on an Intranet server or wherever it makes the most sense to you. Be sure that the data source setup of the page that the wizard creates is accessible from the location where you would like to save the page.

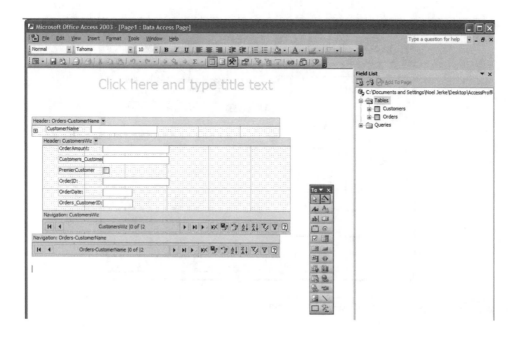

FIGURE C-4   Data Access Page—Design view

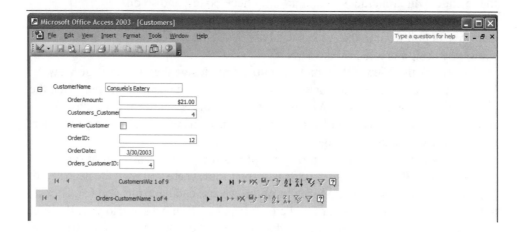

FIGURE C-5   Data Access Page—Page view

Building Pages with Tables and Charts

One of the more powerful features of Data Access Pages is the ability to build pages with PivotTables and PivotCharts. In Appendix B, we review the basics of building each. Those same techniques can be followed when building Data Access Pages.

Open up a new Data Access Page in Design view. From the toolbar select the Office PivotTable control, and then draw a new control on the page layout. Your page should look like Figure C-6.

Now we are ready to begin building the layout of the PivotTable. First, right-click the PivotTable and select Object Properties. Select the All tab on the dialog. Go to the DataMember option. Select the CustomerOrders-PivotTable query, and then close the dialog.

Now, right-click on the PivotTable again. Go to the Field List option and select it. The Field List for the PivotTable pops up. Now drag the CustomerName from the field list to the Row Fields area. Your screen should look like Figure C-7.

Next, drag the Quarters field option from the OrderDate by Month and drag it to the Column Fields drop area. Then drag the OrderAmount to the Totals or Details area.

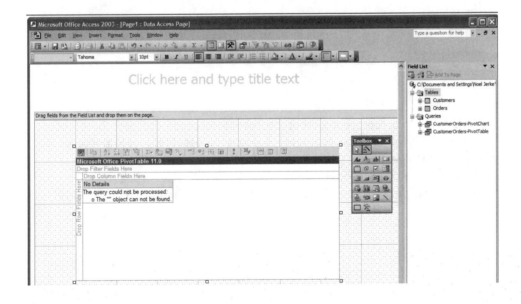

FIGURE C-6   Data Access Page with PivotTable control

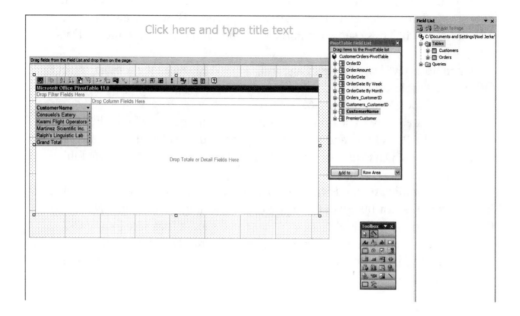

PivotTable with CustomerName set

Select the OrderAmount details in the PivotTable screen and click the AutoCalc button on the PivotTable toolbar. Select Sum on the list. The sum of the order amounts is then generated. Your screen should now look like Figure C-8.

Now, select File | Save and save the page as PivotTable. Switch to the Page view or choose the Web Page Preview option. The PivotTable is then displayed in

| FIGURE C-8 | Final PivotTable design |

the web page. Note that users of the page can still make changes to the PivotTable. They can add new fields, do new calculations, drill into details, and so on. Figure C-9 shows the page in the browser.

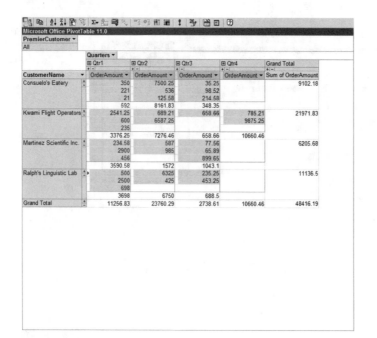

FIGURE C-9 Data Access Page with the PivotTable

PivotCharts can be created by following the same set of steps. Once the page is built, users can build charts with the data bound to the chart. Figure C-10 shows an example PivotChart in the web browser.

The chart types can be changed, the data can be filtered, and so on, just as if we were working directly in Access.

TIP *If you are using the examples provided on the web site, then you will likely need to regenerate the web pages so they will have the proper references.*

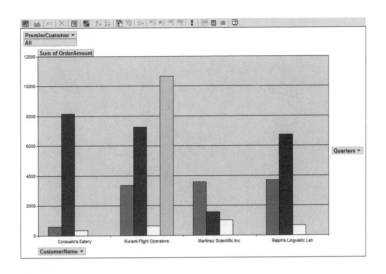

FIGURE C-10   Data Access Page with the PivotChart

Data Access Pages Summary

Data Access Pages are a great way to bring your Access data to end users. If the end user does not have Access loaded and you need to keep the data centralized, then Data Access Pages can provide you with useful options. With the easy-to-utilize and familiar design tools provided in Access, creating them becomes a straightforward proposition.

Index

INTERNATIONAL CONTACT INFORMATION

AUSTRALIA
McGraw-Hill Book Company
Australia Pty. Ltd.
TEL +61-2-9900-1800
FAX +61-2-9878-8881
http://www.mcgraw-hill.com.au
books-it_sydney@mcgraw-hill.com

CANADA
McGraw-Hill Ryerson Ltd.
TEL +905-430-5000
FAX +905-430-5020
http://www.mcgraw-hill.ca

**GREECE, MIDDLE EAST, & AFRICA
(Excluding South Africa)**
McGraw-Hill Hellas
TEL +30-210-6560-990
TEL +30-210-6560-993
TEL +30-210-6560-994
FAX +30-210-6545-525

MEXICO (Also serving Latin America)
McGraw-Hill Interamericana Editores
S.A. de C.V.
TEL +525-1500-5108
FAX +525-117-1589
http://www.mcgraw-hill.com.mx
carlos_ruiz@mcgraw-hill.com

SINGAPORE (Serving Asia)
McGraw-Hill Book Company
TEL +65-6863-1580
FAX +65-6862-3354
http://www.mcgraw-hill.com.sg
mghasia@mcgraw-hill.com

SOUTH AFRICA
McGraw-Hill South Africa
TEL +27-11-622-7512
FAX +27-11-622-9045
robyn_swanepoel@mcgraw-hill.com

SPAIN
McGraw-Hill/
Interamericana de España, S.A.U.
TEL +34-91-180-3000
FAX +34-91-372-8513
http://www.mcgraw-hill.es
professional@mcgraw-hill.es

**UNITED KINGDOM, NORTHERN,
EASTERN, & CENTRAL EUROPE**
McGraw-Hill Education Europe
TEL +44-1-628-502500
FAX +44-1-628-770224
http://www.mcgraw-hill.co.uk
emea_queries@mcgraw-hill.com

ALL OTHER INQUIRIES Contact:
McGraw-Hill/Osborne
TEL +1-510-420-7700
FAX +1-510-420-7703
http://www.osborne.com
omg_international@mcgraw-hill.com

Sound Off!

Visit us at **www.osborne.com/bookregistration** and let us know what you thought of this book. While you're online you'll have the opportunity to register for newsletters and special offers from McGraw-Hill/Osborne.

We want to hear from you!

Sneak Peek

Visit us today at **www.betabooks.com** and see what's coming from McGraw-Hill/Osborne tomorrow!

Based on the successful software paradigm, Bet@Books™ allows computing professionals to view partial and sometimes complete text versions of selected titles online. Bet@Books™ viewing is free, invites comments and feedback, and allows you to "test drive" books in progress on the subjects that interest you the most.